The Law Firm of 2030
How the future law firm might look

EDITED BY ALEX DAVIES

Commissioning editor
Alex Davies

Managing director
Sian O'Neill

The Law Firm of 2030: How the future law firm might look
is published by

Globe Law and Business Ltd
3 Mylor Close
Horsell
Woking
Surrey GU21 4DD
United Kingdom
Tel: +44 20 3745 4770
www.globelawandbusiness.com

The Law Firm of 2030: How the future law firm might look

ISBN 978-1-83723-085-3
EPUB ISBN 978-1-83723-086-0
Adobe PDF ISBN 978-1-83723-087-7

Contents

Executive summary

The legal profession stands on the precipice of transformative change. *The Law Firm of 2030: How the future law firm might look* delves into the dynamic and rapidly evolving landscape of law, offering a visionary glimpse into what the future holds for legal practitioners. From the integration of artificial intelligence and cutting-edge technology to the evolution of people management and workplace culture, we'll cover the critical areas that will shape the future of legal practice.

Our opening chapter by Joanne Brook introduces in brief the concepts and why it is necessary for lawyers to think about how law firms need to change. Joanne considers the paradox of increasing access to on-point data that can assist lawyers with data-overload that can lead to decreased productivity and an ever-increasing workload, coalescing in larger law firms that leave small generalists out of the loop and niche firms needing to really push specificity, expertise, and empathy.

The chapter considers, by reference to the rest of the book and inputs from other contributors, how this can be addressed so that practitioners can reclaim space to innovate for better outputs and ensure law remains a profitable business, people-led where it needs to be, and tech-led where it is best deployed. The chapter also flags the regulatory and compliance position that lawyers increasingly face and the competition human-lawyers face from unaccredited suppliers and AI advisors and whether this is a threat or an opportunity.

The book thereafter is split into four parts. The first part looks at AI and legal technology.

Harry Borovick kicks us off by navigating the ethics of AI and legal practice. Introducing, implementing, applying, and fully leveraging AI can create great opportunities within legal practice. It can also be a quagmire of complex ethical considerations with a balance to be struck between what best serves the practitioner, the client, the courts, and wider society. In examining the ethics of AI in legal practice, chapter two considers practical instances where a balance may be struck between business and legal upsides vs ethical risks, where net positive outcomes are achievable for the most stakeholders.

Chapter three, by Jelena Schidzig, examines how autonomous AI systems are transforming legal practice. Moving beyond today's fragmented legal tech landscape of tools requiring constant human direction, she introduces systems capable of operating autonomously within an organization's infrastructure. This represents more than a technological advancement – it reveals how legal practice will actually function in the future. The innovation marks a significant leap beyond traditional API integration and basic prompt engineering, creating an intelligent layer that truly understands and acts on legal data (underlying evidence) while building upon existing operations and institutional expertise and rule of law. As these systems adapt to and learn from established legal practices, they reshape how legal services are delivered and consumed. Jelena's chapter demonstrates how this evolution toward autonomous operations is already changing the practical reality of legal work, offering insights into how lawyers will deliver services in the future.

Chapter four by Colin Levy explores the critical interplay between artificial intelligence, client confidentiality, and the evolving nature of legal work. It provides a dual perspective – addressing present-day challenges and forward-looking innovations – to guide legal professionals in navigating the integration of AI without compromising ethical standards or the human touch.

Readers will gain insights into safeguarding sensitive data in an era of technological complexity, the importance of maintaining high-quality, hybrid work products through AI-human collaboration, and strategies for building trust with clients while embracing innovation. Colin's chapter concludes with a visionary look at how AI will shape the law firm of 2030, offering practical steps to prepare for an AI-enhanced future that prioritizes confidentiality, accountability, and excellence.

Chapter five, by Martin Martinoff, looks at technological innovation and the evolution of professional legal practice. The legal profession is no longer revered as the fortress of precedent and parchment. It is no longer just a story of tradition. It is becoming a tale of transformation, where silicon and code are as vital as statute and case law. In the coming years, the law firm as we know it might not merely adapt to technology – it might be reborn through it. In his chapter, Martin explores that alchemy – a fusion of human ingenuity and technology that promises to redefine not just *how* lawyers work, but *who* they are as professionals, *what* they deliver, and, most importantly, *why* they matter in a world racing toward informational complexity. The catalysts for this transformation are obvious – relentless client demands, spiraling costs, and a growing flood of new players who rewrite the rules, including tech start-ups, alternative legal service platforms, and even larger software giants.

Part 2 looks at people and culture in the law firm of 2030.

Maria Govis' chapter explores the key trends shaping the world of work from 2025 to 2030, including generational shifts in the workforce and technology-driven transformation. She covers how these trends influence workspace culture, leadership structures, wellbeing at work, talent attraction and retention, and the need for up- and re-skilling. The chapter also offers personal strategies to help legal professionals build careers that align with their values, ensuring a meaningful and fulfilling work life.

Chapter seven then looks at how to manage generation diversity in the law firm of 2030. Law firms are experiencing an increasing level of generation-related impacts within the workplace. This phenomenon is driven by demographic changes, technological advancements, and evolving workplace expectations. Baby Boomers are retiring in large numbers, Generation X has stepped up and often leads with Millennials now forming the largest workforce segment, and Generation Z is redefining career growth and workplace culture. Generational diversity, maintains David Laud, presents a series of challenges for law firm owners. These challenges include succession, recruitment, retention, adoption of technology, and differing attitudes toward work–life balance. Having a strategy to manage generational diversity is key and explored in this chapter, along with case studies and practical examples illustrating how firms are adapting their leadership approach. Generational diversity is an opportunity for innovation and competitive advantage rather than a problem to be managed. Law firms that embrace change will be better positioned for future success.

In chapter eight, Martin Martinoff outlines the strategic capabilities law firms must build to succeed in a technology-driven future. Drawing on insights from Innovate UK's Next Generation Services program, he examines how leaders can respond to changing client demands, evolving regulations, and shifting workforce expectations. The chapter reframes capability-building as a firm-wide priority – encompassing digital fluency, ethical innovation, agile leadership, and client-centric service design. Martin offers a forward-looking roadmap for firms to not just adapt to change but lead it, aspiring for collaboration in innovation, excellence, and impact.

Chapter nine then looks at the socially responsible legal practice. Historically, the legal profession has been characterized by high stress, long hours, and competitive work environments – factors that contribute to elevated rates of burnout, anxiety, and attrition in the industry. Efforts to break away from these traditional norms – such as the rise of alternative employment models like the consultant model – reflect a growing desire for healthier, more sustainable ways of working in the legal sector. Two major forces are driving change, says Aoife Greally – a societal shift toward valuing wellbeing, understood as a holistic combination of mental, physical, and emotional health, and the rise of technology that is reshaping workflows and enabling greater flexibility. Together, these forces are creating new opportunities for law firms to redefine their cultures and improve both individual experiences and organizational performance. By 2030, firms that actively invest in fostering cultures of wellbeing will create workplaces that attract top talent, improve retention, and deliver better client outcomes. This chapter explores how law firms can cultivate such environments, focusing on redefining what success means, leveraging technology, and embracing leadership accountability.

Part 3 looks at finance and operations.

The law firm of 2030 will have practical complexities to navigate including profitability, pricing, and capacity due to advances in AI technologies in the legal practice space. Chapter 10 by Chantal McNaught outlines how profitability and pricing intersect, and why it is of equal importance to consider law firm capacity when setting pricing and measuring for profitability. This chapter first addresses pricing methodology, noting that whilst in some cases time-based billing will have its place, this will be usurped by more client-centered modes of billing. Then, profitability is addressed as billing modes shift, and measures of profit-per-equity-partner are likely to adapt. Finally, Chantal looks at how AI capacity will influence both pricing and profitability, which is an important aspect of the law firm of 2030 not to be ignored.

The legal marketplace has undergone dramatic changes over the past decade, impacting how legal services are delivered. Law firms and corporate legal departments (CLDs) have been increasingly challenged to find new ways to create operational effectiveness and efficiencies at their companies to either save money or to grow market share and profitability. All the extracurricular activities unrelated to the practice of law have come to be known as the "business of law" and regardless of whether it is carried out in-house or externally at a law firm, much of the responsibility for managing and overseeing the business side of legal services has now fallen on the shoulders of the legal operations professional. Chapter 11 by Richard Brzakala examines the growing importance of the legal operations professional in the legal marketplace and how both law firms and corporate legal departments have embraced them as an invaluable and critical resource in their business strategy.

Part 4 then looks at risks and opportunities.

Chapter 12, by Jenifer Swallow, looks at the changing landscape for ESG and the future for which law firms will need to prepare. As geopolitics reshapes regulatory and policy agendas, so demand, risk, and opportunity shift and businesses must respond. The fundamentals of environmental, social – or better said, societal – and governance considerations that have taken hold over the last decade will morph across the next. ESG as it was is dead. In its place we will see a re-prioritization around growth and security, with new language, technologically-led frameworks of governance, and expectations of society alongside. The implications for clients, law firms, and their people are significant.

The focus of chapter 13 is governance in the context of ethics, and the infrastructure necessary to meet ethical duties in legal practice. Jenifer Swallow looks at how lawyers can support clients with the same in decision-making and deployment to the future.

In chapter 14, Wayne Hassay looks at how law firms can rebrand for the future. For over a century, law firms have clung to traditional naming conventions – think Jones, Smith & Smith or the infamous fictional Dewey, Cheatem & Howe. Traditionalists believe these naming conventions carry a sense of importance, legacy, and are even a method to ensure professional responsibility. Keep in mind, these methods were established at a time when the only way to find a lawyer was through his signage downtown, and everyone's and everything's reputation was tied to a surname. However, in today's world of branding and consumer engagement, these conventional names no longer resonate with modern clients. Law firm names often feel distant and impersonal, reinforcing the perception that lawyers are aloof and disconnected from the very people they serve. While personal injury firms may not be the ideal model to emulate – often relying on bold, and at times overly aggressive, tactics – most legal practices have been slow to adopt any branding strategy at all. To complicate matters further, some jurisdictions still prohibit the use of trade names and significantly limit advertising, curtailing firms' ability to modernize their branding strategies. In contrast, industries such as technology, healthcare, and finance have fully embraced branding as a powerful tool to create meaningful connections with consumers. They invest heavily in developing identities that reflect their values, resonate with emotions, and align with contemporary expectations. It is time for law firms to rethink their approach to branding and client engagement. To stay competitive, law firms must evolve, crafting relatable and recognizable brands that authentically reflect their mission, values, and the communities they serve, starting with their name and extending to every aspect of their marketing strategy. The question is no longer whether firms should change. The question is, how quickly can they pivot to remain relevant in an increasingly dynamic marketplace? The urgency is clear – in just a few years, non-lawyer competitors, armed with modern branding strategies, consumer-focused engagement, artificial intelligence, and unencumbered by arcane professional responsibility rules, threaten to marginalize traditional law firms. Those unwilling to adapt risk being left behind in an industry that is rapidly transforming

Data-driven decision-making is only going to be come more prevalent in the law firm of 2030. The power of predictive analytics in law firm strategy is discussed in chapter 15 by Mori Kabiri, who explores how law firms can leverage historical and real-time data to forecast case outcomes, manage resources, and enhance client satisfaction. The chapter looks at the practical steps that can be taken to implement predictive analytics, including key KPIs and data governance principles, before looking at ethical considerations, such as managing bias in AI systems and ensuring privacy and security.

In chapter 16, Kassi Burns, Olga V. Mack and Adam Rouse explore how the legal profession must transition from a "picture" mindset (static, point-in-time data) to a "movie" approach (dynamic, continuously evolving information). Using this powerful analogy, their chapter demonstrates how legal professionals must adapt their practices, technologies, and thinking to thrive in the increasingly dynamic data environment of 2030. The chapter begins by examining how legal data has traditionally been treated as static "pictures" – discrete contracts, precedents, and filings frozen in time. Next it addresses the limitations of "picture thinking" when applied to modern legal evidence. The chapter explores the legal implications when evidence exists as a continuous flow rather than discrete documents, addressing questions of authenticity, admissibility, and interpretation that arise when lawyers must work with "movies" rather than "pictures." The authors track the evolution of e-discovery from its origins in static document collection to today's emerging paradigm of dynamic data capture, examining the technologies and methodologies that enable legal professionals to "film" rather than merely "photograph" electronic evidence. The traditional client relationship has centered around periodic "portraits" – formal updates, quarterly reports, and milestone meetings that provide static snapshots of matter status. The chapter explores how dynamic data transforms these relationships into ongoing "documentaries," with continuous information sharing through client portals and real-time dashboards. Dynamic data enables a shift to "motion studies" that capture the full temporal dimension of legal situations. The authors conclude by providing a roadmap for legal professionals to transition from "picture takers" to "movie directors" of legal information, preparing them for the dynamic data reality of 2030 while maintaining the profession's core values of accuracy, reliability, and trustworthiness.

Chapter 17 then looks at data use and misuse. Brian Fox outlines the growing imperative for organizations to gain comprehensive control over their data in an increasingly complex and regulated landscape. He emphasizes a major mindset shift – technology is not the end but a conduit for data, and true value comes from transforming raw data into reliable information. Companies must now demonstrate accountability for data accuracy, ownership, and ethical use, as stakeholders – from regulators to consumers – expect transparency, precision, and control. In the chapter, Brian lays out a two-part strategy: first, put some structure around your existing data using tools like data catalogs, lineage tracking, and quality monitoring. Second, simplify your data systems by rethinking and rebuilding messy, outdated data flows using modern approaches like Data Mesh, Knowledge Graphs, or even starting afresh with streamlined reporting environments. With better tools and smarter thinking, law firms must get control. Legal teams have a big role to play here, helping tie all this to compliance and turning data governance into a strategic advantage, especially as AI becomes more central to business.

Jane Allen then looks at the geopolitical environment in which law operates. Chapter 18 explores the evolving role of legal leaders amid an era of heightened geopolitical volatility, deregulation, and shifting global norms. Once relatively insulated, legal functions now face mounting pressure to adapt -balancing efficiency with risk, modernizing operations through technology and alternative service models, and navigating complex ethical and reputational challenges. As the Rule of Law erodes in some regions and brand perception becomes more intertwined with legal choices, leaders must reassess risk tolerance, support lawyer wellbeing, and engage more strategically with the C-suite. Looking ahead to 2030, the legal profession is poised to become more tech-enabled, multidisciplinary, and central to corporate leadership – better equipped to both endure disruption and restore order when the pendulum eventually swings back.

Joanne Brook returns for our concluding chapter, which collates responses from a range of businesses to the following five questions:

- Which professional advisors do you instruct regularly?
- What matters do you engage legal advisors for the most?
- What do you dislike about engaging lawyers?
- What do you consider the biggest challenge to your business in the next five years?
- What do clients want from the law firm of 2030?

The chapter takes a client-centric approach to addressing the question of what the law firm of 2030 looks like and how it operates and provides services. Joanne draws on the results of the poll and research from other sources to show what businesses and professionals engage lawyers for and, drawing on the answers to this research, identifies how that is likely to change in the coming years. The chapter considers the "coming storm" and disruption that is inevitable in the profession as the landscapes of business, politics, policy, environment, and human engagements change to meet the needs of clients as advisors and in the wider profession as a whole. The areas of technology that are most likely to impact the profession are considered by asking technology businesses:

- "What new technology do lawyers need?"
- "What new technology will impact professional advisors the most?"
- "Can technology replace lawyers?"

Using answers to these questions, the chapter summarizes how lawyers can adapt their practices, adopt new procedures, anticipate client needs, and give them what they want for the law firm of 2030.

About the authors

Jane C. Allen is a PwC partner in the legal business solutions practice. For nearly 30 years she has focused in the legal, regulatory, and compliance domain, at the intersection of supporting corporate legal functions in applying more efficient project management, better processes and automation, and leveraging technology and data – in defensible manners. In recent years, her efforts have focused on legal function transformation and organizational design, including leveraging GenAI, emerging regulation management and inquiry response, remediation efforts, knowledge management, information governance, and contract management. Past experience includes global investigations, e-discovery and forensics, and other crisis response matters. Prior to PwC, Jane led a litigation support boutique supporting in-house and external counsel in a variety of regulatory proceedings and litigation matters.

Harry Borovick is general counsel and AI governance officer at Luminance, which provides advanced AI for the processing of legal documents. As well as working at the forefront of the development of AI for legal operations, Harry lectures at Kings College London and Queen Mary University London on applied legal AI and AI ethics. Harry currently sits as an AI advisor to CiArb, previously contributed to Globe Law and Business' *Legal Operations in the Age of AI and Data*, and most recently published his book, *AI and The Law: A Practical Guide to Using AI Safely*.

Joanne Brook is a solicitor who qualified as the web was launched and has been a legal technologist ever since. She advises innovators across the creative sectors from software developers to theater producers and from AI and VR developers to artists who distribute NFTs. She focuses on helping clients achieve commercial solutions to previously not-considered legal issues that arise from developing and using their technology. Critically, she helps to protect and license their intellectual property rights to ensure business expansion and growth in a fast-paced market. Prior to becoming a legal consultant, she was a partner at a West End law firm and a boutique City law firm before that. She describes her view of the digital revolution and use of new technologies as being somewhere between sitting in the jump seat with a supersonic test pilot, in awe as the engines roar, and calmly evacuating the plane whilst wearing a parachute and hi-vis, carrying a laptop and inflating a lifeboat. In all that, she feels privileged to continue to advise passionate, smart, and more creative people than herself on a daily basis. Joanne is an intellectual property professional expert for Lexis Nexis and an author of IP and data management precedents for various professional publications. She regularly contributes legal insight to the legal press and lectures on technology and new law.

Richard Brzakala has over two decades of experience in the legal operations field. He is a published author, and a frequent participant and contributor to various legal media outlets, executive roundtables, webinars, podcasts, and discussion forums on topics related to legal operations strategy and outside counsel management.

Kassi Burns is a senior attorney at King & Spalding, LLP, based in Texas. As an attorney with over ten years of experience working with AI and machine learning in litigation, Kassi's career has advanced by always being curious and following technology innovations. In addition to a growing collection of publications on topics related to AI, Kassi is actively engaged in thought leadership through her podcast focused on the impact of emerging technologies to our professional and personal lives, *Kassi &*. She is an executive board member of the Academy of Court-Appointed Neutrals, a member of the Sedona Conference Working Group 13 (AI & the Law) Steering Committee and is Secretary and member of the State Bar of Texas Legal Practice Management Committee. Kassi is an active member of various legal organizations and affinity groups, where she enthusiastically advocates for emerging technology awareness and education.

Brian Fox is a PwC partner focused on sustainable data governance. For over 25 years, Brian has helped Fortune 500 clients across industries define and achieve goals in data quality, data governance, information management, complex data analysis, regulatory remediation, and many other objectives involving complex interconnected data flows and processes. Brian's work helps clients develop and mature data quality programs that address critical risks, combine the efforts of various departments managing data risk, and bring organizations in line with their peers. Brian's background is as a technologist serving the financial services industry in a variety of data-related regulatory contexts. He has substantial experience in the application of advanced data analytics to regulatory matters, including customer remediations, privacy compliance, population validations, and technology-enabled file review efforts that require the analysis of high-volume unstructured data. Expertise includes the extraction and analysis of data from applications, data warehouses, external vendors and other sources, as well as experience with regulatory engagement on pursuing and achieving sustainable data quality for the most critical and high-risk reporting objectives.

Maria Govis is a legal technology expert within global legal business services at KPMG. She has four years of experience consulting and leading large-scale digital transformation projects for legal and compliance departments, with a particular focus on workflow automation and AI for law. She played a key role in a life sciences corporation's transformation initiative recognized with a Financial Times Innovative Lawyers 2021 and 2022 Award. She holds a law degree from the University of Düsseldorf, Germany, and a prior degree in translation and interpreting from Moscow State University, which included an academic stay at the University of Basque Country, Spain. With this background, she is fluent in English, German, Spanish, Brazilian Portuguese, and Russian. Maria's personal interests and research focus on workspace culture, organizational management, and the future of work.

Aoife Greally is the people business partner for EMEA and APAC at Clio. In this role, she champions workplace wellbeing and fosters a culture of support and inclusivity. Clio is the world's leading provider of cloud-based legal technology, empowering law firms to work more efficiently while improving access to justice. Aoife is dedicated to developing initiatives prioritizing mental health, work–life balance, and employee engagement. She advocates for creating environments where employees feel valued, heard, and empowered to thrive. Aoife actively collaborates with leadership to implement policies that support sustainable workloads, flexible working arrangements, and access to mental health resources. She believes that a healthier workplace benefits individuals and drives greater innovation, productivity, and long-term business success. At Clio, Aoife plays a key role in ensuring that the company's people-first culture extends across regions. She makes a tangible impact on the wellbeing of legal professionals and the teams that support them through strategic programs, open conversations, and proactive support systems, helping to shape the future of workplace wellbeing in the legal and technology industries.

Wayne Hassay is the managing partner of Maguire Schneider Hassay LLP (MSH), a full-service law firm based in Columbus, Ohio, focused on the People's Law segment. He is recognized for his longstanding commitment to client-centered legal services and for leading MSH's innovation strategy, particularly in the application of technology and scalable service models designed to broaden access to justice. His work highlights the value of legal service plans and subscription-based models as effective, sustainable mechanisms for serving underserved populations. Wayne writes and speaks regularly at the intersection of legal ethics, technology, and branding, with a particular focus on how law firms can modernize while remaining grounded in professional responsibility. His guiding philosophy is that legal services should be high-quality, affordable, and accessible – meeting the practical needs of both clients and the lawyers who serve them.

Mori Kabiri is an author and a recognized expert in legal operations, legal data analytics, and technology for corporate legal departments and law firms. His book, *Legal Operations KPIs*, has gained international recognition and has been translated into multiple languages. Beyond authorship, Mori contributes to the field through thought leadership – writing articles, publishing research papers, and co-authoring books. Mori is a strong advocate for introducing technology, data, and AI into law school curricula, recognizing these as essential tools for future lawyers. On the business front, Mori leads exclusive Legal Operations KPIs workshops, courses, and forums, bringing this critical subject to legal organizations worldwide. His hands-on approach and deep industry expertise drive innovation, making him a sought-after speaker at leading industry events. Over the past two decades, Mori has designed and implemented transformative legal technologies, including ELM, CLM, BI, and RFP platforms for large international corporations. He is currently the CEO of InfiniGlobe LLC, a legal operations consulting firm based in Newport Beach, California.

David Laud has held executive roles within law firms across the UK over the past 25 years. He's currently serving as chief operating officer at Latimer

Hinks. He spent a decade with Thomas Cook FX, where he led the launch of MoneyGram. As an author, David has published three books covering law firm management, two offering guidance on digital marketing and his most recent delving into managing generational diversity. When time permits, he hosts the "Insight with HReSource" podcast, featuring conversations with business leaders, entrepreneurs, and HR professionals, providing listeners with inspiration and insights.

Colin S. Levy is a legal tech author, educator, and writer. He explores innovation in the legal landscape while empowering professionals to navigate this dynamic space as general counsel for Malbek, a leading CLM provider. He is committed to growing the legal tech community through advisory roles, investments in emerging technology, and ongoing analysis as a columnist for *Today's General Counsel*. Colin serves as a judge for the American Legal Technology Awards and is the author of *The Legal Tech Ecosystem* and the editor of Globe Law and Business' *Handbook of Legal Tech*.

Olga V. Mack is a visionary legal technology entrepreneur, board director, and digital transformation expert dedicated to modernizing legal operations through AI. As a CEO and strategist, she has led legal innovation at Fortune 500 companies, pre-IPO start-ups, and legal tech ventures, including building AI-powered tools that enhance compliance, risk management, and operational efficiency. A Fellow at CodeX, the Stanford Center for Legal Informatics, and the Generative AI Editor at *law.MIT Computational Law Report*, Olga is a thought leader on AI adoption in the legal and nonprofit sectors. She has authored multiple books, including Globe Law and Business' *Product Counsel: Advise, Innovate, and Inspire*, and writes for *Above the Law* and *ACC Docket*. With a passion for making legal services more accessible and functional, she helps mission-driven organizations leverage AI to streamline compliance, protect data, and scale their impact.

Martin Martinoff is innovation lead – Next Generation Professional and Financial Services at Innovate UK. With graduate degrees in policy and management and research into organizational studies and innovation, Martin brings over a decade of sector experience to the fore, driving innovation and thought leadership in professional and financial services. As the innovation lead of the transformative Innovate UK program, he fuses design, technology, and policy to help advance the legal and fintech sectors. His efforts, particularly in building organizational capacities, foster critical thinking and creativity in innovation. From spearheading initiatives like the Open Design Studio and Future Firms, he brings valuable insights on overcoming digital technology adoption challenges in professional services firms.

Chantal McNaught is a PhD in Law candidate at Bond University, Gold Coast, Australia, focusing on "How lawyers can navigate the conflicts between law as a profession and law as a business". She holds law degrees from Bond University and the Australian National University. Admitted as a lawyer to the Supreme Court of New South Wales and the High Court of Australia, Chantal practiced as a solicitor and migration agent in Queensland. With interest in the intersection of technology and law, Chantal transitioned into legal marketing and legal technology. Now residing in Auckland, Aotearoa New Zealand, she serves as the manager for client success at LEAP NZ, focusing on enabling law firms with AI-powered legal technology. Chantal's expertise in leveraging AI and legal technology offers a fresh perspective on enhancing efficiency, profitability, and innovation within law firms.

Adam Rouse is the director and senior counsel, e-discovery operations, for Walgreen Co. Adam advises internal and external counsel concerning e-discovery and legal hold issues across a wide variety of commercial, regulatory, and employment matters. Additionally, Adam coordinates with the global compliance team to facilitate data collection and analysis for global compliance efforts. He also drives the adoption of new and emerging legal technology within the legal department. Adam was nominated to Relativity's inaugural AI Visionary group and named a finalist for an AI Innovation award. He continues to speak and write about the adoption of advanced AI technologies across industries and is a founding member of Legal Data Intelligence Model, an initiative started to break down information silos and encourage data driven legal practice. Adam earned an LLM in Space, Cyber, and Telecommunications Law from the University of Nebraska and continues his interest in space and rocketry with Central Illinois Aerospace, launching amateur rockets throughout the year.

Jelena Schidzig develops advanced AI systems that transform how legal professionals deliver their services and manage risk and compliance. Her innovations include specialized graph neural networks that provide comprehensive legal risk assessment and LLM applications with reasoning layers that autonomously process evidence across jurisdictions, with recent projects implementing these technologies for German law. Uniquely positioned at the intersection of technology and law, Jelena holds degrees in both computer science engineering and law, the latter from Stetson University and German institutions. As a legal risk and compliance director with experience spanning five continents, she has established new methodologies that fundamentally enhance how organizations analyze and respond to litigation, regulatory, and compliance challenges. Jelena is a managing partner of Legal Quant PLLC and the founder of Legal Quant Germany, where she leads innovative projects applying AI to legal practice across jurisdictions. In both industry and academia, she creates AI tools that support sustainable administration of justice while teaching advanced legal risk management methods. Her pioneering application of mathematical principles to legal analysis has established frameworks that enable AI systems to effectively understand and navigate the complex relationships inherent in legal practice.

Jenifer Swallow advises and coaches tech founders, GCs, and policy makers on legal and strategy matters. With a background in high growth environments, she is formerly general counsel at the fintech unicorn Wise Plc, product and human rights lead at Yahoo! EMEA, and CEO of the government-backed organisation LawtechUK. She has won multiple awards, including for her work in governance and ethics and is on the advisory board of the Post Office Project, is a member of the sub-committee of the statutory body the OPRC looking at digital justice, and contributes to a range of initiatives towards the transformation of legal services for society.

Chapter 1:
Where do we go from here?

By Joanne Brook, Lionshead Law

"Mirror, signal, maneuver"

"Mirror, signal, maneuver" is the mantra we use before pulling out into a stream of traffic. This book is about the profession embarking on a journey, so let us start by looking in the rearview mirror, set out our intention, and begin the maneuvers required for the move we are about to make.

As provision of legal services is transformed by technology and a shifting geopolitical landscape, the practices that provide "law" need to rapidly move into a new phase of delivery and adoption of methods of creating new output. This is a book that has been a long time in contemplation and for which the time is now right to present. *The Law Firm of 2030* considers the practice of law within professional firms in the future, why it is necessary for lawyers to think about this now, and provides a guide for how change can be undertaken and expectations exceeded.

This introduction provides a guide to each chapter in this work, with insights into why the topic is necessary and how each of a multitude of issues that will arise for a law firm in 2030 can be resolved. By reference to the rest of the book and inputs from other contributors, we look at how changes can be anticipated and addressed so that practitioners can reclaim space to innovate for better outputs and ensure law remains client-engaged and people-led where it needs to be and tech-led where that is best deployed in the law firm of the future.

The Rule of Law as a warning, not an instruction

The Rule of Law is a fundamental principle of legal practice and pervades every entry point to law. The Rule of Law requires transparency and it needs to be retained, even if that seems to come at the cost of organizational and technological innovation. Our current court system (and common law, precedent, and statute that provides the framework for trial, judgement, and sentencing) provides for humans to interpret and advise on law and regulation and predict outcomes from disputes based on the evidence and human presentation of it. A human judge hears facts, considers arguments and evidence, and provides a reasoned verdict at trial. Questions can be asked of a judge and an appeal is possible based on review of the facts, new evidence, and application of the law by the deciding judge. Ultimately, the determination of a legal outcome is administered by a person who shares the human experience with all of the people in the justice pipeline.

As legal systems move from human managed to "black box", and AI legal systems are created with unidentified, potentially unmediated, and partisan training data, which use proprietary algorithms to make determinations on the outcome of legal matters, we lose the critical "human element" of law and we must ask what we gain from what we give up. The fears of lack of understanding of the judicial process, lack of empathy from the algorithmic judge, and lack of transparency in decision-making may coalesce to undermine justice if adjudication by algorithm is perceived as less trustworthy than human decisions and we relinquish the element of justice being "seen to be done" that is so fundamental to the Rule of Law. Without the feeling of involvement in the system, there could be a fundamental loss of confidence in the statute and regulations those decisions uphold, and ultimately in the social contract that conformity with Law requires if order is to be maintained, all for the sake of expediency. AI-made law and judgements also raise interesting questions about "Who owns Law?". If statute is drafted by AI, legal decisions are made by tech and those systems are proprietary, who owns the output decisions and, by definition, "the Law"? Whilst it is easy to forget jurisprudence in our day-to-day professional practice, those whose lives are spent working within the law are clearly the best placed to consider these issues and reflect on them.

In part 1, on AI and legal technology in the law firm of 2030, Harry Borovick begins our journey by navigating the ethics of AI and legal practice. He considers some complex ethical considerations, suggesting that a balance is to be struck between what best serves the practitioner, the client, the courts, and wider society. This debate is one that is more than just about the ethics of non-human legal decision-making. Traditional programming required a human to input commands and logic to determine a process or set of rules that the computer followed in its problem-solving operations. In AI, the logic and commands are driven by machine learning. These may be supervised learning (where the system is provided with labelled data and the computer identifies and "learns" patterns to collate data within known parameters), or unsupervised learning where data is input and the system is instructed, in essence, to "make of this what you will". The outputs are the results of its "learning". Predictive models can map human behavior based on massive datasets that would take a human several lifetimes to experience and observe and lend themselves to the "pre-crime" of science fiction and the "default due" but as yet inchoate of credit agencies that makes headlines and uncomfortable reading about what we still consider to be "our personal data".

Jelena Schidzig then introduces us to systems capable of operating autonomously within a law firm environment. She presents a roadmap for how legal practice will actually function in the future, where autonomous systems create an intelligent layer that truly understands and acts on genuine legal data, while building upon existing operations and institutional expertise and the rule of law. Jelena's chapter demonstrates how this evolution toward autonomous operations is already changing the practical reality of legal work and offers insights into how lawyers will deliver services in the future.

It is right that Colin Levy goes on to explore how integrating AI must be undertaken so as not to compromise the ethical standards that are the bedrock of law. As we enter the *"post-professional society"* that Richard and Daniel Susskind anticipated in *The Future of the Professions*[1] where *"technology has transformed the work of human experts",* Colin provides vital insights into how AI–human collaboration can work and provides strategies for building and retaining trust with clients without compromising the Rule of Law.

Timelines flatten the space between years, but their linear perspective is sometimes helpful when it comes to matters as pliable as time. When I look at pace of change on a timeline, the year I qualified (1996) is as close to the launch of the world wide web in 1993 as a newly qualified lawyer in 2025 is to the launch of ChatGPT in 2022. Both of these events have been transformational in the legal profession. Introduction of the web meant the democratization of knowledge, where every piece of information uploaded could be accessed. The launch of Google in 1998 meant that information was tagged and made searchable and retrievable in seconds. ChatGPT is described as providing "democratization of language"[2] by enabling a user to use conversational prompts to instruct it to complete various tasks and write to order in any style it is instructed. As knowledge *and* language are the basis of legal practice, these two pillars have been eroded significantly by technology and the legal profession must consider how it needs to transform in order to remain relevant in a world where professional expertise and erudition can be achieved by machines.

Martin Martinoff then shifts our focus from one of tradition and reverence towards lawyers to one of dynamic operations by a profession that has redefined and repositioned itself. He foresees how the law firm as we know it might not merely adapt to technology, but be reborn through it. In this chapter, Martin explores the fusion of human ingenuity and technology that promises to redefine not just how lawyers work, but who they are as professionals, what they deliver, and, most importantly, why they continue to matter in a world racing toward informational complexity.

Part 2 of the book looks at people and culture in the law firm of 2030. With the alchemical interface of humans and machines considered, Maria Govis moves the discussion on to explore the key trends that are shaping the working environment from 2025 to 2030, including generational shifts in the workforce and technology-driven transformation. She covers how these trends influence workplace culture, leadership structures, wellbeing at work, talent attraction and retention, and the need for upskilling and reskilling. Crucially, this chapter presents personal strategies to help legal professionals build careers that align with their values, ensuring a meaningful and fulfilling work life in the new realms of legal practice post-2030.

In any business that is undergoing transformation, the needs of the next generation must be considered if the business is to survive and thrive. The law firm of 2030 isn't just about "PeopleLaw" or "BigLaw", legal engineers or data researchers – it is the sum of the people who choose to enter and remain in the profession and drive it forward.

David Laud then looks at how to manage generational diversity in the law firm in 2030 and beyond. Law firms are experiencing an increasing level of generation-related impacts. This phenomenon is driven by demographic changes, technological advancements, and evolving workplace expectations. Baby Boomers stepped away from work in the "Great Resignation" post the global COVID-19 pandemic and are still leaving in large numbers. Generation X has stepped up and often leads, with Millennials now forming the largest workforce segment, whilst Generation Z is redefining career growth and workplace culture in the ranks. Succession, recruitment, retention, adoption of technology, and differing attitudes toward work–life balance all present challenges for law firms and having a strategy to manage generational diversity is key. This chapter explores those challenges as well as providing case studies and practical examples illustrating how firms are adapting their leadership approach.

With the SRA-regulated sector growing considerably more slowly than the non-SRA regulated sector,[3] it is time to consider whether the value of training for a regulated environment is reduced. In the era of self-regulating contracts and autonomous judgments, will lawyers need the traditional skills of research, document interrogation, and drafting when all of these services are readily available to clients from legal services that fall outside the regulated sector? The question of whether professional regulation constrains innovation is outside the scope of this book, but it is a valid question for law firms to ponder for future innovation and growth and when they are considering longer term how they will structure themselves under new practice regimes.

With this in mind, Martin Martinoff looks at how we can build capabilities for the tech-driven law firm. Looking at how legal education is evolving to prepare the next generation of lawyers for a technology-driven landscape, he also reflects on the need for continuous professional development to be adaptable enough to keep pace with rapid technological change. Martin examines how leaders can respond to changing client demands, evolving regulations, and shifting workforce expectations, aspiring for collaboration in innovation, excellence, and impact.

Aoife Greally wraps up this section by looking at the socially responsible legal practice. High stress, long hours, and competitive work environments historically contribute to elevated rates of burnout, anxiety, and attrition in the industry as well as the "lost to law" practitioners unable to balance external commitments with these work expectations. Efforts to break away from these traditional norms – such as the rise of alternative employment and consultancy models – reflect a growing desire for healthier, more sustainable ways of working in the legal sector. These shifts create new opportunities for law firms to redefine their cultures and improve both individual experiences and organizational performance.

Part 3 looks above and below the line in finance and operations. With lawtech start-ups now firmly embedded within both PeopleLaw and BigLaw firms, and non-legal practitioners and venture capital investing in law, Chantal McNaught outlines how profitability and pricing intersect, and why it is of equal importance to consider law firm capacity and technology scale-up when setting pricing and measuring it for profitability. This chapter addresses pricing methodology, noting that whilst Susskind believes *"Hourly billing will fade away in the 2020s as the dominant charging mechanism"*[4] because *"clients prefer to know how much their legal bills will be"*, time-based billing will be usurped by more client-centered modes of billing. Then, as billing modes shift, profitability and measures of profit-per-equity-partner have to adapt. As hourly rates die, lock step will enter its demise.

The method of consumption of legal services as well as the growth of the marketplace has already been transformed, and changes will continue incrementally for the foreseeable future. As business practices require operational effectiveness and efficiencies to save money or to grow market share and profitability, all activities unrelated to the practice – the "business of law" – now fall on the shoulders of the legal operations professional. Richard Brzakala examines the growing importance of the legal operations professional as director in the theatre of law and how both law firms and corporate legal departments have embraced them as an invaluable and critical resource in their business strategy.

We conclude our book by looking at risks and opportunities for legal professionals. As geopolitics reshapes regulatory and policy agendas, so demand, risk, and opportunity shift and businesses must respond.

Jennifer Swallow looks at the changing landscape for ESG and the future for which law firms will need to prepare. She posits that ESG, as it was, is dead, and in its place we will see a reprioritization around growth and security, with new language, frameworks of governance, and expectations of society alongside those. In this chapter, Jenifer considers the significant implications this shift brings for clients and law firms. Continuing her exploration of "new" ESG obligations, in chapter 13 she extends our thinking on the ethics infrastructure of legal practices.

Wayne Hassay then takes us through law firm branding and consumer engagement. Looking at naming traditions and conventions, he considers how law firm names often make practitioners feel distant and impersonal, reinforcing the perception that lawyers are aloof and disconnected from the people they serve. His call to action is for the future law firm to develop an identity that reflects its values, resonates with emotions, and aligns with contemporary expectations of its consumers. He questions how quickly lawyers can pivot in their branding and respond to the challenges of non-lawyer competitors with focused branding strategies, consumer-focused engagement, artificial intelligence, and no regulation.

Everyone reading this book will recognize that data-driven decision-making by computer (rather than the amassed experience and learning of a legal team) is going to become more prevalent in law firms as we move through this decade into the next one. With this in mind, the power of predictive analytics in law firm strategy is discussed by Mori Kabiri, who explores how law firms need to leverage historical and real-time data now and in the future to forecast case outcomes, manage resources, and enhance client satisfaction. This chapter signposts the practical steps that can be taken to implement predictive analytics, including key KPIs and data governance principles, before looking at ethical considerations, such as managing bias in AI systems and ensuring privacy and security.

Kassi Burns, Olga V. Mack, and Adam Rouse advocate for legal professionals to adapt their practices, technologies, and thinking to thrive in the increasingly dynamic data environment for 2030. In their chapter, they explain the need for legal professionals to transition from a "picture" mindset (static, point-in-time data) to a "movie" approach (dynamic, continuously evolving information) and, using this powerful analogy, examine the limitations of "picture thinking" (contracts, precedents, data bundles frozen in time) when applied to modern legal work.

Brian Fox then looks at data use and misuse, outlining the growing imperative for organizations to gain comprehensive control over their data in an increasingly complex and regulated landscape. Brian maintains that technology is not the end but a conduit for data, and true value comes from transforming raw data into reliable information.

Jane Allen then invites us to consider the geopolitical environment in which law operates. Chapter 18 explores the evolving role of legal leaders amid an era of heightened geopolitical volatility, deregulation, and shifting global norms. As the Rule of Law erodes and brand perception becomes more intertwined with legal choices, leaders must reassess risk tolerance, support lawyer well-being, and engage more strategically with the C-suite. Looking ahead to 2030, the legal profession is poised to become more tech-enabled, multidisciplinary, and central to corporate leadership – better equipped to both endure disruption and restore order when the pendulum eventually swings back.

Finally, I return to present the concluding chapter, which collates responses from a range of businesses to the following five questions:

1. Which professional advisors do you instruct regularly?
2. What matters do you engage legal advisors for the most?
3. What do you dislike about engaging lawyers?
4. What do you consider the biggest challenge to your business in the next five years?
5. What do clients want from the law firm of 2030?

Drawing on the results of the poll and research from other sources to show what businesses and professionals engage lawyers for, the final chapter reevaluates the "coming storm" and disruption that is inevitable in the profession as the landscapes of business, politics, policy, environment, and human engagements change to meet the needs of clients as advisors and in the wider profession as a whole.

Using answers to these questions, the chapter summarizes how lawyers can adapt their practices, adopt new procedures, anticipate what clients want, and give clients what they *need* from the law firm of 2030.

References

1 Richard and Daniel Susskind, *The Future of the Professions: How Technology Will Transform the Work of Human Experts*, 2015, OUP.

2 Nuria Talayero-San-Miguel, Head of Digital Public Policy, Telefonica, www.telefonica.com/en/communication-room/blog/chatgpt-the-democratisation-of-written-language/

3 Technology And Innovation In Legal Services, www.sra.org.uk/globalassets/documents/sra/research/full-report-technology-and-innovation-in-legal-services.pdf

4 *Tomorrow's Lawyers: An Introduction to Your Future*, Richard Susskind, p. 181.

Part 1:
AI and Legal Technology

Chapter 2:
Navigating the ethics of AI and legal practice

By Harry Borovick, general counsel and AI governance officer, Luminance

Why humans matter

The nuances of human interaction remain central to the delivery of good legal services. Whether it is the ability to dig into questions or complex issues, the ability to understand context outside of the words spoken or the facts provided, or understanding the subtlety of human stress (typically in legal matters for all parties), AI systems are a long way off the capabilities of a competent or effective human.[1] Providing an experience equal to that of interacting with a human is unlikely by 2030, even if AI systems are rapidly approaching (and may exceed) the on-paper technical proficiency of many lawyers, particularly at scale. This will likely remain the case, even when digital avatars give end users or practitioners the *impression* of interacting with a human.

Applying AI in legal practice

The applications of artificial intelligence in law are varied and remain in the nascent stages of adoption. When considering the application of AI to legal practice:

> *"The reality, as most legal professionals know, is that the daily work of a litigator varies tremendously from that of a transactional lawyer. Even within similar areas of legal practice, the day-to-day can be diverse."*[2]

For example, within practice areas that can be broadly described as "transactional", the vast majority of work carried out by a commercial real estate lawyer involves distinct and specialized tasks compared to the work of a capital markets lawyer, an employment lawyer, or even a real estate finance lawyer. Within litigation, many of the tasks faced daily by a criminal defence lawyer in a small legal practice will be almost unrecognizable compared to those handled by a civil litigator in a large law firm, even if there are similarities regarding the high-level principles of the work.

That said, many tasks remain the same across legal practice areas. Lawyers still mostly work at desks, send emails, make notes, research case law and/or statutes, interpret guidance, analyse legal documents, and deliver an output of some kind to an end client. That end client may be a colleague within the same company or a third party.

Many responsibilities also remain the same. Therefore, for legal practitioners and law firms, when considering how to navigate the legal risks and ethical challenges of the future, it is worth starting with first principles and understanding that the primary duties of most lawyers remain as follows:[3]

- Duty to the courts;
- Duty to the client;
- Duty to the profession; and
- Duty to oneself and wider society.

For simplicity, this chapter will not extensively deliberate what it means to act with "good ethics" – this is far too subjective. Instead, we can use these four duties as the de facto ethical framework, and determine whether behaviour or actions are likely to be "ethical" based on how courts and regulators have previously spoken, published, acted or enforced on legal practitioners, as well as the providers and end-users of AI systems.[4]

Navigating ongoing ethical challenges

For legal practitioners developing, deploying, or offering AI systems to serve their clients, it may be hard to know where to begin in terms of practical guidance that can be applied across multiple legal practice areas. At the date of publication, this remains a major challenge – particularly where international elements affect either the location of the practitioners or their client base.

Looking to well-established regulatory guidance or internationally recognized risk management frameworks is a practical first step in setting up an AI risk management approach within a legal practice. Ethical issues should not be considered separately from AI risk management; rather, they should be at the core of balancing practical opportunities against tangible and intangible AI risks.

Beyond regulatory compliance, law firms should proactively consider ethical challenges posed by AI systems in legal practice, even in the absence of strict legal or regulatory requirements. A non-exhaustive list of key considerations includes:[5]

- *Transparency*. The potential need, or absence of need, for clients to understand when and how AI is being used in their cases or transactions.
- *Accessibility*. Whether clients are best served, and access to justice is best achieved, by removing human elements in provision of legal services (e.g. where the only affordable advice may be AI-generated) and how best to deliver that service safely.
- *Bias and fairness*. AI models trained on biased, insufficiently diverse, or excessively broad but unrefined legal data can drive, perpetuate, or cause disparities in legal outcomes.
- *Confidentiality and data security*. AI tools that interact with client data must adhere to appropriate security standards to ensure that privileged or sensitive information remains protected.
- *Human oversight*. While AI can enhance efficiency, final legal advice or decisions should always involve human judgment to maintain professional integrity, unless this materially conflicts with the other considerations and would cause detriment (notably if the human oversight pushes the cost of access to legal services out of reach).

Even recognizing that some ethical risks remain unknown within a legal practice is itself a positive step, as it demonstrates an understanding that the level of ethical risk is difficult to quantify. But, practically, legal practices need *somewhere* to begin – ideally, right now. So, what framework should be used?

The National Institute of Standards and Technology (NIST), part of the US Department of Commerce, produces one of the best-established frameworks for AI risk management and deployment. This framework[6] is designed to be relatively sector-agnostic and provides a strong foundation for legal professionals integrating AI into their practice. It is also well-suited, arguably better than any other internationally-respected framework, as a starting point for considering how to build, maintain, and enforce guardrails for ethical conduct by users and deployers of AI in legal practice. Between now and 2030, the AI Risk Management Framework is likely to be updated, and competing (or even, better) frameworks may become widely used. But for now, this chapter will lean on this framework to set out a four-part strategy for practically navigating the use and impact of AI on legal services.

Its four core components (Govern, Map, Measure, Manage) are heavily simplified below, but in each case it is critical to break these down into practical realities.

1. Govern

What it means

Building a culture within an organization that prioritizes risk management, with clear processes, policies, guidance, and reporting across the entire lifecycle of a company's AI usage, whether for internal or external purposes.

In practice

Committees: Establish AI ethics committees within firms to oversee AI applications.

Training and competence: Encouraging new or existing staff to take on roles of AI governance. Practically, they should do so when appropriately educated so firms paying/supporting staff to engage in academic or professional training courses and certifications is sensible. Many such courses already exist, and a whole new market of AI governance training is springing up. Reputable courses such as those provided by the IAPP,[7] various universities, or even tech companies can also be attractive to employees as a career-enhancer.

Policies: Develop AI governance policies that align with professional legal ethics. Many companies and legal practices have developed AI governance policies, or are considering doing so. It is critical to not create rigid policies in a vacuum that neglects to consider existing regional and international professional standards (e.g. SRA guidance in the UK, CIaRB guidance for arbitrators, ABA guidance in the US, etc.).

Transparency: Actively encourage client-facing and internal transparency in AI decision-making, particularly when AI tools assist in legal analysis or case prediction. Whether it is appropriate, or perhaps even legally required, to make transparent disclosures to third parties, such as the court or the counterparties, will be a matter of law and regulatory guidance that varies between jurisdictions (but definitely something to bear in mind).

2. Map

What it means

Conducting an initial assessment of AI usage, opportunities, and risks to effectively govern AI deployment. This is essential to build the initial understanding of how AI usage within a legal practice aligns with ethical and legal standards.

In practice

Legislation, regulation, and guidelines: Identifying applicable or relevant legal and ethical frameworks, e.g. human rights legislation such as the European Convention on Human Rights, bar/legal practice codes of conduct such as the SRA Code of Conduct, data privacy legislation such as the GDPR, customer-specific legal frameworks such as DORA (in terms of hard law), or guidance by regulators such as the FCA and SEC.

Appropriate applications: Identify legal tasks where AI can improve efficiency while managing ethical compliance.

- This should be done systematically (overlapping with the "manage" stage of the NIST AI Risk Management Framework below).
- Common applications of AI in legal practice include:[8]
  - Document review and management;
  - Contract negotiation;
  - Evidence analysis;
  - Case evaluation;
  - Drafting of legal documents (e.g. legal letters, filings, and opinions);
  - Legal research;
  - AML/KYC management;
  - Case management; and
  - Billing.
- In future, AI in legal practice may more commonly include many more complex applications such as:
  - Case success probability analysis;
  - Auto-negotiation of negotiations, settlements and disputes; and
  - Low-value/low-risk judicial operations and judgments.

Bias: Recognising the potential biases within AI systems and implementing measures to mitigate them. Quite simply, AI systems are built on data. Where that data is reliant on particular subsets of data, it may be more prone to bias. Bias can be good. It is important to recognise that bias isn't always bad (a bias can be trained into an AI system to give a desired or advantageous outcome, such as the way a contractual clause's risk should be considered).

The negative impacts of bias in AI systems is materially aggravated where the output creates a greater risk to individual rights and freedoms or systematically discriminates against individuals or groups of individuals.[9]

As an example – with respect to access to justice:

- A legal practice may be entirely meeting its duties (1-4 set out earlier in this chapter) if it uses an AI system to assess the probability of success in a case, and therefore whether it should take on that case, if it can be relatively confident that the AI system is not providing biased evaluation based on the individual characteristics of the potential client (such as ethnicity, religion, or other personal characteristics of this kind). The probability that the legal practice is acting within its duties is increased if it has properly "mapped" the risks of bias within the AI system's data or at least recognised the potential for bias. Practically, this can be as simple as having a clear understanding of where the training data comes from (e.g., is it generalist data or a specialist data set to minimise risk). Without mapping such risks, they cannot be addressed or mitigated.
- If the legal practice decides not to provide legal representation for an individual and that decision was based solely or materially on the AI system's determination, without any human mapping of, or mitigation of, biases by the system, it is unlikely that it is acting justly and within its duties.

Oversight: Assessing the extent of human oversight required to maintain legal integrity in AI-assisted tasks is critical to success in deploying AI systems in a manner that complies with overriding legal duties.[10] Once potential legal frameworks, use cases, and bias risks have been mapped, it is then appropriate to determine and plan for how much human oversight is productive to usage of AI in an ethical manner. For example, it is relatively easy to predict that full AI automation (rather than augmentation/acceleration and then verification by a human) of legal research and the provision of a legal opinion or court filing on that basis is not acceptable in the eyes of the courts, clients, the wider profession, or society as a whole.

There have been numerous cases of lawyers reprimanded for "use" of unverified legal cases that do not exist. While that kind of incident is likely to become less common due to increasing sophistication and accuracy of the underlying technology, it remains a strong illustration of what is expected of a good legal practice. Courts, clients, and the wider profession expect that when legal practitioners act for clients they are doing so while applying genuine professional expertise and appropriate human oversight. Therefore, mapping where that oversight is best applied (and how/when), is critical for successful usage of AI in legal practice – both practically and ethically.

3. Measure

What it means

Using both quantitative and qualitative metrics to assess AI performance, risks, successes, and failures. These metrics should tie back to initial mapping efforts to ensure effective ongoing governance.

In practice

NOTE: Some ethical or social considerations are very hard to audit, track, validate, measure, or cross-compare in a meaningful way. Even when somewhat possible, these are at fixed moments in time and can change rapidly. Most notably, AI systems (as with lots of technology) have a significant environmental and social impact. While that is potentially easier to consider at the "map" stage, it is very hard to say with certainty what the environmental cost to using AI tools may be – particularly at scale, when applied across a wide variety of tasks. This does not mean that environment impacts or other ethical issues (e.g. the sources of training data) should not be measured at all, but it is important to be realistic regarding the challenges of accurate assessment.

Audit and track: Legal practices should periodically audit AI performance and AI gains.

AI performance in tasks

This includes by comparison to other AI (or non-AI) systems that might be tested as benchmarks, and/or by comparison to human performance. It is important to recall that while AI outputs may vary, if they are acting with visible/auditable logic (rather than as a total black box) they are likely over time to be more consistently accurate than humans.

This means that AI systems *should* be less variable in that the differences that might be seen between humans due to experience (e.g. the quality of comprehension and presentation of legal advice between a paralegal and a partner). So, the benchmark against humans should not be on a few minor tasks, but rather, tasks at scale (ideally with a fair level of quantity).

Considering bias and fairness as part of the audit of the AI systems is critical to the assessment, rather than simply looking at qualitative data.[11] For example, when asking an AI system to analyse the probability of success in a case, it isn't just the accuracy of the probability that matters but whether it achieved that understanding through an unethical or unfair analysis of evidence or participants within the case data or its own training data.

AI gains

Measuring the value of an AI system is not simply limited to auditing the performance, accuracy, and biases. The tangible translation of the usefulness of the system to the legal practice should also be measured – i.e. hours saved, cost efficiencies, and qualitative feedback on employee and customer satisfaction.[12]

Calling back to the duty that legal practices have to their profession and society as a whole – happier legal practitioners (due to greater support at work, reduced stress, better work–life balance, access to higher quality work) and happier customers (whether due to potential reduced cost or greater speed) is good for everyone.

It is important to note that there is an ethical tightrope to walk – a legal practice that measures greater efficiencies isn't automatically driven or incentivised to share that knowledge with a client. The legal practice may simply wish to retain the cost and time efficiencies without passing this on to clients. Alternatively, it may wish to beat slower-moving legal practices (in terms of technology-based efficiencies) and offer more competitive or fixed pricing. Whether it is ethically necessary or "right" to disclose such efficiencies and advantages is subjective, but what is unequivocal is that customers inevitably and continuously expect increasing quality of service delivery and the cheapest reasonable/available pricing, and there will always be a level of pushback on this by private legal practitioners. In future, we may see regulators insisting that AI-based tech in the delivery of legal services is required or recommended, but that would seem unlikely. A lawyer today does not expect to have to disclose to their clients that they gained efficiency and saved cost/time by using a word processor instead of a pen and paper.

Validate: Implementing feedback loops where human lawyers check AI-generated outputs is essential. Whereas "Audit" refers to the effects of the technology as a whole, validation refers to granular output quality and accuracy. There is a significant potential landmine for legal practitioners who may increasingly rely on AI-generated outputs in the provision of legal advice and services.

This is a core reason why "augmentation" rather than "automation" by AI makes far more sense for the vast majority of legal services delivered to clients. This will become particularly complex as "agentic" AI becomes more common (AI systems capable of autonomously carrying multiple tasks or solving multiple related problems without the need for human intervention or instruction at each step). As the technology continues to develop at incredible pace, the capabilities and accuracies of AI systems will improve and it is inevitable that greater reliance on AI systems grows until it is a relative norm for many tasks (though, likely not all).

The ethical unknown is the extent to which each legal practice, or legal regulator, will be able to feel comfortable relying on autonomous and semi-autonomous systems in delivery to clients, where the legal practice would still remain on the hook for the deliverables, outcomes, and potential consequences.

Cross-compare: Once audit and validation are well-established within a legal practice, the positive consequence is the ability to then engage in far more detailed, rigorous, and accurate cross-comparison of AI systems, as well as their abilities to be effectively used by humans.

Practically, this usually means engaging in periodic RFPs (tender processes) open to relevant technology providers, where the questions posed can be meaningful and tailored to that legal practice's needs. It can also mean easy filtering of irrelevant technology, providers with poor reputations, or simply things that are too expensive for a tangible return on investment.

4. Manage

What it means

Allocating and adapting resources and responsibilities to continuously monitor and adjust AI governance strategies. Effective AI governance, particularly when social and ethical challenges are dynamic, requires ongoing training, policy updates, and accountability frameworks to maintain the adoption or use of AI systems in a manner that is beneficial, ethical, and legally compliant.

In practice

Policies: As discussed when considering the "govern" pillar of the NIST AI Risk Management Framework, a legal practice cannot expect its employees to always know what is right/wrong or create ethical and legal risk, if this isn't codified. Creating and regularly updating AI policies is crucial. AI governance and ethical risk management policies should evolve alongside emerging legal and technological developments. Policies should cover internal guidelines for the use of AI systems. However, they should also be clear and distinguish where risks are greater, or ethical considerations are more complex, when used for the benefit or detriment of third parties. They should be simple to understand in plain English, e.g. "Do not use AI systems of any kind that have not been approved by the internal IT team – list of approved systems and tools can be found here: [...]".

Policies should, most of all, be concise. Long policies = unread policies. However, it is also sensible to provide more detailed and specific policies and guidance for targeted use cases. What is an appropriate level of detail for use-case specific policies will depend on the sophistication of the intended users. Importantly, such policies should be drafted for the least sophisticated potential user, rather than the most sophisticated, to maximise cross-practice adherence.

Training systems: Legal practices should deliver or procure periodic and ongoing training in AI ethics, data security, and regulatory compliance. Access to training should be available, or even mandatory, to all employees of legal practices. However, it is appropriate or even preferable that the training is tailored to the different practical needs and operational risks related to specific employees.[13] Ideally, this should also connect to relevant policies that have been implemented – for example, with respect to HR teams that may only provide an internal-facing service within a law firm. They can still compromise a firm's reputation by using AI systems in a manner that would breach internal policies, the law, or may be perceived as unethical (automated, biased, or discriminatory candidate selection for promotion or new jobs).

To see real engagement from employees, it is advisable for legal practices to invest in AI certification programs and workshops such as those mentioned when considering the "govern" pillar of the NIST AI Risk Management Framework. This not only means that employees should be up to date on responsible, ethical, and legal use of AI systems, but will have a certification to publicly demonstrate that understanding. This type of visible certification can significantly increase attendance and engagement for employees by giving them a semi-permanent/permanent token that may be desirable on their CV.

Accountability: Clear accountability mechanisms should be in place to address AI-generated errors. Law firms must define who is responsible when an AI tool produces incorrect legal advice or biased outcomes, ensuring that human oversight remains central to decision-making.[14]

Conclusion

As law firms integrate AI into their practice, ethical considerations should be at the forefront of decision-making. AI is already able to improve efficiency, reduce costs, and enhance legal research, but it also introduces risks related to bias, transparency, and accountability. This is a democratised effect – benefiting one-person legal practices and law firms with thousands of lawyers.

Without reasonable ethical oversight, AI-powered systems in legal services may inadvertently reinforce systemic biases, break client confidentiality, or produce inaccurate conclusions. Therefore, legal practices must be proactive in selecting AI applications that align with both legal and ethical standards. This involves not only implementing AI responsibly but also educating legal professionals on the potential ethical pitfalls associated with its use. Fostering a culture of ethical awareness, firms can better position themselves to navigate the complex intersection of law and technology.

The NIST AI Risk Management Framework is just one ethical and legal framework that can be applied. Such frameworks provide legal practices and the professionals within them with guardrails for assessing AI-related risks and establishing practical mechanisms that uphold professional integrity.

A systematic approach helps legal practices to mitigate ethical concerns while leveraging AI to support their work. However, ethics is not just about regulatory compliance – it is about preserving trust and fairness in the legal system and the legal profession. Legal services rely on confidence that legal processes are conducted with integrity, irrespective of the technology involved. As AI adoption grows and the technology continues to evolve in capability, legal practitioners must remain pragmatic but vigilant in balancing innovation with their fundamental responsibilities to the courts, their clients, the legal profession, and society as a whole.

References

1 Montresor Legal General Counselling (2025). *AI and the Law with Harry Borovick.* www.youtube.com/watch?v=wBiPXoJXhwc

2 Schmelzer, R. (2024). Your Next Lawyer Might Be A Bot: Game-Changing AI Trends In Law. www.forbes.com/sites/ronschmelzer/2024/12/26/your-next-lawyer-might-be-a-bot-game-changing-ai-trends-in-law

3 Solicitors Regulation Authority (2019). *SRA Code of Conduct for Solicitors, RELs and RFLs.* www.sra.org.uk/solicitors/standards-regulations/code-conduct-solicitors

4 Merken, S. (2024). *Lawyers using AI must heed ethics rules, ABA says in first formal guidance.* www.reuters.com/legal/legalindustry/lawyers-using-ai-must-heed-ethics-rules-aba-says-first-formal-guidance-2024-07-29

5 GOV.UK (2019). *Understanding artificial intelligence ethics and safety.* www.gov.uk/guidance/understanding-artificial-intelligence-ethics-and-safety

6 NIST AI RMF Playbook (2022). www.nist.gov/itl/ai-risk-management-framework/nist-ai-rmf-playbook

7 Iapp.org (2025). *Artificial Intelligence Governance Professional.* http://iapp.org/certify/aigp/

8 Fredrik Filipsson (2024). Top 15 Real-Life Use Cases For AI In the Legal Industry. https://redresscompliance.com/top-15-real-life-use-cases-for-ai-in-the-legal-industry

9 Melchionna, L. C. (2023). *Bias and Fairness in Artificial Intelligence – New York State Bar Association.* https://nysba.org/bias-and-fairness-in-artificial-intelligence/?srsltid=AfmBOor712r-o4jBybQWQZx6-jlCZ6kzbLeNLzk1pX4CIgC41CBTqkME

10 LexisNexis (2018). *Generative AI: The importance of human oversight in the law.* www.lexisnexis.co.uk/insights/generative-ai-the-importance-of-human-oversight-in-the-law/index.html

11 Müller, V. C. (2020). *Ethics of Artificial Intelligence and Robotics.* Summer 2020 ed. Stanford Encyclopedia of Philosophy. https://plato.stanford.edu/entries/ethics-ai

12 sdi (2024). *Five Ethical Issues of AI in the Modern Workplace.* www.servicedeskinstitute.com/resources/five-ethical-issues-of-ai-in-the-modern-workplace

13 White, S. (2022). *How AI is reshaping the future of legal practice.* www.lawsociety.org.uk/topics/ai-and-lawtech/partner-content/how-ai-is-reshaping-the-future-of-legal-practice

14 Gajjar, D. and Brione, P. (2024). *Artificial intelligence: ethics, governance and regulation.* https://post.parliament.uk/artificial-intelligence-ethics-governance-and-regulation

Chapter 3:
Redefining legal practice – from adaptive intelligence to autonomous operations

By Jelena Schidzig, Legal Quant

Introduction

"What if it were properly arranged?"[1]

While ancient roots of law stretch back millennia, modern legal systems have been profoundly shaped by Enlightenment principles that promised a world where reason would triumph over arbitrary power. These rational foundations, layered upon centuries of legal tradition, created systems designed to discover truth through structured argument and logical analysis. Today, as artificial intelligence reshapes the boundaries of what's possible, legal practitioners find themselves in a position of remarkable irony – clinging to traditions of human judgment while simultaneously demonstrating why those traditions may be insufficient.

Conservative disposition implies a certain ambivalence to change; a profession founded on principles of reason has grown increasingly detached from underlying mathematical and scientific foundations that make rational analysis of complex systems possible. Furthermore, the regulatory domain, charged with the oversight of inherently probabilistic market mechanisms characterized by correlative, rather than strictly deterministic, causal relationships, maintains a persistent adherence to deterministic frameworks in the evaluation of artificial intelligence. This ill-suited application is deemed to be fundamentally deficient in its capacity to adequately apprehend the intrinsic probabilistic nature of artificial intelligence, thereby imposing a material constraint upon the comprehensive assessment of its capabilities and limitations.

This chapter does not merely document how technology is changing legal practice. Rather, it explores a fundamental disconnect. Think of it – the path of traditional legal reasoning was conceptualized and thought over decades versus the mathematical realities of the systems law aims to govern. Beyond the superficial debates about whether AI will replace lawyers lies a more profound question: *What happens when the tools we create understand the complexity of legal relationships better than we do?*

Through examination of emerging autonomous systems built on Transformer architectures, multi-agent frameworks, and purpose-built legal infrastructure, this chapter reveals possibilities that transcend the limitations of current legal technology discourse. These aren't simply faster tools for traditional tasks but potentially new forms of legal intelligence – systems capable of "understanding" not just legal content but professional context, ethical boundaries, and the complex relationships between legal concepts across jurisdictions and practice areas.

What follows is not a celebration of technology for its own sake, nor a defense of tradition against innovation. Instead, it is an invitation to reflect on what legal practice could become when liberated from limitations mistaken for essential characteristics – and a warning about what happens when a profession founded on reason refuses to follow evidence to its logical conclusion.

The current landscape

From decision trees to Gen AI

It is quite interesting how the narrative of technology acceptance in legal practice has evolved during the past decade. The same industry calling the early advocates of machine learning application in the legal domain "legal rebels" based their resistance on principles that were revolutionary when legal systems were established. The irony becomes even more apparent as we observe current generic AI solutions being adopted through productivity tools, creating risks for the very professional standards these tools claim to uphold.

The foundations of our justice systems were built on foundations of reason and enlightenment, guided by idea of a system where truth would prevail through rational thought. It is not quite compelling as to the "how's and why's" the "legal mind" trained on causality principles is in denial of the fundamental science on which causality is based – particularly when the legal practice itself grapples with complex, probabilistic causation in market regulation. The disconnect becomes even more profound when we consider law's essential purpose of market regulation, where indirect causation and systemic effects create probability spaces that mirror the very mathematical foundations of machine learning. How can legal education and practice become so detached from understanding these market dynamics and correlations – the very elements law was designed to regulate, and which inherently operate in probability spaces rather than simple deterministic relationships?

This disconnect is further exemplified in current approaches to AI literacy in legal education. While firms rush to provide prompt engineering workshops and tool-specific training, these superficial adaptations fail to address the fundamental need for understanding AI's scientific and mathematical foundations. Traditional legal curricula, focused on case law and procedural knowledge, leave practitioners ill-equipped to evaluate the capabilities and limitations of AI systems. This creates a paradox where legal professionals are expected to use AI tools competently while lacking the foundational knowledge to assess their appropriateness and implications for legal practice.

The consequences of this knowledge gap manifest clearly in the adoption and implementation of predictive analytics tools. While statistical analysis could enhance legal decision-making, current implementations often reduce complex legal evaluations to simplistic metrics without providing a connected systemic approach. Systems that equate contract values with case values reveal this fundamental misunderstanding of legal assessment complexity. True case valuation demands integration of case merits, procedural considerations, and evolving legal interpretations – yet current predictive tools present these as isolated features without providing systemic perspective. This fragmented approach, stemming from insufficient understanding of both AI capabilities and legal complexity, not only undermines informed client decision-making but also raises fundamental questions about meeting professional standards of competence.

The current legal technology landscape has made significant strides in transforming traditional practice. The integration of LLMs into document management, case tracking, and predictive analytics has markedly improved operational efficiency. These advancements have helped firms reduce billable hours, establish more accurate cost benchmarks, and develop better-informed contingency planning. The industry's growing acceptance of these tools marks an important milestone in the evolution of legal practice.

Notably, while these improvements demonstrate the profession's capacity to embrace technological change, they also highlight areas requiring deeper integration. Current tools, while valuable for specific tasks, still rely heavily on human intervention and prompt-based interactions. This creates bottlenecks and limits the potential for true automation and a systemic approach.

These limitations become particularly critical when considering security implications of legal technology adoption.

Security considerations in legal technology adoption

> *"With the ever-evolving use of technology by lawyers and courts, lawyers must be vigilant in complying with the Rules of Professional Conduct to ensure that lawyers are adhering to their ethical responsibilities and that clients are protected."*[2]

While the legal profession rightfully prioritizes data protection, some proposed solutions may inadvertently create more risks than they resolve. Consider the recent promotion of facial recognition systems for securing legal documents.[3] This approach, while appearing innovative on the surface, raises significant considerations about both security effectiveness and professional obligations.

Biometric data, by its nature, represents identifying information rather than a security mechanism. Using facial recognition for document protection is akin to displaying one's credentials publicly while hoping they remain secure. The immutable nature of biometric data presents unique challenges – unlike compromised passwords or security keys that can be replaced, biological characteristics cannot be changed if breached. While biometric security presents one set of challenges, the increasing adoption of AI-powered tools introduces equally complex security considerations, particularly in how legal information is accessed and processed.

The current deployment of copilots[4] and generic AI tools in legal practice presents serious security and confidentiality risks. While these tools promise improved efficiency through integration with common productivity software, this convenience masks significant data exposure concerns. The use of generic copilots in office applications essentially creates a potential data harvesting channel where sensitive legal information processed through everyday document creation and editing could be captured and utilized beyond the firm's control. This is particularly concerning as such tools, while integrated into standard productivity software, often prioritize broad functionality over domain-specific security requirements. Without security architecture specifically designed for legal information handling, these generic implementations can create systemic vulnerabilities in how sensitive legal data is processed and managed.

Interactions with generic LLM models, particularly those integrated into standard productivity tools, pose significant risks to data security and confidentiality. While these risks can be mitigated through proper system design and implementation to prevent the scraping of user content and interactions, most current commercial offerings don't provide such guarantees. The lack of transparency about how these interactions are stored, processed, and potentially reused makes it essential for legal professionals to carefully evaluate AI tool deployment and consider solutions specifically designed to protect client confidentiality.

These fundamental security risks extend beyond data collection concerns into the realm of information handling and segregation. Current generic tools lack the capability to properly maintain legal document hierarchies, respect jurisdictional boundaries, and handle precedential relationships – creating additional vulnerabilities where sensitive information might be inappropriately mixed or exposed across different matters, clients, and jurisdictions. This structural limitation magnifies the potential security impact of any data exposure.

Retrieval Augmented Generation (RAG) represents an advancement in AI technology that aims to improve accuracy by grounding language model responses in verified documents and data sources. In legal contexts, this technology requires sophisticated understanding of how legal knowledge is structured and accessed. Legal information follows specific hierarchical relationships, with complex interactions between precedents, jurisdictions, and temporal relevance that generic implementations often fail to address. However, these risks can be significantly mitigated through deterministic quote retrieval systems that verify source material after LLM processing.

By implementing unique reference tracking and structured quote verification, organizations can maintain precise control over information flow and ensure source accuracy while protecting sensitive data. Such implementation requires rigorous security protocols including encrypted data storage with granular access controls, secure chunking mechanisms that preserve document context, strict reference management that maintains client confidentiality boundaries, and verifiable audit trails for all information retrievals. Unlike simple prompt anonymization, which provides insufficient protection for sensitive legal information, this deterministic approach ensures that data remains protected throughout the entire processing chain while maintaining its essential context and relationships.

These technical challenges underscore the critical importance of proper

AI governance frameworks. The ISO 42001 standard for AI management systems provides comprehensive guidance for addressing security and operational risks in legal technology adoption. It emphasizes systematic assessment of AI interactions with sensitive data, establishing clear protocols for data access and retrieval, and maintaining documented compliance with professional obligations. The framework becomes particularly crucial when implementing RAG systems and managing copilot interactions with legal documents, as it requires continuous monitoring of AI system behaviors and regular evaluation of their outputs. Yet many current "best practices" in legal tech adoption fall short of these standards, often prioritizing convenience over comprehensive security.

Modern smart card technology, combined with established cryptographic methods, offers a practical approach that aligns with these governance requirements while addressing fundamental security needs. Systems using HMAC-based or time-based one-time passwords (HOTP/TOTP) provide robust security through proven cryptographic algorithms. These methods generate unpredictable tokens without requiring storage of sensitive personal or behavioral data, can function offline, and have undergone extensive security auditing.

Deployment of AI agents as an additional layer on top of these cryptographic foundations represents a more sophisticated approach to security. These agents can detect unusual access patterns, potential security breaches, and anomalous system behavior while maintaining strict privacy protocols. Instead of relying on biometric data for authentication, these AI agents focus on system-level interactions, providing security through comprehensive oversight rather than vulnerable personal identifiers.

This points toward a more comprehensive vision of legal technology integration – one where security isn't an add-on feature but an inherent characteristic of the system design. The legal profession's unique combination of confidentiality requirements, ethical obligations, and complex information hierarchies demands this integrated approach. Such a framework not only aligns with professional obligations and established security principles but also creates a foundation for safe and effective technological advancement in legal practice. This foundational security role of AI agents indicates their broader potential for enhancing legal operations. As we will explore in detail, these agents can represent not just a security layer but a fundamental shift in how legal operations can be managed autonomously while maintaining professional standards and ethical obligations.

The innovation

The foundation for autonomous legal agents builds on significant advances in AI architecture. The evolution from traditional Transformer neural networks to Transformer-2 architectures represents a crucial step toward true autonomous operation. While original Transformers[5] architectures have enabled sophisticated language understanding through attention mechanisms, the novel "Transformer-2" architectures introduce more complex reasoning capabilities through enhanced pattern recognition and relationship modeling – capabilities particularly relevant for legal analysis and decision-making.

Further architectural advancement comes through diffusion transformer models, which enable sophisticated multi-modal processing capabilities. These architectures can simultaneously handle text, image, audio, and motion data, creating possibilities for more natural and comprehensive system interactions. As demonstrated by frameworks like OmniHuman,[6] these models can generate realistic human interactions from minimal input data, opening new possibilities for professional service delivery.

Models built using Titan neural network architecture[7] further advance these capabilities by implementing sophisticated meta-learning frameworks that enable systems to adapt and improve their performance across different legal contexts. This architectural advancement is particularly significant for legal applications, as it allows systems to maintain consistency across different jurisdictions and practice areas while adapting to the specific requirements of each situation.

The self-adaptive Transformer2 (squared)[8] model architecture enables the model to dynamically adjust to different tasks without extensive training by deploying task-specific expert vectors that scale singular values of vector metrics, generating "expert" vectors that are applied based on query type to generate domain-specific answers, utilizing single value decomposition of weight between the components. This approach overcomes the existing limitations of resource intensive "one-shot" fine tuning in traditional LLM architectures, enabling efficient model specializations across different tasks and domains. The application of specialized Transformer2 architecture would be particularly valuable in the legal domain, as it enables different models of thinking required in legal work that could benefit from task-specific expert vectors.

These technical foundations would enable AI agents to move beyond simple pattern matching to understand complex legal relationships and causality chains. The combination of enhanced reasoning capabilities with specialized legal knowledge creates systems that can operate autonomously while maintaining professional standards.

Agents

The system features autonomous AI agents capable of direct system interaction and operation, eliminating the traditional prompt-response loop through a conceptualized adaptive intelligence layer that goes beyond standard API integrations, as demonstrated by existing automated legal service delivery systems that already serve various stakeholders including practitioners and judiciary.[9] Through understanding individual user profiles and workflows, these agents develop sophisticated benchmarks that reflect realistic scenarios, improving the generalization and robustness of algorithms in domain-specific legal operations.

The evolution of agentic AI has progressed from single-modality applications – like coding copilots, document analysis systems, and legal research assistants – to more advanced models capable of learning across multiple modalities of data. Advanced foundation models built with rigorous safety protocols, combined with deep learning architectures like CipherPrune,[10] create an environment capable of addressing the industry's core technical challenges around data anonymization for custom model generation, providing the confidentiality preservation while ensuring predictable and controllable agent behavior, implementing robust security protocols, and aligning computational complexity with learning algorithms for specific legal operations, delivering AI driven automation.

Agent operations in the legal domain

The agents' ability to maintain professional standards stems from built-in governance frameworks that guide their operations. Rather than following simple rule-based protocols, they understand and apply ethical guidelines and professional requirements as integral parts of their decision-making processes. This ensures compliance while enabling adaptive responses to complex legal situations.

To provide transparency in their operations, these agents can demonstrate their reasoning through a "chain of thought" (CoT) process – similar to how a lawyer might explain their legal reasoning in a brief. While CoT offers valuable insights into the decision-making process, recent research by Anthropic[11] on foundation reasoning model Claude 3.7 indicates that CoT monitoring alone has demonstrated limitations in detecting unintended behaviors or faithfully representing all aspects of model reasoning. Therefore, it is advisable for legal agents to have incorporated complementary approaches alongside CoT, such as:

1. External knowledge validation, where retrieved information is independently validated.
2. Consistency checks that compare conclusions across different reasoning paths.
3. Domain-specific reasoning tests designed for legal contexts.
4. Explicit documentation of retrieved sources and their influence on conclusions.

This multi-faceted approach to transparency creates robust verification, making each step of their decision-making explicit, especially in scenarios involving ethical considerations, creating clear, verifiable paths that demonstrate alignment with professional standards. Notably, the transparency established through model architecture would allow legal professionals to understand and validate the agents' decisions while maintaining efficient autonomous operation.

Collaborative operations

Within the system, agents could interact through stable tensor connections that enable real-time information exchange while preserving complex legal relationships. This architectural approach allows agents to maintain jurisdictional boundaries and ethical walls while sharing necessary information for coordinated operations. The graph-based structure naturally maps to legal hierarchies and precedential relationships, enabling sophisticated collaboration without compromising professional obligations, as demonstrated by emerging graph neural network approaches to legal risk assessment.[12]

This hybrid approach could enable agents to maintain sophisticated awareness of legal context while exchanging information in real-time. For example, when analyzing contract portfolios, the system could simultaneously process the contractual language while understanding relationships between different agreements, jurisdictional requirements, and compliance obligations. This architecture could offer organizations a way to handle legal information that respects both the content of documents and their place within the entity-specific legal framework, while maintaining necessary ethical walls and confidentiality boundaries.[13]

The technological foundation of this transformation extends beyond traditional AI architectures. By incorporating advanced human interface frameworks like OmniHuman, which generates realistic human interactions from single reference images combined with motion and audio signals, these systems can provide sophisticated engagement capabilities that match or exceed current professional interaction standards.

This multi-modal approach enables law firms to scale their expertise delivery while maintaining high-quality client interactions. Unlike domain-related chatbots or basic automation tools, these systems can present complex legal analysis through natural, professional interactions that adapt to various contexts – from boardroom presentations to client consultations. The ability to generate consistent, high-quality, human-like interactions from minimal reference data means firms can maintain their professional presence across multiple channels and jurisdictions while ensuring consistent service quality.

When combined with our multi-agent architecture, this creates a comprehensive system in which specialized legal expertise is delivered through sophisticated, natural interactions. Law firms can extend their reach and capabilities without compromising their professional standards or client experience. This isn't about replacing lawyers but rather augmenting their practice with tools that can handle everything from routine consultations to complex advisory work, all while maintaining the professional presence clients expect.

The implications for legal operations are significant. Firms can offer continuous availability for initial onboarding and consultations, provide consistent service across jurisdictions, and scale their expertise without the traditional limitations of human resource availability. This transforms not just how legal services are delivered but also how firms can grow and compete in a global market.

Similarly, the system's capabilities could be extended to Alternative Dispute Resolution and depositions. In these contexts, the system could process real-time information while mapping relationships to existing evidence and prior statements. This could help identify potential litigation status, referencing settlement options in ADR by understanding both explicit positions and underlying patterns, or assisting during depositions by connecting testimony to documentary evidence in real-time. Throughout these processes, the system would maintain appropriate confidentiality boundaries while providing legal professionals with deeper contextual insights.

The potential applications could further extend existing models currently serving practice areas such as regulatory compliance monitoring, intellectual property portfolio management, corporate governance, M&A due diligence, and global supply chain management, with particular emphasis on ESG governance requirements. The system could help organizations maintain visibility across their supply chain operations while ensuring alignment with ESG standards and reporting obligations, connecting contractual commitments with actual governance practices and compliance requirements across different jurisdictions. These exemplify just some of the potential applications where the combination of document processing and relationship understanding could provide value in legal operations.

Autonomous systems

PaaS infrastructure for legal industry autonomy

The true innovation of autonomous platforms such as the PaaS (Platform as a Service) approach extends beyond individual agent capabilities to create a comprehensive, closed infrastructure specifically for the legal industry. Rather than having law firms adapt to generic technology solutions or navigate an ever-growing maze of "innovations", this system would empower the industry to leverage technological evolution moving resiliently forward.

Having a controlled environment allows specialized agents to not only perform legal tasks but actively analyze operational needs and develop tailored solutions. These agents can review existing operations, identify efficiency gaps, and autonomously code the specific APIs and integrations that firms actually need, replacing the requirement for firms to piece together disparate tools or invest resources in learning complex prompt engineering.

This approach fundamentally shifts the relationship between legal practice and technology. Instead of law firms constantly racing to adapt to new tools, the infrastructure adapts to serve the precise needs of legal operations. By providing a closed, purpose-built environment, this will enable the legal industry to leverage technology on its own terms rather than being driven by external tech developments.

This infrastructure approach acknowledges a crucial reality – while the legal industry has belatedly embraced technology, the current rush to adopt various tools without fundamental understanding creates more problems than solutions. Rather than expecting legal professionals to become technology experts or prompt engineers – skills far removed from their core expertise – this PaaS environment would allow them to focus on what they do best: practicing law.

The system bridges the gap created by traditional legal education's lag behind technological advancement. Instead of requiring lawyers to navigate complex technical implementations, it would provide an autonomous infrastructure that adapts to their needs while maintaining professional standards. The sector-specific autonomous systems represent a practical solution to the industry's delayed engagement with technology, offering a path forward that improves rather than disrupts legal practice. This approach also democratizes access to advanced legal AI to smaller firms and solo practitioners that could not afford to build their own proprietary systems that would meet the required level of confidentiality.

However, this technological solution alone cannot address the fundamental challenges facing the legal profession. The industry requires a deeper transformation in professional education and training, one that embraces multidisciplinary approaches and acknowledges the mathematical and scientific foundations underlying modern legal practice.

The current regulatory landscape further complicates this evolution. Large technology vendors, through lobbying efforts, exert disproportionate influence on the legal sector through installed "expert vehicles" practices in reminiscence with universal legal principles and regulatory frameworks established across Western jurisdictions. This creates a disconnect between technological innovation and legal oversight, exacerbated by the preference for political connections over technical expertise in both legal and technology sectors.

While AI has already begun transforming traditional legal tasks like document drafting, research, and predictive analysis, its influence extends increasingly into advisory services. The automation of certain types of proceedings and claims processing could significantly reduce court backlogs and costs, while preserving the attorney's role in complex litigation.

This evolution highlights a critical gap in current legal education. Most newly licensed attorneys lack preparation for handling cases that require understanding of both legal principles and market dynamics. A hybrid approach to legal education, combining AI-assisted learning with practical market analysis and cross-disciplinary understanding, could transform this landscape. This would shift focus from theoretical repetition to developing critical analytical skills through interactive learning experiences and real-world applications.

The future legal education must bridge the gap between traditional legal theory and practical market dynamics to prepare attorneys who can effectively navigate through modern legal challenges.

Impact on legal operations

Transforming legal service delivery, this sector-specific closed infrastructure would enable the standalone automated processing and expert guidance to be integrated with existing e-filing systems and court communications. The automated development of custom domain related APIs disseminated though sector-own scalable platform infrastructure for legal expertise delivery would provide in-house departments with continuous access to domain-specific counsel at fixed costs.

The autonomous nature extends beyond basic automation to intelligent orchestration of legal processes, including practice areas such as alternative dispute resolution and mediation. This proactive approach could also help in-house counsels to prevent costly litigation through early access to expert guidance, while maintaining professional standards through systematic oversight.

Such infrastructure also enables law firms to develop customized service delivery platforms that scale their expertise efficiently. Access to consistent, accessible legal guidance helps prevent disputes and maintain compliance across industries while keeping costs predictable. This systematic approach to legal service delivery will transform how firms operate and interact with clients.

This innovation will fundamentally change how legal operations are managed. By eliminating manual configuration and integration requirements, organizations can focus on strategic legal work rather than technical implementation. The system's ability to self-manage and optimize operations reduces overhead while increasing reliability and efficiency.

The integration of self-adaptive architectures, complete feedback loops, and domain-specific expertise creates possibilities that go far beyond what current solution offerings can accomplish. The autonomous nature of the system extends beyond basic automation, encompassing intelligent decision-making and resource allocation. This technological advancement will also lead toward more efficient service delivery and better utilization of legal resources that varies significantly between cases and practices across jurisdictions and organizations.

The future legal professional

The legal profession stands at a transformative crossroads, though many practitioners remain unaware of its magnitude. Recent high court decisions[14] highlighting missed deadlines and compromised client interests due to digital incompetence reveal just how wide the gap has grown between technological capability and professional practice. This disconnect is not merely a matter of adaptation but points to a fundamental question of what it means to be a legal professional.

The emergence of autonomous legal operations systems doesn't signal the obsolescence of human lawyers but rather demands a profound evolution in their role. Tomorrow's legal professional will transition from being primarily a technical executor of legal processes to becoming a strategic architect of legal solutions. This shift requires not just new skills but a new mindset altogether.

As autonomous systems increasingly handle document management, research, drafting, and analysis, legal professionals will develop entirely new competencies. The most successful will combine traditional legal expertise with strategic vision, emotional intelligence, and system orchestration capabilities. They will focus their human judgment on novel legal challenges, complex negotiations, and precedent-setting cases that require creative approaches beyond algorithmic resolution.

This evolution will demand a restructuring of traditional legal career paths. The profession may see the emergence of specialized roles combining legal expertise with technical and business acumen – legal system architects who design frameworks for AI-assisted operations, legal data strategists who understand both legal principles and information architecture, and human-machine collaboration specialists who excel at augmenting autonomous systems with human insight. The conventional progression through document review and routine advisory work will give way to more direct engagement with complex problem-solving and strategic counsel.

For legal education, this transformation necessitates more than adding isolated technology courses to traditional curricula. Future lawyers will need multidisciplinary training that connects legal principles with their mathematical and scientific foundations. They must understand not just what the law says but how complex systems, probability spaces, and causal networks function within the environments law seeks to regulate. This educational shift may create new specializations that combine legal knowledge with complementary fields like data science, behavioral economics, and complex systems theory.

Mid-sized and specialized firms may discover new competitive advantages as technology democratizes access to sophisticated legal tools, reducing the scale advantages previously held by larger firms. This could foster more diverse practice models focused on specific industries or legal challenges where human creativity and judgment remain essential differentiators.

The profession will also need to reconsider its value proposition and billing models. When autonomous systems can provide routine legal services efficiently, the traditional hourly billing model becomes increasingly difficult to justify. Legal professionals will demonstrate value through their ability to handle complex, multifaceted challenges requiring human judgment, creative problem-solving, and strategic thinking rather than through time spent on routine tasks.

The most successful legal professionals in this new landscape won't be those who grudgingly adapt to technological change but those who enthusiastically embrace it as an extension of their capabilities. They will recognize autonomous systems not as competitors but as powerful tools that allow them to focus on the most intellectually challenging and socially meaningful aspects of legal practice.

This transformation will elevate rather than diminish the importance of legal expertise, creating a profession where lawyers operate more like strategic advisors and system architects than technical processors of legal information. By embracing this evolution, the legal profession can increase its impact, handling more complex challenges and serving broader populations while maintaining the highest standards of professional service.

Beyond adaptation – evolutionary acceleration

While the legal profession debates whether and how to adapt to technological change, a more fundamental transformation has already begun. This isn't merely about better tools for familiar tasks but an evolutionary acceleration that could redefine what it means to provide legal services – and what it means to be a legal professional.

The evidence of this acceleration surrounds us but often goes unrecognized. While many practitioners struggle with basic digital competence, system architects are building autonomous legal agents capable of sophisticated pattern recognition across diverse legal domains and jurisdictions. While law schools add isolated "legal tech" courses to traditional curricula, Transformer-2 architectures are developing capabilities that raise new questions about what parts of legal reasoning are uniquely human.

This evolutionary acceleration will not be evenly distributed. In the short term, it will create unprecedented advantages for early adopters while rendering traditional practice models increasingly unsustainable. In the medium term, it will likely drive consolidation in routine legal services while creating new opportunities for specialized expertise that augments rather than competes with artificial intelligence. Over longer timeframes, it may reshape our understanding of legal education, professional licensing, and even the meaning of legal advice.

For individual practitioners, the implications are both liberating and demanding. Liberation comes from offloading routine tasks to systems that can perform them with greater accuracy and consistency. The demands come in developing new skills focused on system orchestration, cross-disciplinary integration, and judgment in cases where autonomous systems identify multiple valid legal approaches.

For legal institutions, this acceleration creates both opportunities and threats. Courts that embrace autonomous systems could dramatically reduce backlogs and improve access to justice; those that resist may find themselves increasingly irrelevant as alternative dispute resolution mechanisms leverage these capabilities to provide faster, more consistent outcomes.

As of March 2025, Transformer-2 utilizing CipherPrune architectures have demonstrated advanced capabilities in document analysis, precedent evaluation, legal reasoning, inconsistency identification, and authority allocation – domains previously considered uniquely human. These systems could function effectively as neutral analytical tools for judges, serving as digital analogues to special masters.[15] Operating as procedurally neutral instruments that assist without displacing judicial authority, these systems can prove particularly valuable in complex litigation – cryptocurrency disputes, fraudulent transfer cases, leveraged buyout litigation, D&O liability matters, pre-filing liability management transactions, mass tort estimations, environmental litigation, intellectual property disputes, cybersecurity matters, and e-discovery processes – effectively supporting judicial case management. The petition of bankruptcy judge Michael Kaplan to amend Federal Rule of Bankruptcy Procedure (FRBP) 9031[16] highlights a growing recognition that complex cases entering bankruptcy require specialized assistance beyond traditional judicial resources. The specific areas he identifies, such as massive discovery volumes, technical subject matter expertise, complex electronically stored information (ESI) management, privilege determinations, and claims and fee reviews, perfectly align with strengths of Transformer-2 architectures.

By implementing technologies as digital analogues to the "court appointed neutrals", Judge Kaplan envisions, bankruptcy courts could address the very concerns his petition raises about costs, complexity, and compensations that traditional special masters' appointments entail. This specialized system assistance would provide necessary analytical support, expanding access to expertise otherwise unavailable in resource-limited judicial context while avoiding lobbying concerns and financial burdens associated with human special masters. Simultaneously, these systems would serve as neutral aids to judges considering independent human neutral appointments, providing quality control assurance that case administration is actually improved, which might be particularly valuable when judges lack subject matter expertise to effectively oversee masters themselves.

Implementation requires jurisdiction-specific methodological frameworks, ensuring fundamental procedural fairness principles remain operative regardless of technological infrastructure. Integration decisions necessitate domain-specific calibration with continuous assessment against both efficiency metrics and substantive justice parameters.

Law schools that recognize this isn't merely about adding technology courses, but fundamentally reimagining legal education to address both technical competencies and ethical considerations skills lawyers must develop in an increasingly AI-augmented profession, may produce graduates uniquely positioned to thrive and better navigate this evolving professional landscape. Those that don't may find their value proposition increasingly questioned.

Ultimately, the question isn't whether legal practice will evolve in response to autonomous systems – it's whether the profession will consciously direct this evolution or merely react to changes imposed from outside. Those who understand this as an opportunity for Renaissance rather than replacement will not only survive the transition but help define what comes next – a legal system in which human and artificial intelligence work in concert to deliver justice with unprecedented scale, consistency, and fairness.

The future belongs not to those who can adapt fastest, but to those who can reimagine most boldly. We have moved beyond the point where simply keeping pace with change is sufficient – the opportunity now lies in actively shaping that change. This pivotal moment offers unprecedented potential for those willing to think expansively about what legal services can become and how they can better serve the evolving needs of clients and society.

The time for adaptation has already passed. The age of legal renaissance has begun.[17]

References

1 Oakeshott, Michael. *On Human Conduct*. Clarendon Press, 1975.

2 ABA Standing Committee on Ethics and Professional Responsibility, Formal Opinion 512, Generative AI Tools.
www.americanbar.org/content/dam/aba/administrative/professional_responsibility/ethics-opinions/aba-formal-opinion-512.pdf

3 International Legal Technology Association (ILTA), Workshop introducing the "practical steps for deploying facial recognition while maintaining compliance and trust", ILTA Evolve 2025. www.iltanet.org/live-events/evolve

4 ILTA Evolve 2025, Workshops: Microsoft Corporation.

5 Google Research, Attention Is All You Need, Vaswani et al., 12 June 2017.
https://proceedings.neurips.cc/paper_files/paper/2017/file/3f5ee243547dee91fbd053c1c4a845aa-Paper.pdf

6 ByteDance Research, X. Ma, J. Wang, W. Wei, Covariate Adjusted Response Adaptive Design with Delayed Outcomes, 3 February 2025. https://arxiv.org/abs/2502.01062

7 Google Research, A. Behrouz, P. Zhong, V. Mirrokni, Titans: Learning to Memorize at Test Time, 23 December 2024. https://arxiv.org/abs/2501.00663.

8 Sakana AI Research, Q. Sun, E. Cetin, Y. Tang, Transformer – Squared: Self-Adaptive LLMs, 24 January 2025. https://arxiv.org/abs/2501.06252

9 Legal Quant development, https://lclerk.de

10 ICLR 2025, Conference Paper, Y. Zhang, J. Xue, M. Zhen, M. Xie, M. Zhang, L. Jiang, Q. Lou, CipherPrune: Efficient and Scalable Private Transformer Inference, 24 February 2025. https://arxiv.org/pdf/2502.16782

11 Anthropic Research, Y. Chen, J. Benton, A. Radhakrishnan, J. Uesato, C. Denison, J. Schulman, A. Somani, P. Hase, M. Wagner, V. Mikulik, S. Bowman, J. Leike, J. Kaplan, E. Perez, Reasoning Models Don't Always Say What They Think, 3. April 2025, https://assets.anthropic.com/m/71876fabef0f0ed4/original/reasoning_models_paper.pdf.

12 Legal Quant Research, Legal Risk Hub, 5 August 2024. https://legalriskhub.de

13 Above Law, Joe Patrice, AI Delivers Fresh Nightmares For In-House Counsel, 15 February 2025.

14 German Federal Court of Justice ruling from 14 March 2024, V ZB 2/23 (ECLI:DE:BGH:2024:140322BVZB2.23.0)

15 28 U.S.C. Rule 53 – Masters, United States Code, 2018 Edition, Supplement 5, Title 28 – Judiciary and Judicial Procedure. Comparative judicial practice is available via Federal Judicial Center at: https://judiciariesworldwide.fjc.gov/question/what-special-master

16 Hon. Michael Kaplan, US Bankruptcy Court (D. N. J.). The American Bar Association (ABA) request and recommendation to Judicial Conference of the United States to permit the use of "court appointed neutrals" in proceedings under Bankruptcy Code. www.uscourts.gov/file/78167/download

17 While the concepts and frameworks presented in this chapter contribute to scholarly and professional discourse, the specific expression, methodology, and presentation of these ideas represent the author's original work and intellectual property developed through extensive research and professional experience. This chapter presents conceptual frameworks for academic consideration, and the author welcomes scholarly engagement and discussion. For inquiries regarding potential collaboration or applications, please contact j.schidzig@legal-quant.com.

Chapter 4: The intersection of artificial intelligence and client confidentiality in legal practice

By Colin Levy, general counsel of Malbek, legal tech author and speaker

Introduction

The integration of artificial intelligence into legal practice represents a fundamental transformation of the profession, one that challenges traditional frameworks while offering unprecedented opportunities for enhanced service delivery. As law firms and legal departments increasingly deploy AI systems to analyze documents, predict outcomes, and streamline operations, they confront complex questions about how these technologies interact with core ethical obligations, particularly the duty of client confidentiality. This intersection between technological capability and professional responsibility creates novel challenges that demand careful examination and thoughtful response.

The discourse surrounding AI in legal practice has often gravitated toward extremes – either heralding a revolutionary transformation of the profession or warning of existential threats to its foundational principles. However, the reality lies in a more nuanced middle ground, where actual technological capabilities intersect with practical ethical considerations. This chapter tries to illuminate this intersection, providing a realistic assessment of how current AI technologies affect client confidentiality obligations and offering pragmatic frameworks for addressing emerging challenges.

The technological landscape of modern legal practice

The evolution of AI technologies has fundamentally changed the landscape of legal practice, though perhaps not in the ways often portrayed in popular media. Today's AI systems, while powerful, run through fundamentally different mechanisms than human intelligence. Rather than replicating human cognitive processes, these systems excel at detecting patterns in data and applying sophisticated statistical analysis to produce useful outputs. This distinction proves important for understanding both the potential and limitations of AI in maintaining client confidentiality.

Contemporary AI applications in legal practice primarily use two distinct technological approaches, each with unique implications for confidentiality. Machine learning systems, which have gained considerable prominence, learn patterns from large datasets to make predictions or classifications. These systems power modern document review platforms, enabling rapid analysis of vast document collections while simultaneously creating novel challenges for data protection. In contrast, rules-based knowledge systems encode explicit legal rules and procedures, offering more predictable but less flexible capabilities. These systems often form the backbone of practice management tools that handle sensitive client information.

The practical implementation of these technologies manifests across various domains of legal practice. In document review and due diligence, AI systems analyze contracts and other legal documents at scales previously unimaginable, processing thousands of documents while identifying relevant provisions and potential risks. This capability, while transformative for legal practice, raises important questions about data access and protection. Similarly, AI-powered legal research platforms now offer sophisticated analysis of case law and prediction of litigation outcomes, using sensitive client information in ways that demand careful consideration of confidentiality implications.

The evolution of client confidentiality in the digital age

The duty of confidentiality stands as a cornerstone of the attorney–client relationship, historically developed in an era of physical documents and face-to-face communications. This fundamental duty has evolved significantly as legal practice has moved into digital environments, but the integration of AI technologies presents unprecedented challenges to traditional frameworks for maintaining confidentiality.

The traditional understanding of confidentiality encompassed relatively straightforward scenarios – securing physical documents, controlling access to office spaces, and managing direct communications with clients. However, the digital transformation of legal practice has already required significant evolution in how firms conceptualize and implement confidentiality protections. Electronic communications, cloud storage, and digital document management have required new technical and procedural safeguards, establishing a foundation for addressing AI-specific challenges.

The introduction of AI systems adds more layers of complexity to this evolving landscape. These technologies often require access to vast amounts of data for training and operation, creating scenarios where client information might be used in ways not contemplated by traditional confidentiality frameworks. Moreover, the sophisticated pattern-recognition capabilities of AI systems raise novel questions about potential indirect disclosures through model behavior or outputs.

Core confidentiality challenges in AI implementation

The implementation of AI systems in legal practice presents several fundamental challenges to maintaining client confidentiality. Perhaps most significant is the issue of data access and training. Machine learning systems require extensive datasets to develop their capabilities, creating tension between the need for system effectiveness and the duty to protect client information. This challenge manifests in multiple dimensions, from the initial selection of training data to the ongoing improvement of AI models through use.

Consider, for example, a document review system that learns to identify privileged documents. The system's effectiveness depends on exposure to many examples of privileged communications, yet each such example represents sensitive client information that must be protected. This creates complex questions about data usage, retention, and cross-matter contamination that traditional confidentiality frameworks may struggle to address.

Technical vulnerabilities present another important challenge. AI systems introduce novel attack vectors and potential security risks that must be carefully managed. Model inference attacks, where sophisticated adversaries might reconstruct sensitive information from model outputs, represent a particularly concerning threat. Similarly, the distributed nature of many AI systems, often involving cloud-based processing and third-party vendors, creates more points of potential vulnerability.

Developing a practical framework for AI implementation

The challenges presented by AI implementation in legal practice require a comprehensive framework that addresses both technical and procedural parts of confidentiality protection. This framework must bridge theoretical understanding with practical implementation, making sure technological sophistication does not compromise ethical obligations. The development of this framework requires careful consideration of both system architecture and organizational processes.

At the technical level, the implementation of AI systems demands a sophisticated approach to data protection that goes beyond traditional security measures. The architecture of these systems must incorporate multiple layers of protection, beginning with fundamental considerations of data segregation and access control. For example, law firms implementing document analysis systems must consider not only how to secure the immediate document repository but also how to protect the derivative data generated through AI analysis. This might involve creating isolated computing environments for different clients or matter types, implementing sophisticated encryption protocols that protect both raw data and AI-generated insights, and developing comprehensive audit trails that track both direct data access and indirect information flows through AI systems.

The procedural elements of this framework must be equally strong. Organizations must develop nuanced policies that govern the use of AI systems, addressing not only operational aspects but also ethical considerations. These policies should delineate clear guidelines for system usage while maintaining enough flexibility to accommodate the dynamic nature of AI technology. For example, a policy framework might establish tiered access levels for different types of AI analysis, with heightened review requirements for systems processing particularly sensitive client information.

Practical implementation guidelines for AI-enhanced legal practice

The theoretical frameworks surrounding AI and confidentiality must be translated into concrete practices that legal professionals can implement in their daily operations.

Consider the following hypothetical case study that illustrates the complexities of putting AI systems into practice while maintaining client confidentiality.

Case study: Global law firm AI implementation

In 2023, a global law firm with offices across three continents decided to implement an AI-powered document review system for merger and acquisition due diligence. The firm found several critical challenges:

- Multiple jurisdictions with varying data protection requirements.
- Clients in highly regulated industries with strict confidentiality obligations.
- Legacy document management systems containing decades of sensitive client information.
- Teams across different time zones requiring continuous system access.

The firm's experience in addressing these challenges provides valuable insights for developing practical implementation guidelines. Their systematic approach, detailed below, shows how theoretical frameworks can be translated into operational protocols while maintaining rigorous confidentiality standards. This section provides detailed guidance for practitioners seeking to maintain rigorous confidentiality standards while leveraging AI capabilities, incorporating insights from both academic research and practical experience in legal technology implementation.

Data segregation and classification protocols

The foundation of effective confidentiality protection in AI-enhanced legal practice lies in sophisticated data segregation and classification systems.

To illustrate this principle, consider the following hypothetical scenario. A mid-sized law firm handles both healthcare and technology clients. The firm implements an AI-powered contract analysis system and must design appropriate data segregation protocols. Consider three different clients:

1. *Client A:* A healthcare provider with HIPAA-protected patient information occasionally embedded in contracts.
2. *Client B:* A technology start-up with sensitive intellectual property and trade secrets.
3. *Client C:* A retail chain with standard commercial contracts.

This scenario shows why a one-size-fits-all approach to AI implementation fails to adequately protect client confidentiality. The firm developed a tiered classification framework that provides different handling requirements based on data sensitivity.

This framework might include:

- First-tier data representing routine client communications and publicly filed documents, which may be appropriate for general AI processing with standard security protocols.
- Second-tier data encompassing sensitive business information and private client details, requiring enhanced security measures and restricted AI system access.
- Third-tier data including highly privileged communications and strategic documents, demanding the most stringent controls and limited AI processing permissions.

Implementation of this framework requires systematic review processes before data enters any AI system. Organizations should establish clear protocols for data classification, including specific criteria for each tier and detailed procedures for handling edge cases. Regular audits should verify proper classification and adherence to handling requirements.

Technical infrastructure requirements

Legal practitioners must develop robust technical infrastructure to support secure AI implementation.

To illustrate these challenges, consider this hypothetical scenario based on common industry experiences.

At a midsize litigation firm we'll call Anderson & Partners, the implementation of an AI-powered legal research and document analysis system revealed several critical infrastructure requirements. The firm discovered that its existing network architecture, while adequate for traditional legal work, required significant enhancement to support secure AI operations.

First, the firm needed to establish secure processing environments for AI operations. Anderson & Partners first tried to run its AI document analysis system on its general office network, but quickly recognized the need for isolation. It created a separate virtual private cloud environment dedicated to AI processing, with encryption for both data in transit and at rest.

When an attorney needed to analyze sensitive merger documents for a fictional technology client, TechCorp Industries, the documents moved through this secured environment, with all processing occurring in isolated containers that prevented data leakage between matters.

Access control systems proved equally important. The firm developed a sophisticated permissions framework after a near-miss incident where a junior associate almost uploaded privileged documents to a public AI platform. Its new system required multi-factor authentication for AI system access and implemented role-based controls that limited system capabilities based on attorney seniority and matter type. For example, only senior attorneys could allow the training of AI models on client data, while associates had restricted access limited to using pre-trained models.

Comprehensive audit trails became a fundamental requirement after Anderson & Partners conducted a hypothetical risk assessment exercise. Consider its process for handling confidential patent documents – each interaction with the AI system was logged, creating a detailed record of who accessed what information, when, and for what purpose. When a fictional pharmaceutical client, PharmaCare Solutions, later questioned whether its confidential research data had been protected well, the firm could produce detailed records showing exactly how its information had been processed.

Data minimization and processing protocols

The practical implementation of data minimization principles requires careful attention to both technical and procedural safeguards. Returning to our hypothetical firm, Anderson & Partners, consider how it addressed these challenges in day-to-day operations. When handling a complex merger transaction for a fictional technology client, the firm's AI system first requested access to the client's entire document repository for due diligence analysis. This presented an unnecessary confidentiality risk, as many documents had sensitive information irrelevant to the transaction.

The firm developed a sophisticated approach to data minimization that began with careful scope definition. For example, when analyzing employment agreements for its fictional client GlobalTech Solutions, attorneys first identified specific provisions relevant to the transaction. They then created targeted data extraction protocols that gave the AI system only these relevant sections, significantly reducing exposure of sensitive employee information.

System training evolved through careful iteration. Anderson & Partners developed a novel approach to AI model training using a combination of public documents and carefully scrubbed client materials. In one illustrative example, when training its contract analysis system to identify problematic change-of-control provisions, it first used publicly available SEC filings to establish baseline capabilities. Only after confirming the system's accuracy did it introduce carefully selected and anonymized client documents for enhanced training.

Incident response in practice

Effective incident response requires more than theoretical frameworks – it demands practical, tested protocols that can be implemented under pressure. Consider how Anderson & Partners handled a hypothetical near-miss event. During routine system tracking, its technology team discovered that its AI document analysis system had inadvertently included metadata from privileged communications in its training dataset.

While this fictional scenario didn't result in an actual breach, it triggered the firm's incident response protocols. The response team immediately isolated the affected system parts and began a comprehensive review of all

AI training data. They discovered that the system had been keeping document metadata that should have been stripped during preprocessing, creating a potential confidentiality risk.

The firm's response showed several key principles of effective incident management. First, it maintained transparent communication with affected clients, providing clear explanations of the potential risk while avoiding technical jargon. For its fictional client, HealthCare Systems Inc., this meant explaining how the metadata retention might have theoretically exposed certain parts of its communication patterns, while emphasizing that no actual confidential information had been compromised.

Training and compliance integration

Professional development in an AI-enhanced legal practice requires sophisticated integration of technical training with ethical compliance. Anderson & Partners developed what it termed "integrated learning pathways" that combined practical system training with deep consideration of ethical implications. Consider its approach to training new associates – rather than treating AI system training and ethical compliance as separate topics, it developed scenario-based learning modules that addressed both simultaneously.

In one hypothetical training scenario, associates were presented with a complex document review task for a fictional pharmaceutical client. The exercise required them to use the AI system effectively while identifying potential confidentiality risks. For example, they needed to recognize when the AI system's pattern-matching capabilities might inadvertently connect seemingly unrelated documents in ways that could reveal confidential strategy information.

The firm's training program emphasized practical application through carefully constructed scenarios. When introducing new AI capabilities, such as automated contract analysis, the training included both technical instruction and ethical consideration. Associates learned not just how to run the system but also how to critically evaluate its outputs for potential confidentiality concerns. For example, they worked through a hypothetical scenario where the AI system found patterns across multiple client matters, requiring them to assess whether using these insights would violate confidentiality obligations.

These integrated training approaches helped attorneys develop what Anderson & Partners called "technological judgment" – the ability to effectively leverage AI capabilities while maintaining rigorous ethical standards. Its experience, while fictional, shows how firms can successfully bridge the gap between technical capability and professional responsibility.

The firm's incident response framework, developed through this hypothetical experience, addressed several critical areas. When a potential document misclassification was detected in a fictional corporate client's materials, the response team could immediately isolate the affected AI system parts, preventing any further data exposure. The firm's documentation protocols enabled it to quickly identify all potentially affected clients and matters, while its communication templates helped with prompt and appropriate notification to necessary parties.

Most importantly, each hypothetical incident contributed to system improvement. When the firm discovered that its AI system occasionally mishandled certain types of financial documents, it used this information to enhance its classification algorithms and strengthen its data handling protocols. This continuous improvement process, while fictional, illustrates the dynamic nature of AI security requirements in legal practice.

1. *Secure processing environments.* Organizations should establish isolated computing environments for AI processing of confidential information. These environments should implement end-to-end encryption, strict access controls, and comprehensive logging of all system interactions. Virtual private clouds dedicated to specific clients or matter types can provide more segregation of sensitive data.
2. *Access control systems.* Implementation of role-based access control systems must go beyond traditional binary permissions to incorporate AI-specific considerations. These systems should manage not only direct user access but also AI system permissions, including granular controls over which systems can access specific data sets and for what purposes.
3. *Audit trail implementation.* Comprehensive logging systems must track not only direct data access but also AI system interactions with confidential information. These logs should capture both successful and attempted access, system configuration changes, and data transformations performed by AI systems.

Operational protocols for AI system usage

Daily operations involving AI systems require careful attention to several key areas:

1. *Data minimization practices.* Legal practitioners should implement strict data minimization protocols when using AI systems. This includes:
   - Analyzing whether AI processing is truly necessary for specific tasks.
   - Limiting data inputs to only essential information.
   - Regularly purging unnecessary data from AI systems.
   - Implementing automated data retention and deletion schedules.
2. *System training and validation.* When training AI systems on client data, organizations must:
   - Use synthetic or anonymized data for initial system training whenever possible.
   - Implement rigorous validation processes before processing actual client data.
   - Maintain separate training and production environments.
   - Regularly audit system outputs for potential confidentiality breaches.
3. *Vendor management.* For organizations using third-party AI solutions, comprehensive vendor management protocols should include:
   - Detailed security assessments of vendor systems and practices.
   - Clear contractual provisions regarding data handling and confidentiality.
   - Regular audits of vendor compliance with security requirements.
   - Established procedures for data retrieval or deletion upon contract termination.

Incident response and recovery

Organizations must develop comprehensive incident response plans specifically addressing AI-related confidentiality breaches.

These plans should include:

1. Detection protocols:
   - Automated tracking systems for unusual AI system behavior.
   - Regular analysis of system logs and access patterns.
   - Clear criteria for identifying potential breaches.
   - Established channels for reporting concerns.
2. Response procedures:
   - Immediate containment actions to prevent further data exposure.
   - Investigation protocols to determine breach scope and impact.

   - Communication templates for client notification.
   - Documentation requirements for regulatory compliance.
3. Recovery and improvement:
   - Procedures for system restoration and data recovery.
   - Analysis protocols to identify root causes.
   - Processes for implementing lessons learned.
   - Updates to security protocols based on incident analysis.

Training and compliance programs

Effective implementation requires comprehensive training programs that address both technical and ethical considerations:

1. Technical training staff members require regular training on:
   - Proper use of AI systems and security features.
   - Data classification and handling procedures.
   - Recognition of potential security risks.
   - Proper documentation practices.
2. Ethical awareness training should emphasize:
   - Professional responsibility implications of AI use.
   - Recognition of potential ethical conflicts.
   - Decision-making frameworks for ethical challenges.
   - Documentation requirements for ethical considerations.

Documentation and review procedures

Organizations must maintain comprehensive documentation of their AI-related procedures and regularly review their effectiveness:

1. Documentation requirements:
   - Detailed system configuration records.
   - Processing logs for confidential information.
   - Training materials and completion records.
   - Incident response documentation.

2. Review procedures:
   - Regular audits of system usage and compliance.
   - Periodic review of security measures.
   - Assessment of training effectiveness.
   - Updates to procedures based on emerging threats.

Navigating professional responsibility in an AI-enhanced practice environment

The integration of artificial intelligence into legal practice requires a sophisticated reconceptualization of professional responsibility obligations. While the main duties of competence, diligence, and confidentiality remain unchanged, their practical implementation demands nuanced understanding of how AI systems interact with traditional ethical frameworks. To illustrate these complexities, consider the hypothetical case of a large corporate law firm, Blackstone & Reed, as it grapples with evolving professional obligations in an AI-enhanced practice environment.

When Blackstone & Reed implemented an AI-powered due diligence system for mergers and acquisitions work, the firm confronted novel questions about the intersection of professional judgment and automated analysis. In one illustrative scenario, the AI system flagged an apparently routine change-of-control provision in a target company's contracts as potentially problematic, contradicting initial human review. This fictional situation exemplifies the complex interplay between technological capability and professional responsibility – while the AI system showed superior pattern recognition in identifying the problematic clause, the ultimate interpretation required sophisticated legal judgment that no current AI system could provide.

The duty of competence in this context extends beyond traditional legal knowledge to encompass understanding of AI systems' capabilities and limitations. For example, when Blackstone & Reed's AI system analyzed a complex cross-border acquisition agreement, it did not recognize certain jurisdiction-specific nuances in contract interpretation. This hypothetical scenario highlights why attorneys must maintain enough technological literacy to identify potential gaps in AI analysis while preserving their core focus on legal knowledge.

The question of client communication presents particularly nuanced challenges in an AI-enhanced practice environment. Consider how Blackstone & Reed approached client disclosure regarding AI usage in document review for a fictional pharmaceutical client, GlobalHealth Pharmaceuticals. The firm developed a comprehensive communication framework that balanced technical detail with practical understanding, explaining both the efficiency benefits and potential limitations of AI-assisted review. This approach exemplifies how firms can fulfill their ethical obligations while maintaining clarity in client communications.

Professional oversight of AI systems demands sophisticated frameworks that integrate technological capability with legal judgment. In our hypothetical firm, this manifested in a multi-layered review process for AI-generated analysis. For example, when reviewing a large portfolio of intellectual property licenses for a technology client, the firm implemented what it termed "calibrated oversight" – a system where the level of human review scaled with both the complexity of the agreements and the confidence level of the AI analysis.

The evolution of professional responsibility in this context extends to novel questions about attribution and accountability. Consider a scenario where Blackstone & Reed's AI system missed an important liability provision in a complex financial agreement. This hypothetical situation raises important questions about professional liability. How should responsibility be assigned between the attorney, the firm, and the AI system vendor? The firm's approach to this challenge involved developing sophisticated protocols for documenting both AI and human review processes, creating clear accountability frameworks while maintaining practical efficiency.

Training requirements present another critical dimension of professional responsibility in AI-enhanced practice. Blackstone & Reed's experience shows how firms must balance technical training with fundamental legal judgment. Its hypothetical training program integrated practical AI system instruction with sophisticated ethical considerations, ensuring attorneys understood not just how to run AI tools but also how to critically evaluate their outputs within the broader context of professional obligations.

The question of ethical AI use extends beyond individual matters to encompass broader questions of practice management. For example, when Blackstone & Reed discovered its AI system showed potential bias in analyzing certain types of commercial agreements, it faced complex decisions about system change and client disclosure. This fictional scenario illustrates how firms must develop sophisticated frameworks for addressing systemic AI issues while maintaining its professional obligations.

Risk management in this context requires integration of traditional legal ethics with novel technological considerations. Consider how Blackstone & Reed approached conflict checking in AI-enhanced practice – its systems needed to account not just for traditional client conflicts but also for potential issues arising from AI system training data and cross-matter learning. This hypothetical example shows how firms must evolve traditional ethical frameworks to address emerging technological realities.

The question of oversight presents another critical dimension of professional responsibility. While AI systems can enhance efficiency and accuracy in many legal tasks, they cannot replace professional judgment. Attorneys must develop systematic approaches to reviewing AI outputs and maintaining appropriate human oversight of automated processes. This oversight function requires not only technical understanding but also careful consideration of how to integrate AI capabilities with traditional legal judgment.

Future trajectories and strategic considerations

As AI technology continues to evolve, legal practitioners must maintain a forward-looking perspective while grounding their approach in current realities. The trajectory of AI development suggests increasing sophistication in natural language processing and predictive capabilities, which will probably create both new opportunities and novel challenges for maintaining client confidentiality. Understanding these potential developments enables proactive rather than reactive approaches to confidentiality protection.

The regulatory landscape surrounding AI in legal practice remains dynamic, with various jurisdictions developing different approaches to governing these technologies. Law firms must track these developments while maintaining flexibility in their implementation frameworks. This requires developing scalable approaches to AI integration that can adapt to evolving regulatory requirements while maintaining consistent protection of client information.

The strategic implications of AI integration extend beyond immediate operational considerations to encompass broader questions about the future of legal practice. Firms must consider how AI capabilities might reshape client expectations and service delivery models while making sure technological advancement does not compromise core professional values. This strategic planning requires careful balance between innovation and tradition, leveraging new capabilities while preserving essential parts of the attorney–client relationship.

The intersection of artificial intelligence and client confidentiality represents a critical frontier in legal practice, demanding thoughtful integration of technological capability with ethical duty. Success in this domain requires developing sophisticated frameworks that address both technical and professional challenges while maintaining focus on fundamental duties to clients. As AI technology continues to evolve, the legal profession must maintain its commitment to client confidentiality while adapting its approaches to meet emerging challenges.

The path forward requires ongoing attention to both technological developments and ethical implications. Legal practitioners must develop and maintain robust frameworks for protecting client information while leveraging AI capabilities to enhance service delivery. This balance demands continuous evaluation and change in approaches, making sure technological advancement serves rather than compromises professional obligations. Through careful attention to these considerations, the legal profession can harness the benefits of AI while upholding its fundamental ethical commitments.

Looking to 2030 – the future of AI-enhanced legal practice

The integration of artificial intelligence in legal practice is poised to undergo significant transformation by 2030, reshaping how firms deliver legal services while maintaining their core ethical obligations. This analysis examines key developments we might expect to see, illustrated through carefully constructed hypothetical scenarios that show both opportunities and challenges.

The evolution of the hybrid intelligence practice

By 2030, leading law firms will probably operate as hybrid intelligence practices, where AI systems and human legal knowledge work in carefully orchestrated collaboration. To illustrate this evolution, consider how a hypothetical firm, Global Law Partners, approaches complex international transactions. Its AI systems conduct comprehensive initial due diligence across multiple jurisdictions, identifying potential regulatory conflicts and business risks. However, the firm maintains strict protocols making sure strategic interpretation and client counsel remain exclusively human responsibilities.

The firm's matter management system shows how this hybrid approach might function in practice. When handling a fictional cross-border acquisition for TechGlobal Industries, the system automatically implements jurisdiction-specific compliance protocols while attorneys focus on strategic negotiation and relationship management. This arrangement shows how technology may enhance rather than replace core legal judgment.

Specialized AI models and practice integration

Practice-specific AI models will probably emerge by 2030, each designed to address legal domains while maintaining rigorous confidentiality standards.

For example, Global Law Partners uses specialized systems for its intellectual property practice that understand complex patent documentation across multiple technical fields. These systems maintain sophisticated safeguards against cross-matter contamination while enabling deeper technical analysis.

The evolution of these specialized systems shows the potential for AI to enhance specific practice areas while preserving ethical obligations. When the firm handles sensitive intellectual property matters for its fictional pharmaceutical client, BioPharma Solutions, its AI system automatically implements enhanced security protocols and maintains strict data segregation between matters.

Enhanced ethical frameworks and controls

Ethical frameworks will probably evolve significantly to address increasingly sophisticated AI capabilities. Global Law Partners has developed what it terms "dynamic ethical protocols" that automatically adjust security measures based on matter sensitivity, jurisdiction, and client requirements. This adaptable approach shows how technical capabilities might evolve to support rather than challenge ethical obligations.

The firm's approach to confidentiality protection illustrates this evolution. Its systems use advanced encryption and access controls that automatically adapt to changing circumstances. When handling sensitive merger negotiations for a fictional technology client, its system automatically implements enhanced data protection measures without requiring manual intervention.

Professional development and AI literacy

By 2030, sophisticated understanding of AI capabilities and limitations will become fundamental to legal practice. Global Law Partners maintains ongoing professional development programs that combine technical knowledge with ethical consideration. These programs help attorneys understand not just how to use AI systems but how to critically evaluate their outputs and implications.

The firm's training approach shows how technical and ethical considerations might be integrated. New attorneys take part in sophisticated simulation exercises that combine practical system usage with complex ethical scenarios. This preparation helps them develop what the firm calls "technological judgment" – the ability to effectively leverage AI capabilities while maintaining rigorous professional standards.

Client communication and trust

Maintaining client trust will remain paramount as AI capabilities advance. Global Law Partners maintains sophisticated yet accessible communication protocols about its AI usage, helping clients understand both capabilities and limitations. This transparency helps maintain confidence while setting realistic expectations about AI's role in legal service delivery.

The firm's approach to client communication shows how transparency might evolve. When discussing AI usage with clients, it provides clear explanations of how systems support its practice while emphasizing the primacy of human judgment in strategic decisions. This balance helps maintain client confidence while ensuring realistic understanding of AI's role.

Strategic implementation considerations

The successful integration of AI in legal practice by 2030 will likely depend on several key factors.

First, firms must develop sophisticated governance frameworks that address emerging capabilities while maintaining rigorous confidentiality protections. Global Law Partners shows this through regular review and updating of its AI protocols, ensuring it remains current with technological advances while preserving ethical standards.

Second, professional development must prepare attorneys for an increasingly technological practice environment while preserving core legal judgment. The firm's training programs show how technical knowledge and professional judgment might be integrated effectively.

Finally, firms must maintain unwavering focus on client service and confidentiality as fundamental principles guiding technological advancement. This requires careful balance between innovation and responsibility, making sure technological capabilities enhance rather than compromise professional obligations.

The evolution of AI-enhanced legal practice through 2030 presents both opportunities and challenges for the profession. While AI capabilities will probably advance significantly, successful practices will be those that maintain focus on human judgment, ethical responsibility, and client trust. The experience of our hypothetical firm suggests that thoughtful integration of AI technology can enhance legal practice while preserving its essential character as a profession built on trust and judgment.

Success in this evolved landscape will require ongoing commitment to both technological literacy and ethical practice. Firms must continue developing sophisticated frameworks for AI governance while investing in professional development that prepares attorneys for an increasingly technological practice environment. Most importantly, they must maintain unwavering focus on client service and confidentiality as fundamental principles guiding technological advancement.

Chapter 5:

Technological innovation and the evolution of professional legal practice

By Martin Martinoff, Innovation lead – Next Generation Professional and Financial Services, Innovate UK

The alchemy of law and technology

The legal profession is no longer revered as the fortress of precedent and parchment. It is no longer just a story of tradition. It is becoming a tale of transformation, where silicon and code are as vital as statute and case law. In the coming years, the law firm as we know it might not merely adapt to technology – it might be reborn through it. In this chapter, I want to explore that alchemy – a fusion of human ingenuity and technology that promises to redefine not just *how* lawyers work, but *who* they are as professionals, *what* they deliver, and, most importantly, *why* they matter in a world racing toward informational complexity. The catalysts for this transformation are obvious – relentless client demands, spiraling costs, and a growing flood of new players who rewrite the rules, including tech start-ups, alternative legal service platforms, and even larger software giants.

Yet, to fully understand how the profession is evolving, we need to search beneath the surface of this seismic shift for the questions that few have dared to ask. What might happen when the tech tools of law outpace the minds that build them? Could technology amplify justice, or would it merely magnify efficiency? And what does it mean to be a professional lawyer when a machine might know more than you ever will?

Recent research tells us a compelling story for AI adoption in the UK law firms – from the cautious two-thirds of the largest firms a few years ago, to almost all by the end of 2024, as reported by the latest UK Law Firms Survey by PwC.[1] GenAI, ignited by ChatGPT, spurred a torrent of investment in technology as strategic for 90 percent of the top 100 UK firms, who are now trialing tools. Another clear signal that technology isn't a sideline is the shifting budgets – IT spend per user at the biggest firms leapt 11.4 percent in 2024 to £16.6k.[2] These trends are spreading among smaller practices as more affordable, cloud-based AI tools are levelling the playing field and bringing a provocative possibility for smaller and boutique firms to outmaneuver behemoths not through scale, but through agility and imagination.

One way to look at the historical evolution of law firms is as compliance-driven organizations – hierarchical, risk-averse, with a business model anchored by the billable hour. While the early technology (typewriters and word processors) might have tremendously improved efficiency, they left the essence of legal practice untouched. That essence, steeped in human judgment and lawyer-centric norms, resisted change with a tenacity that bordered on defiance. The partnership model, with its collegial yet conservative bent, slowed innovation, often prioritizing short-term profits over long-term bets. The early change in this paradigm came with the normalization of paralegals and non-legal specialists, with document management systems and automation software. What we are seeing today with AI is not just streamlining of the sector but its reshaping. Routine tasks could easily vanish into algorithms to free lawyers for the creative, the strategic, the truly human tasks. Many predict that this evolution is inevitable and that soon lawyers will partner with AI as naturally as they once paired with junior associates.

We need to push beyond the obvious productivity gains like faster document reviews, sharper research, and slicker contracts. While many tech solutions focus on how AI can turbocharge workflows, it is fair to ask whether the evolution should be in speed or scope. Imagine an AI that doesn't just draft a contract but anticipates the negotiation, modelling outcomes based on real-time market shifts or a client's unspoken priorities. Or consider a system that doesn't merely predict litigation success but rewrites legal strategies to pre-empt societal trends – say, climate litigation or digital rights – before they hit the courts. These lines of thinking could be the next frontier, and they will force us to ask questions like, Will lawyers become curators of AI's expertise and brilliance, or will AI become the silent senior partner?

Such transformation would not come without tension, rooted in the very economics of professional labor. The billable hour is wobbling as AI tools slash time on tasks once billed by the minute. Firms are pivoting to new and alternative models like fixed fees, subscriptions, and even AI-powered legal scalable platforms. An important dimension of this transformation of AI slashing costs is that it could unlock justice for those priced out of the system, turning legal services into a utility rather than a luxury.

Successful law firms will be defined by their leadership. Leadership that is not fixed on rigid hierarchies but on agile, tech-savvy structures where decisions come from the client-centered functions, not the corner office. As Lee Bryant of Post*Shift describes it,[3] law firms could become "programmable organizations" where multi-agent AI coordinates work like software, flattening silos and amplifying responsiveness. Successful firms will not just adopt tech, they will orchestrate human and machine in harmony.

Of course, innovation and tech adoption come with risk – from data breaches and confidentiality lapses to algorithmic bias AI hallucinations. The Solicitors Regulation Authority and Law Society underscore this – technology can't outrun accountability. Indeed, it is a real concern that AI systems could codify inequality faster than humans can correct it. Similarly, efficiency could distance lawyers from the empathy that justice demands.

Within a decade, the UK legal sector could lead this blend of law and technology, with a thriving ecosystem of elite firms, nimble start-ups, and regulatory agility. But leadership is about imagining and with this chapter we should dare to ask what's next.

AI and lawtech – driving transformational change

The legal profession in the UK is a proving ground for AI and lawtech and innovation is rewriting the rules of practice. In the past year alone, law firms have sprinted from cautious curiosity to near-total embrace of AI, propelled by client demands, competitive pressures, and the dazzling possibilities unleashed by the generative AI boom post-ChatGPT. While back in 2015, when lawyers reading Susskind's *The Future of Professions* were skeptical of "robot lawyers", today technology isn't just an option. It is what separates trailblazers from the laggards.

A number of factors contribute to this shift from hesitation to hyperdrive – from client expectations and impatience to cost squeezes, from the GenAI explosion after ChatGPT's 2022 debut. Clients, fed up with slow turnarounds and hefty bills, started expecting the kind of slick, tech-driven service they'd seen in banking or retail. Certainly, GenAI promised a future where legal work could be swift, affordable, and precise – drafting contracts, summarizing briefs, and researching legal context in a blink. Within a year of ChatGPT's launch, 90 percent of the UK's top 100 law firms had jumped on the generative AI bandwagon, up from a modest 55 percent the year before.[4] AI changed from a "nice-to-have" into a "must-have".[5]

This shift isn't just about keeping up, it is about standing out, and law firms, big and small, are pouring resources into AI as a strategic lifeline. The Law Firms' Survey 2024[6] paints the picture – 67 percent of the top ten firms have rolled out Microsoft Copilot, with 30 percent of the top 100 using it widely and 45 percent testing it out. Meanwhile, 23 percent of top firms are crafting bespoke AI tools with their own data. AI isn't a sideline experiment anymore – it's the new backbone of legal competitiveness.

Practical AI applications – rewriting the legal playbook

AI isn't here to tinker around the edges – it's rewiring the very circuits of legal work. From sifting mountains of documents to predicting courtroom outcomes, it's turning grind into gold. Let's break it down.

Document review and e-discovery

Gone are the days when junior lawyers drowned in document stacks – AI has flipped that. The UK Serious Fraud Office's use of RAVN[7] during the Rolls-Royce corruption probe is the poster child – 30 million documents, 600,000 reviewed daily, compared to a human's measly 3,000. That's an 80 percent cut in manual slog, with fewer mistakes to boot. Law firms are cashing in too. Slaughter and May's Luminance[8] pilot for M&A due diligence let lawyers "read" hundreds of pages per minute, shifting their focus from grunt work to deal-making.[9] Even smaller players are in on it – Freyda, backed by Innovate UK's NGPFS Program, brings low/no-code AI to the table, echoing RAVN's prowess by making document review a breeze for firms of all sizes. This isn't just faster – it's smarter, slashing time and costs while boosting accuracy.

Legal research and predictive analytics

Legal research used to be a marathon of digging through case law and statutes. Now, advanced platforms scour databases in seconds, while natural language processing lets lawyers ask plain-English questions and get draft memos in minutes. But the real magic is predictive analytics – AI that mines litigation data to forecast outcomes or judge leanings. Tabled Technologies' Libra.law, funded by the NGPFS Program, nails this, using refined datasets to deliver razor-sharp insights. Imagine a litigator tweaking their pitch based on a judge's hidden patterns, or a firm advising clients with data-backed confidence. This is law moving from gut instinct to calculated strategy, and AI is the compass.

Document generation and automation

Drafting standard documents – contracts, wills, loans – once ate up hours. AI is making that history. Clifford Chance's CC Dr@ft automates everything from derivatives to loan agreements,[10] ensuring consistency and compliance at warp speed. Errors drop, time shrinks, and lawyers get to flex their brains on the tricky stuff. Genie AI, from the NGPFS Program, mirrors this, slashing drafting time with AI precision, while Ordli automates family legal docs, syncing with the Office of the Public Guardian effortlessly. This isn't about replacing lawyers – it's about turbocharging them, turning routine tasks into quick wins so they can tackle the big leagues.

Client service and AI chatbots

Clients don't wait – and AI ensures they don't have to. Chatbots now handle the basics – answering FAQs, triaging cases, even offering simple guidance, all 24/7. The Law Firms 2024 Survey suggests that about half of UK firms are using AI interfaces to keep clients in the loop, meeting the demand for instant, transparent service. Legal Utopia, another NGPFS-funded project, uses AI to give clients real-time peeks into firm operations, boosting responsiveness without burning out staff. It's a win-win – clients feel heard, and lawyers dodge the admin trap, focusing on meatier work instead.

Legal analytics and strategic insight

Of course, AI isn't just about doing – it's about knowing. By crunching vast datasets, it spots trends in cases, contracts, or regulations that humans would miss. Litigation teams can tailor arguments to a judge's track record, while corporate lawyers stay ahead of regulatory curves. Trustestate's AI probate tool, funded by the NGPFS Program, does this brilliantly, analyzing data for strategic edge. Picture a firm that doesn't just react to change but predicts it, advising clients before trouble brews. This is law as a proactive force, powered by AI's knack for turning raw info into goldmine insights.

These illustrations paint the new normal. AI could automate 30-40 percent of tasks in some practice areas, with drafting and data extraction already showing a 40 percent quality bump.[11] In big cases – like murder trials – document review that took weeks now takes days. The Law Firms' Survey 2024 backs this up – a third of top 100 firms see 16 percent of their work as automatable, and 80 percent peg at least six percent. Productivity is soaring too – 19 percent of top firms report gains, while 83 percent of the top ten expect more client work thanks to AI. This is law reimagined, where efficiency meets excellence.[12]

The ethical tightrope

AI's brilliance comes with baggage. Privacy risks loom large – most firms fret over cloud-based cyber threats and many have faced supply chain attacks. Bias in algorithms, "hallucinations" spitting out nonsense, and the loss of human touch are real worries too. The Solicitors Regulation Authority is blunt – delegate to AI all you want, but the buck stops with you. Firms are stepping up – governance committees and innovation chiefs are now common, keeping tech in check. A number of NGPFS-backed projects like Mimica tackle privacy head-on with GDPR-compliant design, while Libra.law curbs hallucinations with curated data. Still, the big questions linger. Can AI be fairer than us? And how do we keep the law human when machines take the wheel?

The future hinges on more than tech adoption and AI deployment. It is about innovating wisely, ethically, and with a spark of humanity that no algorithm can mimic. As we hurtle toward 2030, the firms that master this balance will lead the pack, proving that in law, as in life, the best tools don't just change the game – they redefine it.

Rethinking the legal business model

In discussions with both established law firms and tech start-ups, one sentiment is shared – the legal industry is at a crossroads. The wave of tech innovation, the rise of AI, and the shift in client demands for transparency are tearing the economic foundations of the law profession. The system in which time was the ultimate metric of value is virtually dismantled by AI's ability to shrink hours-long tasks into minutes. Firms are being forced to rethink how they continue to make money, how they evolve and innovate without imploding. Many firms are also thinking about how they organize themselves to survive in a world where technology calls the shots.

From billable hours to scalable products and services

One way to describe this seismic shift is the move from billable hours to scalable services. To navigate the innovator's dilemma, firms need to adapt structures and leadership for the AI age. The model of billing for hours of work cannot cope with clients, fed up with ballooning costs and murky invoices, who are clamoring for transparency and predictability. Such demands could be met by AI tools – routine grunt work, like document review or basic contract drafting, once billed at hourly rates, can now be handled by algorithms in a fraction of the time. About a third of UK law firm leaders believe that some 20-25 percent of their current billable work could be automated in the near future.

This isn't a minor tweak – it's a wake-up call. Time no longer equals revenue, value does. Therefore, firms are pivoting to fixed fees, subscriptions, and outcome-based billing. Such models prioritize results over clock-watching. AI is the engine behind this shift, turning one-off services into scalable, repeatable products. Imagine contract review platforms or litigation prediction tools not as back-office aids, but as standalone offerings that generate steady income streams. The Law Firms' Survey 2024 backs this up – just under half of the top 100 firms expect generative AI to save at least ten percent of chargeable hours, while over 50 percent of mid-tier firms foresee pricing pressure as clients push for cost-effective solutions. It is important to note this isn't just about cutting costs – it's also about redefining how legal services are delivered. We have seen this first-hand from the Innovate UK's funded projects – from a subscription model that delivers AI-driven contract drafting as a service (fast, reliable, and client-friendly) to rolling out subscription tiers that provide scalable access to legal tools, embodying the move to value-based billing. These aren't just experiments, they're glimpses of a future where law firms operate like tech companies, with products that scale beyond the constraints of the hourly grind.

This shift could have a broader societal impact, too. By automating commoditized tasks, AI slashes the cost of some legal services, thus opening doors for those priced out of the traditional system. Such innovations could potentially provide some element of a route into the justice system that people aren't able to access at the moment. Therefore, innovating firms are not just rethinking revenue – they are reimagining access to legal services. Equally, junior lawyers, freed from drudge work, can shift to complex, client-facing roles that AI cannot replicate, enhancing both firm value and client outcomes.

Overcoming the innovator's dilemma

I can't not pay tribute to the late Clay Christensen in this high-stake game of innovation in law. Adopt AI too slowly, and you're left in the dust; adopt it too fast, and you risk gutting your own revenue. This is Christensen's innovator's dilemma in a nutshell – how do you embrace tech that disrupts the very model keeping you afloat? The traditional leverage structure, where junior associates grind out billable hours on low-level tasks, is under siege as AI takes over that work.

The argument is that firms that crack this puzzle would turn disruption into dominance. Slaughter and May is a case study in getting it right. It did not just buy into AI, it invested in it, taking a stake in Luminance, a due diligence platform, and launching Collaborate, an in-house tech incubator. Through Collaborate, it mentors legal tech start-ups, testing and refining tools in real time. Its approach is not about building everything itself – it is about partnering with innovators. Oxford University research[13] points to an "emerging culture" of such collaborations, predicting that by 2030 these partnerships will produce AI products tailored to legal precision. Slaughter and May's approach shows one way to innovate without torching your bottom line. It is about blending tech with tradition, not against it.

Smaller firms are also in the game with affordable, off-the-shelf AI tools – like cloud-based contract analysis platforms. Even small-scale innovations could help level the playing field for a sole practitioner who could tackle workloads that once demanded a team and could potentially compete with Magic Circle giants on efficiency and cost. The Law Firms' Survey 2024 notes that 23 percent of top 51-100 firms are already using tools like Microsoft Copilot, proving that innovation isn't exclusive to the elite. Insights from NGPFS program's Innovation Adoption Accelerators TiPS and Innovate Finance[14] confirm that this democratization could spark a wave of innovative boutique and virtual firms. Such shifts could reshape the legal market as smaller players punch above their weight.

An important lesson of the work of these two adoption accelerators, led by academic partners, is that tech alone would not cut it. The billable-hour mindset and traditional way of work are ingrained in firm culture, which stifles change. Overcoming the inertia and resistance demands a mental overhaul, where AI is seen as a partner, not a threat. Legal Utopia,[15] another NGPFS success story, nails this balance. By teaming up with the Competition and Markets Authority (CMA), it's innovating responsibly, ensuring tech aligns with ethical standards and market needs.

Adapting law firm structures and leadership

We can reasonably expect that the law firm of tomorrow would not just act differently but would look differently. Technological innovation thrives on agility, not rigid hierarchies. The old pyramid, with partners lording over associates, is crumbling under the weight of a tech-driven market. Successful firms prioritize responsiveness – aligning operations with what clients need, not what tradition dictates. Multi-agent AI could take this further, enabling non-hierarchical set-ups where work flows like software, coordinated seamlessly between humans and machines. Picture a "programmable organization" – less bureaucracy, more adaptability. The NGPFS program is already paving the way. Collaborative Conveyancing,[16] one of its projects, automates property enquiries, turning a clunky process into a streamlined, client-centric service. It's a microcosm of what's possible – tech making firms leaner and more agile.

But structure is only half of the picture – leadership seals the deal. The Law Firms' Survey 2024 highlights this shift – 50 percent of top ten firms prioritize cost reduction, while 100 percent are planning transformations to harness technology. These aren't tweaks – they're bold moves by leaders who see AI as a competitive edge, not a cost center. Similarly, smaller firms, though cautious or modest about AI investment, are experimenting with tools like Copilot. Such strategies are not simply about keeping up. They are redefining what leadership means in a tech-first world. For many law firms the question is not whether they will adapt, but how fast and with what vision. Those who champion innovation over inertia will shape the future.

Navigating regulatory and ethical frontiers in a tech-driven legal sector

As AI and lawtech are reshaping the UK legal profession, firms face a stark choice – innovate or stagnate, but never at the cost of trust. While AI solutions promise streamlined workflows, sharper insights, and broader access to justice, they bring regulatory and ethical challenges that demand understanding and careful navigation. From securing client data in cloud systems to addressing algorithmic bias to ensuring accountability and explainability for AI-driven decisions, these issues are critical to a firm's survival.

Data privacy and cybersecurity – the new battleground

Over the past few years, cloud-based and AI tools have transformed legal practice but they have also made data privacy and cybersecurity top priorities. Client confidentiality, once guarded in physical files, now resides on external servers, heightening risks. The SRA mandates GDPR compliance and robust data protection, regardless of AI's complexity, which might complicate oversight. It is widely accepted in the sector that a data breach does not just violate regulations – it erodes trust. This sentiment is shared by almost all the top 100 firms, ranking cyber risks as a major concern,[17] with increasing cybersecurity budgets. Increasing numbers of firms are facing supply chain attacks, exposing AI ecosystem weaknesses.

Algorithmic bias and accountability – AI's double-edged sword

Another challenge around adoption of AI solutions is any algorithmic bias where flawed data could skew outcomes and taint legal advice. A growing concern are the "hallucinations" in GenAI models that can generate confident yet false results. A US lawyer's ChatGPT-crafted brief citing non-existent cases serves as a warning.[18] In the UK, the SRA and Law Society insist that AI can assist, but lawyers retain responsibility. "The human must stay in control" is the profession's mantra. And firms do embed oversight into their processes, like using curated legal datasets to reduce hallucinations, ensuring AI enhances rather than supplants judgment. For litigation teams or corporate functions, this is vital as clients demand fairness and precision, not faulty automation. Therefore, firms that prioritize transparency and human review not only mitigate risks but also gain credibility, leveraging ethical AI as a market advantage.

Regulatory agility – compliance as strategy

It is only fair to recognize that the regulatory landscape is complex and while the UK encourages AI innovation, the EU's AI Act tightens rules, creating a tangible challenge for firms with cross-border clients. We can see firms building internal governance and AI committees, heads of innovation, and CTO positions with the ambition to align tech with ethics. The Law Society's AI framework[19] pushes for transparency and bias testing. For strategic firms, agility in compliance becomes a foundation for growth, not a barrier. Those who anticipate regulatory changes, rather than merely react, will lead the field.

Ethical evolution – a living commitment to responsible innovation

More firms realize that adopting AI isn't a one-off choice – it's an ongoing technological commitment and a strong ethical component. Firms must ensure systems remain transparent and adaptable. This might involve testing outputs, auditing datasets, and training staff to catch errors. As the systems become more complex, these tasks will be more demanding, but the reward is trust – from both clients and regulators. The way to think about this is that firms embracing such ethical rigor do not just prevent ethical missteps – they define responsible innovation. Furthermore, by investing in governance and ethical AI, firms do not just weather the tech revolution but they shape it, delivering value while upholding the profession.

Embracing the future of legal practice

As technology is ushering in a new era it is sweeping away tradition, taking the legal profession to a crossroads. From AI and automation to a vibrant ecosystem of legal tech start-ups, tech innovation, tools, and platforms are redefining the who, what, and how of legal services. This transformation is not simply about adopting new solutions. It is underpinned by strategic and responsible innovation while tackling ethical and regulatory challenges. As this chapter has shown, the evolution of legal practice sets the stage for chapter eight, where we'll explore the human skills that will empower lawyers to excel in this tech-driven future and organizational capabilities that the sector would need. Technology will redefine lawyers as tech-proficient, data-savvy problem-solvers skilled in advocacy and empathy. Experts emphasize that unlearning learned helplessness is key to expanding what's possible in law firms. This mindset shift – embracing continuous learning over outdated habits – will drive success.

The UK's leadership opportunity

The UK legal sector is poised to lead this revolution, with elite firms, a thriving tech ecosystem, and regulatory agility. But this advantage isn't guaranteed – it requires vigilance. With other global legal markets racing to integrate technology, the UK must lead through continuous innovation. This transformation demands bold leadership. Pioneer firms must see AI as a catalyst for reimagining practice, asking, If you could instantly reshape your firm with technology, what would you build? Leadership here means setting the pace while upholding ethical standards.

A future of promise and responsibility

Technology is now the heartbeat of legal evolution. The UK, with its heritage and tech ecosystem, can lead globally by 2030. Initiatives backed by programs like NGPFS showcase its commitment to responsible innovation. This is a chance to redefine justice, widen access, and elevate the human role in a tech-driven world. It's up to the profession to chart this course with courage, creativity, and commitment to professionalism.

References

1 www.artificiallawyer.com/2024/10/22/top-firms-dont-fear-genai-but-others-do-pwc-survey/

2 www.pwc.co.uk/press-room/press-releases/research-commentary/2024/law-firm-performance-surpasses-expectations-with-continued-growt.html

3 https://postshift.com/from-pyramid-to-platform/

4 www.lexisnexis.co.uk/research-and-reports/generative-ai-survey-h2-2024.html

5 https://itbrief.co.uk/story/ai-to-transform-uk-law-firms-with-96-adoption-rate

6 www.pwc.co.uk/industries/legal-professional-business-support-services/law-firms-survey.html

7 www.computerweekly.com/news/252438919/SFO-expands-use-of-AI-after-successful-trial-in-Rolls-Royce-investigation

8 www.slaughterandmay.com/news/luminance-launches-with-backing-of-invoke-capital-and-in-collaboration-with-slaughter-and-may/

9 www.slaughterandmay.com/news/luminance-launches-with-backing-of-invoke-capital-and-in-collaboration-with-slaughter-and-may/

10 www.lawsociety.org.uk/campaigns/lawtech/features/clifford-chance-lawtech-showcase

11 www.clio.com/resources/legal-trends/2024-report/

12 www.pwc.co.uk/press-room/press-releases/research-commentary/2024/law-firm-performance-surpasses-expectations-with-continued-growt.html

13 www.law.ox.ac.uk/sites/default/files/migrated/ai_final1097.pdf

14 https://iuk-business-connect.org.uk/wp-content/uploads/2025/01/Innovate-UK-Next-Generation-brochure.pdf

15 www.legalutopia.co.uk/

16 https://collaborativeconveyancing.co.uk/

17 www.pwc.co.uk/industries/legal-professional-business-support-services/law-firms-survey/risk-and-resilience.html

18 www.reuters.com/legal/transactional/lawyer-used-chatgpt-cite-bogus-cases-what-are-ethics-2023-05-30/

19 www.lawsociety.org.uk/contact-or-visit-us/press-office/press-releases/law-society-new-ai-strategy-the-three-is

Part 2:
People and Culture

Chapter 6:

The key trends shaping the world of work from 2025 to 2030

Maria Govis, manager (CLM operative), global legal business services, KPMG LLP

Introduction

The legal profession does not exist in isolation. Societal, technological, and economic shifts shape the world of work globally, and the legal industry is no exception. This chapter explores key trends shaping the workplace from 2025 to 2030, including generational shifts in the workforce and technology-driven transformation. It examines how these trends will impact the legal profession by 2030, covering workspace culture, leadership structures, well-being at work, talent attraction and retention, and the growing need for upskilling and reskilling. It also offers personal strategies to help legal professionals build careers that align with their values, ensuring a meaningful and fulfilling work life.

Generational shifts reshaping workplace dynamics

Generational differences can feel like a clichéd topic but understanding them helps make sense of relationships across many dimensions – family dynamics, marketing strategies, political and voting behavior, and, of course, the workspace.[1] When discussing generations, researchers typically refer to social generations, i.e. groups of people born around the same time who share similar cultural experiences and have lived through the same significant events. This section explores the characteristics of the generations currently in the workforce and outlines emerging trends for each of them.

Baby Boomers (born 1946-1964)

The Baby Boomers[2] are a particularly large generation that have dominated leadership roles across industries for decades. Of the last five US presidents, four — Clinton, Bush, Obama, and Trump – have been Boomers. In the US, data even suggests that the sheer size of this generation delayed leadership opportunities for Generation X (born 1965-1979).[3] By 2030, Boomers will be

66 and older, retiring in large numbers, and opening up leadership positions for the next generations.

Generation X (born 1965-1979)

Often described as the "in-between" generation, Gen X sits between two cohorts[4] that have been more culturally prominent. By 2030, its members will be between 51 and 65 years old, holding senior positions across the legal industry. Gen X is commonly known for its resilience and adaptability. It is the last generation to grow up in an analog world and had to learn digital technology as adults – unlike younger generations who are digital natives. When it comes to career progression, Gen X tend to favor long-term stability over frequent "job-hopping", a trend that has only gained traction in more recent years.

Millennials (born 1980-1994)

Alongside Gen X, Millennials will also be in leadership positions by 2030. At that point, they will be between 36 and 50, marking the peak years of their careers. Unlike previous generations, Millennials are generally less focused on career "at all costs". Instead, they prioritize purpose-driven work, mental wellbeing, and work–life balance. This shift in values is expected to influence leadership styles, a topic explored later in this chapter.

Generation Z (born 1995-2012)

Currently dominating entry-level roles, Gen Z will be well into their careers by 2030, playing a key role in shaping workspace norms. Law firms and their hiring teams are already aware of this shift.[5] As a fully digital-native generation, Gen Z amplifies many traits associated with Millennials. They value independence, flexibility, and continuous learning. They also expect organizations they work for to take clear stances on social and ethical issues.

Shifting leadership styles

Generational dynamics in the workplace are at a turning point in the 2020s.

The idea that younger generations – particularly Gen Z – "don't want to work" is a reductionist and misleading generalization. Legal professionals seek intellectual challenge and professional growth, which is one of the main reasons people choose to study and work in law in the first place. This remains true for younger cohorts.

However, they also expect to have work environments that support and motivate them to do their best work. With Boomers retiring in the 2020s, younger generations are driving shifts in the workspace culture.

Different generations have varying perspectives[6] on what good leadership means. In recent years, the trend has shifted towards empathy-focused leadership.[7]

Research shows that for leaders to be effective – especially among younger generations – demonstrating growth "at all costs" is no longer enough, as such an approach is often followed by high turnover rates and disengagement. Instead, what is increasingly valued is empathy, active listening, and fostering a genuinely inclusive work environment with healthy interpersonal relationships.[8] In corporate legal careers, this shift means that young employees will seek out leaders who offer more than just impressive quarterly results. They will gravitate towards seniors who actively contribute to a healthy, inclusive workplace and demonstrate genuine investment in their teams' growth – not just on paper.

Rethinking talent attraction

Beyond empathetic leadership, attracting top talent will require offering incentives that align with Millennials' and Gen Z's values. The traditional idea of a legal career – long hours in exchange for high salaries, a corner office and a path to partnership – is becoming less appealing to younger generations. Their priorities are shifting toward different incentives.

Purpose and meaning in work

One of the strongest values for Millennials and Gen Z is purpose-driven work. According to Deloitte's 2024 survey, nine out of ten Millennials and Gen Z workers consider purpose in their jobs to be very or somewhat important.[9]

While the desire for meaningful work is not unique to younger generations, what sets them apart is their increased willingness to walk away from employers or assignments that do not align with their values. By contrast, Gen X has generally been more inclined to prioritize stability and long-term career progression within a chosen organization. This shift highlights the need for law firms and in-house legal teams to rethink how they articulate their values and purpose. Staying attractive to young talent will require more than just competitive salaries – it will mean demonstrating a broader mission beyond shareholder value and profit maximization.

More young legal professionals will seek out values-driven organizations that focus on social impact and ethical responsibility, rather than treating them as an afterthought.

The legal industry is already struggling to attract young talent. In the past seven years, Germany has seen a ten percent decrease in licensed attorneys.[10] Data in this country also shows a significant number of women opting for in-house legal roles instead of practice as attorneys, potentially reflecting concerns about work–life balance and workspace culture within law firms. More broadly, there is growing evidence of a declining interest among young legal professionals in pursuing Big Law careers, including the partnership track.[11]

The question of struggling to find a meaning in a Big Law career is not new.[12] Ultimately, it is a deeply personal question, shaped by individual circumstances. However, the fact that younger generations are "revisiting" this question – and often coming to less favorable conclusions – poses a challenge for Big Law's long-term talent strategy.

Flexibility and remote work

When it comes to attracting young professionals, flexibility – both in working hours and location – is a key incentive. This includes not only flexible working hours (within the constraints of the legal industry), but also remote or, at the very least, hybrid work arrangements. Since the end of the pandemic, there has been a strong push to return to the office for at least part of the week. The results of this return have been mixed[13] – while in-person work has fostered collaboration and team connection, it has also led to declined productivity for some. Still, organizations that allow employees to decide when to come to the office and when to work remotely will be more attractive to younger professionals.

For the newer generations in the workforce:

> *"The best companies aren't families... They're there to provide healthy, fulfilling work environments so that when workers shut their laptops at a reasonable hour, they're the best husbands, wives, parents, siblings, and children they can be."*[14]

Wellbeing at work

Closely tied to purpose, meaning, and work–life balance is workplace wellbeing. Research suggests that professionals who find little meaning in their work are more likely to have mental health issues.[15] Younger workers increasingly expect employers to prioritize mental health. This includes not only fostering a supportive and inclusive workplace culture but also offering concrete benefits, such as mental health coverage in companies' healthcare plans. This trend will be particularly interesting to watch in the legal industry, where mental health has long been stigmatized. As generational shifts in leadership take hold, they may finally drive much-needed changes in how mental wellbeing is perceived and addressed within the profession.

Talent retention and career progression

Given the trends discussed above, expectations around talent retention and career progression are evolving. Both employees and employers will need to adapt to shifting career models and leadership structures.

Flattening of hierarchies

Millennials and Gen Z generally prefer flatter hierarchies, where leaders work alongside employees as part of a team. The long-term trend of increasing individualism – reaching its peak with Gen Z's approach to work – has led to a questioning of traditional authority structures. This mindset shift is also reflected in how Millennial managers tend to operate today. Many naturally adopt a more collaborative leadership style, aligning with younger employees' expectations of openness and shared decision-making.

Rethinking career progression

Economic uncertainty and shifting career values mean that fewer Millennials and Gen Z professionals are drawn to the traditional, decades-long partnership track at law firms. This is a stark contrast to previous generations, many of whom would spend 20+ years at the same firm. As a result, both firms and individuals may need to rethink leadership progression altogether. While companies may explore new organizational strategies beyond the traditional partnership model, individual professionals are increasingly carving out their own alternative career paths.

Individual-level career shifts

Fractional counsel roles

Where the regulation allows it, more legal professionals, instead of committing to full-time, in-house roles, are opting to provide project-based legal support to small and mid-size companies that do not have enough legal work to justify employing an in-house legal counsel, but that still need legal assistance. This model offers legal professionals flexibility and control over chosen clients, and can be particularly appealing to those who want to reconcile career ambitions with family and personal priorities.

Non-linear career paths

Another growing trend is career fluidity among younger generations – not just job-hopping, but industry-hopping. Millennials and Gen Z prioritize continuous learning and skill development, and today's economic climate, combined with the rise of alternative legal careers, makes non-linear career progression increasingly common.

Instead of following a straight path from associate to partner, legal professionals are now moving between law firms, in-house roles, legal tech companies, alternative legal service providers, and fractional counsel positions. These shifts are no longer seen as career missteps, but as intentional, strategic moves aligned with evolving skills and interests.

Company-level structural shifts

Self-management models

While not a new concept, a self-management approach may gain traction in the coming years as Millennials and Gen Z push for flatter hierarchies. Unlike the individual-driven career progression shifts above, self-management represents a structural transformation at the company level. This model challenges the idea of power as a scarce commodity within organizations, where traditional structures often lead to office politics and fierce competition for few available promotions.[16] Instead, the self-management model operates on the premise that people can do their best work and stay motivated in an environment of trust, autonomy, and shared responsibility.

This approach involves distributed leadership, advisory-based decision-making rather than hierarchical power, and the freedom and responsibility to define one's own role and scope of work. In such an environment, careers emerge organically from people's interests and presented opportunities. Self-management is far from an easy, idealistic solution. The approach requires radical collaboration and a steep learning curve for everyone involved. It demands strong communication, trust, and a deep commitment to collective decision-making.

Technology-driven business transformation

Technological advancements, particularly generative artificial intelligence (GenAI), are reshaping how tasks are performed across industries. While the legal sector is often considered slow to adopt new technology, there is no denying that GenAI will have a significant impact on this industry. By 2030, legal professionals will rely even more on process automation and AI-powered tools to handle routine tasks. While AI will not replace legal professionals, it is expected to take over many of the most repetitive activities within legal practices.

This will reshape job roles, with paralegals and legal clerks being among those most affected. Workforce projections already reflect this transformation – the World Economic Forum's (WEF) Future of Jobs 2025 Report has, for the first time, listed "paralegals, legal assistance, legal secretaries, and legal officials" among the fastest-declining jobs for 2025-2030.[17]

As technology reshapes legal work, experienced and early-career professionals will need to adapt to remain relevant in a transforming industry. The key challenges will revolve around upskilling and reskilling of the workforce and redefining early-career legal roles to accommodate these changes.

Growing need for upskilling and reskilling

As noted in the WEF's Future of Jobs Report, "technological advances are expected to drive skills change more than any other trend over the next five years".[18] The same report projects that nearly 40 percent of existing skill sets across the global workforce will become outdated or require transformation between 2025 and 2030. In a workforce of 100 people, it would mean that 59 would need re-training by 2030 to remain employable.

Despite this pressing need, there is currently a lack of proven models for scaling effective reskilling programs.[19] This is a challenge that law firms and other legal professionals must address in the coming years.

Rethinking early-career legal roles

Traditionally, law school graduates would start their careers performing legal research, drafting documents, and handling administrative tasks – many of which are now increasingly performed by means of technology. This raises critical questions in the coming years:

- How will junior lawyers gain foundational legal experience if technology is increasingly handling many of those entry-level tasks?
- What alternative career pathways and new models of legal career progression may emerge, beyond the ones described above?

Growing levels of burnout and workplace disengagement

The legal profession is known for its demanding nature. High ethical expectations, high stakes, and a notoriously poor work–life balance contribute to its reputation as a tough field. In this environment, burnout among legal professionals has become a global issue.[20] The 2021 International Bar Association (IBA) report[21] found that one in three lawyers in 124 jurisdictions said their work negatively or extremely negatively impacted their wellbeing.

More recent data from Bloomberg Law's 2024 Attorney WellBeing Report[22] paints a similar picture. In the second half of 2023, surveyed US legal professionals reported feeling burned out almost half the time at work, with female attorneys affected more (53 percent) than male attorneys (41 percent). For 2024, respondents reported experiencing disrupted sleep (56 percent), anxiety (55 percent), depression (29 percent), and unhealthy coping behaviors, such as increased alcohol use (14 percent). The same report also indicates that by the end of 2023, nearly half (48 percent) of surveyed attorneys admitted to actively seeking or being open to new job opportunities.

Closely linked to burnout is workspace disengagement – a broader corporate trend that extends beyond the legal industry. Gallup's 2025 annual report[23] revealed that only 31 percent of surveyed US employees felt engaged at work, the lowest level in a decade. The most cited reasons included:

- Unclear performance expectations;
- Poorly defined roles;
- Dissatisfaction with the organization; and
- Lack of connection to the company's mission or purpose.

Another key issue is the expectation to check parts of themselves at the door[24] – the need to put on a professional persona that may feel disconnected from the authentic self.

The decline in workplace engagement is closely linked to the generational shifts discussed earlier. According to Gallup's report, workers under 35 have experienced the sharpest drop in engagement levels, reinforcing the need for workplace culture shifts that prioritize wellbeing, clear purpose, and clear career progression.

Studies show[25] that lawyers who feel valued primarily for their financial contributions tend to have worse health outcomes than those who perceive their work as meaningful and aligned with their broader professional growth trajectory.

Reframing this trend – taking ownership of career satisfaction

To end this chapter on a constructive note, it is important to emphasize that – regardless of workplace trends – we, as individuals, have agency over our careers.

In an environment where continuous reskilling and even career changes are becoming more of a norm than an exception, staying in tune with our needs, values, and aspirations is key to professional growth and adaptability. There are numerous methods for career planning and assessing personal job satisfaction. One approach that has personally helped me is applying design-thinking principles to career planning. This framework offers a practical way to be intentional about shaping your legal career, particularly when feeling stuck or disengaged.

While design thinking methodology is not the universal, "one-size-fits-all" solution that it is sometimes portrayed to be, its principles can be highly effective when reevaluating career direction and experimenting with new possibilities. A great starting point for this approach is Bill Burnett and Dave Evans' Designing Your Work Life.[26] It introduces some of the key design thinking principles, putting them in a career development context.

Reframing

Reframing is one of the core principles of design thinking, which involves shifting the way we perceive a situation or a problem, allowing us to acquire new perspectives and explore different approaches. An effective example is how we might reframe feeling stuck in a job:

Original belief: "I am unhappy and feel trapped in my current work situation."

Reframe: "I am competent and capable of making it work anywhere. My current situation is good enough – *for now* – and I will take small, intentional steps to change it."

By shifting focus from frustration to agency, reframing helps move us towards practical, solution-oriented action.

Setting the bar to action low

Another key design thinking principle is bias to action – taking small, proactive steps to solve a problem. For lawyers, this can be particularly challenging, as they are trained to deliver to the highest standards – both in law school and in client work. However, the perfectionist mindset can keep us stuck, forcing us to prefer no action to imperfect action. The suggested solution is to lower the bar. Instead of feeling overwhelmed by the scale of a potential career shift, start with small, manageable steps. This is the same principle used in habit formation – start small, stay consistent, and progress will follow.

In a legal career context, this could mean:

- Reading up on a legal field of interest;
- Having informal conversations with professionals in a career path or legal area you're considering switching to; and
- Exploring possible changes and adjustments within your current role, before making any big moves.

Prototyping

Closely tied to bias to action is prototyping – testing an idea in small, low-risk ways before committing to a major shift.[27]

This approach is particularly helpful when considering career changes or reskilling – for example, transitioning into a new legal practice, moving from a law firm to a government agency (or vice versa), or exploring alternative legal career paths.

A prototype in this context could involve:

- Collaborating on a project with colleagues in the department or practice field you're considering switching to;
- Taking an introductory course in the new area (before committing to graduate or masters programs); or
- Seeking out short-term, on the side projects that align with your interests.

By testing new ideas before making drastic changes, prototyping reduces uncertainty and builds confidence in career transitions.

Storytelling

Storytelling is a powerful career tool, playing a critical role in everything from job interviews to business development. We constantly use storytelling to:

- Present ourselves to recruiters in a compelling way;
- Build relationships within our professional networks; and

- Communicate our companies' values to prospective clients and employees.

A successful career is, at its core, a story – one that we shape through our experiences and choices, and how we present them to the world. The key is to make this story convincing, compelling, and inspiring – not just for others, but for ourselves.

Storytelling is particularly valuable in non-linear career paths, where legal professionals may transition between different focus areas or industries. A well-crafted narrative can help process these pivots, showcasing them for what they are – intentional, strategic, and exciting, rather than disjointed or random.

The principles outlined in this section – reframing, lowering the bar to action, prototyping, and storytelling – are just one approach to being intentional about career planning. While no single method is a perfect fit for everyone, these tools can help overcome feelings of disengagement. It is possible to consistently work on creating a professional path aligned with personal values and aspirations. It is up to us to take ownership of our careers and stay adaptable.

Conclusion

The world of work is complex, and the coming years will not be easier to navigate – from economic and geopolitical uncertainties to the effects of technological advancements. These shifts create both workplace insecurity and opportunities for reskilling and career reinvention.

This chapter has explored generational differences and how they shape workplace dynamics, particularly as younger generations take on a more significant role in the workforce. It is easy to fall into generalizations and finger-pointing from all sides when discussing generational shifts. However, differences do not have to be divisive. Instead, they can be an opportunity for learning, growth, and collaboration – with each generation contributing unique strengths and perspectives. In the demanding legal field, where burnout and workplace frustrations are common, my key message is this. If you're disengaged or unhappy – whether in your current role, workplace, or your overall career direction – change is always possible. You don't have to wait for the legal industry to evolve before taking meaningful personal action. You have the power to shape your own career, right now, within your sphere of influence.

References

1 Twenge, Jean M., *Generations*, Simon and Schuster, 2023.
2 Eurostat, Population structure and ageing, February 2025. https://ec.europa.eu/eurostat/statistics-explained/index.php?title=Population_structure_and_ageing
3 Twenge, Jean M., *Generations*, Simon and Schuster, 2023.
4 European Parliament, *Demographic Outlook for the European Union*, 2002, ISSN 2600-5255
5 Hinchee, J., *The 37-Year-Olds Are Afraid of the 23-Year-Olds Who Work for Them*, October 2021. www.nytimes.com/2021/10/28/business/gen-z-workplace-culture.html
6 Pearce, N., Leading the Six-Generation Workforce, April 2024. https://hbr.org/2024/04/leading-the-6-generation-workforce
7 PhD Brower, T., *Empathy Is The Most Important Leadership Skill According To Research*, September 2021. www.forbes.com/sites/tracybrower/2021/09/19/empathy-is-the-most-important-leadership-skill-according-to-research/
8 Harvard Business Review, Rometti, G., Sutton, R., Rao H., Zaki J., *HBR's 10 Must Reads 2025: The Definitive Management Ideas of the Year*, Harvard Business Review, 2025.
9 Deloitte, 2024 *Gen Z and Millennial Survey*, 2024. www.deloitte.com/global/en/issues/work/content/genz-millennialsurvey.html
10 Dahmen, D., *New Figures on the Legal Market: The Downward Trend Continues*, May 2024. https://rsw.beck.de/aktuell/daily/meldung/detail/anwaltsmarkt-weniger-rechtsanwaelte-mehr-unternehmensjuristen-anwaeltinnen-frauen
11 Miller, J., *Big Law Firms Fall Out Of Fashion with Idealistic Gen Z*, May 2023. www.ft.com/content/c4c8a5fb-bee7-4e9a-81da-cb6255285619
12 Sharbaugh, T., *Is It Possible To Find Meaning In BigLaw?* October 2022. www.legalevolution.org/2022/10/is-it-possible-to-find-meaning-in-biglaw-336/
13 Deloitte, 2024 *Gen Z and Millennial Survey*, 2024. www.deloitte.com/global/en/issues/work/content/genz-millennialsurvey.html
14 Fried, J., Heinemeier Hansson, D., *It Doesn't Have to Be Crazy at Work*, HarperCollins Publishers, 2018.
15 Twenge, Jean M., *Generations*, Simon and Schuster, 2023.
16 Laloux, F., *Reinventing Organizations: A Guide to Creating Organizations Inspired by the Next Stage of Human Consciousness*, Nelson Parker, 2014.
17 World Economic Forum, *Future of Jobs Report 2025*, January 2025.
18 *Ibid.*
19 Harvard Business Review, Rometti, G., Sutton, R., Rao H., Zaki J., *HBR's 10 Must Reads 2025: The Definitive Management Ideas of the Year*, Harvard Business Review, 2025.
20 Tufvesson, A., *Can A Global Push Alleviate Lawyer Burnout?* November 2024. https://lsj.com.au/articles/can-a-global-push-alleviate-lawyer-burnout/
21 International Bar Association, *Mental Wellbeing in the Legal Profession: A Global Study*, October 2021.

22 Bloomberg Law, 2024 *Attorney Wellbeing Report: The Divide Between Health and the Legal Industry*, September 2024. https://news.bloomberglaw.com/bloomberg-law-analysis/analysis-report-highlights-risks-of-poor-attorney-well-being

23 Harter, J., *US Employee Engagement Sinks to Ten-Year Low*, January 2025. www.gallup.com/workplace/654911/employee-engagement-sinks-year-low.aspx

24 Laloux, F., *Reinventing Organizations: A Guide to Creating Organizations Inspired by the Next Stage of Human Consciousness*, Nelson Parker, 2014.

25 Sharbaugh, T., *Is It Possible To Find Meaning In BigLaw?* October 2022. www.legalevolution.org/2022/10/is-it-possible-to-find-meaning-in-biglaw-336/

26 Burnett, B., Evans, D., *Designing Your New Work Life*, Knopf Doubleday Publishing Group, 2021.

27 *Ibid.*

Chapter 7:
Managing generational diversity

By David Laud, chief operating officer, Latimer Hinks

This chapter explores the challenges and opportunities of managing a generationally diverse workforce, offering practical strategies for fostering collaboration, minimizing friction, and building an inclusive, future-ready legal practice.

The generational shift in law firms

The legal profession, often viewed as a bastion of traditions, conservative approaches to management, and meticulously pressed suits, now stands at the cusp of an unavoidable evolution. For centuries, law firms have been run via hierarchical, structured systems where trainees could only look in awe at those who'd worked their way up the ladder, aspiring themselves to one day make partner. This ascent to the hallowed seat at the top table required an investment of many years, typically being committed to the same firm. However, the landscape of law firms is shifting dramatically as a result of demographic changes, technological advancements, and the changing expectations of new generations entering the workforce.

As Baby Boomers (1946-1964) reach retirement age, they leave behind leadership roles and decades of institutional knowledge. Meanwhile, Generation X (1965-1980) has moved into senior leadership positions, tasked with balancing tradition and innovation. Millennials (1981-1996), now the largest segment of the workforce, continue to challenge conventional notions of work, pushing for flexibility, transparency, and purpose-driven careers. And just as firms began adapting to Millennials, along came Generation Z (1997-2012), digital natives with an entirely new approach to career growth, workplace technology, corporate ethics and expectations of diversity and inclusion.

According to the Pew Research Center,[1] Millennials became the largest demographic in the workforce in the US from 2019, comprising over 35 percent of employees, while Generation Z is projected to make up more than

30 percent by 2030. Meanwhile, Baby Boomers, who once made up the backbone of legal leadership, are reaching retirement age in huge numbers. The Alliance for Lifetime Income found that 11,200 Americans will turn 65 every day through 2027.[2] Over the past ten years the figure has been a steady 10,000. Economists have referred to this phenomenon as "Peak 65". With improving nutrition, health and fitness, and desire to continue to contribute to society and their bank balances, not all 65-year-olds retire on their birthday. The implications for law firms are significant – without strategic adaptation, firms risk losing key talent, struggles with succession planning, and failing to create an inclusive culture that appeals to the modern workforce.

The generational shift is about more than just numbers – it's about fundamental differences in how people approach work, leadership, communication, and career progression. Older generations were shaped by stability and hierarchy, whereas younger generations operate in a fast-paced, digital-first world with an emphasis on flexibility, collaboration, and continuous learning.

A 2024 Deloitte study of Gen Z and Millennials[3] highlighted that work–life balance and flexibility remain paramount. The study attributes this to a fundamental shift in workplace expectations – younger employees prioritize career growth, purpose, and workplace culture over mere job security. This is a wake-up call for law firms, who have historically operated under rigid, hierarchical structures with long working hours and an "earn your stripes" mentality.

The law firms that will thrive in 2030 will be those that embrace generational diversity, rather than resist it. Those that fail to adapt risk falling behind in talent acquisition, client engagement, and essentially retention. Clients will also match the generational profile of the firms and as a consequence expect their legal counsel to reflect modern values, technological fluency, and adaptability. Law firms must recognize that generational diversity isn't a problem to be managed – it's an opportunity to be harnessed. A multi-generational workforce offers unique perspectives that can drive innovation, enhance client relationships, and foster a more resilient workplace. The challenge lies in bridging generational gaps, aligning expectations, and creating an environment where every generation can thrive.

Generational characteristics

When managing a multigenerational workforce, it's essential to primarily understand the unique characteristics, expectations, and work styles of each age group. While generational labels can never fully encapsulate the diversity of individuals, they do provide important insights into broader trends that shape workplace behaviors. These differences are often influenced by the economic conditions, technological advancements, and societal values that defined each generation's formative years.

Law firms are currently home to four[4] primary generations – Baby Boomers, Generation X, Millennials, and Generation Z – each bringing their strengths, challenges, and expectations. The ability to recognize and embrace these differences will be crucial in fostering collaboration, reducing conflict, and ensuring a firm's long-term success.

Baby Boomers (1946-1964)

Baby Boomers grew up in a post-war period characterized by economic expansion and stability. Their careers have been defined by loyalty, long hours, and a strong work ethic, with many viewing job security and seniority as signs of success.

Key characteristics:

- Prefer structured, hierarchical workplaces with clear lines of authority.
- Prioritize in-person meetings, phone calls, and traditional communication over digital alternatives.
- Dedicated to their careers, often equating long hours with professional success and having a "live to work" mentality. Despite this, they do know how to kick back and party when the opportunity arises.
- More likely to have spent the majority of their careers at one or two firms.

Boomers have tended to push back against hybrid work models and the younger generation's push for better work–life balance. A Baby Boomer mindset can be guilty of dismissing these calls for improved conditions, seeing them as signs of decreased commitment and disruption to their traditional, structured, and ordered way of working. Despite these differences, Baby Boomers bring invaluable expertise and a deep understanding of client relationships. Rather than viewing retirement as the end of their professional contributions, many are transitioning into advisory or consultant roles. This adjustment in their role opens opportunities for knowledge sharing and mentoring of younger members of staff.

Generation X (1965-1980)

Referred to as the "sandwich generation", Generation X sits between Baby Boomers and Millennials, balancing traditional values with modern work expectations. Having witnessed economic downturns, corporate layoffs, and the rise of technology, Gen X is highly adaptable and independent.

Key characteristics:

- Valued for their strong leadership skills and ability to bridge generational divides.
- Gen Xers often prefer direct communication but are comfortable using email and digital tools.
- Advocates for work–life balance but have an eye on the data and the impact of changes in work patterns on profitability.
- Pragmatic, results-driven, and likely to challenge outdated legal traditions.

Gen X lawyers are often the first adopters of flexible work models in law firms. They value professional autonomy and tend to measure success through results rather than hours worked. Gen X has been instrumental in advocating for alternative career paths in law firms, including part-time partnerships and remote work structures. However, they often feel stuck between older and younger generations, needing to balance tradition with progress.

Millennials (1981-1996)

Millennials, often mistakenly stereotyped as "entitled" or "impatient", have reshaped workplace expectations more than any previous generation. They prioritize purpose-driven work, collaboration, and a healthy work–life balance. Having entered the workforce during economic recessions and rapid technological change, Millennials are highly adaptable and entrepreneurial.

Key characteristics:

- Strong preference for digital communication, such as WhatsApp, Teams, and video calls.
- Value mentorship and frequent feedback rather than traditional annual reviews.
- Prioritize flexibility, hybrid work, and mental wellbeing over rigid career paths.
- Expect clear professional development opportunities and social responsibility from employers.

Millennials make up the majority of law firm associates today, and their expectations are shaping the industry. To retain Millennial talent, law firms must rethink billable hour expectations, introduce flexible work policies, and provide structured mentorship programs. Failure to do so results in high turnover, with firms losing trained associates just as they become most valuable.

Generation Z (1997-2012)

As the first generation to grow up entirely in the digital age, Gen Z lawyers expect seamless technology integration in their work environments. Unlike Millennials, who were instrumental in introducing greater levels of workplace flexibility, Gen Zs are increasingly seeing it as non-negotiable and a deal breaker if not offered by firms.

Key characteristics:

- Strong preference for flexible hours, project-based structures.
- Values authenticity, diversity, and inclusion in workplace culture.
- Prioritizes digital tools, automation, and AI over traditional legal research methods.
- Seeks rapid career progression and continuous learning opportunities.

Having grown up in an environment where the internet and technology generally were at the forefront of so many innovations, Gen Z professionals believe their career success depends on digital literacy. This highlights the importance of tech adoption in law firms – not just for efficiency but for attracting and retaining talent.

A 2023 survey[5] identified that 69 percent of Gen Zs are strong advocates for diversity and inclusion and would therefore seek out employers who offered an inclusive workplace and embraced difference. Additionally, Gen Z is highly entrepreneurial, with many seeking alternative career paths in legal tech, freelance lawyering, and remote consultancy. Firms that fail to accommodate these evolving preferences risk losing top talent to more progressive competitors.

While each generation has unique perspectives, the key to a thriving law firm in 2030 is not about choosing one approach over another – it's about blending the strengths of all generations. By understanding and respecting generational differences, law firms can foster collaboration, reduce turnover, and create a more inclusive, happy and productive workforce.

Challenges of managing a multigenerational workforce in law firms

Having a multigenerational workforce brings numerous benefits, which include diverse perspectives, experience, and skills. Different generations also present unique challenges. The key to navigating these challenges is to recognize the fundamental differences in work styles, communication preferences, career expectations, and attitudes.

Failing to address these generational variances can lead to workplace tension, lack of collaboration, reduction in productivity, and ultimately higher staff turnover. This section explores the primary challenges law firms face in managing generational diversity and offers suggestions to how to overcome them.

Divergent work styles

One of the most common sources of tension between differing age groups in an office environment is the conflict in work styles. Baby Boomers, who grew up in an era of face to face rather than Teams or Zoom meetings, often expect their colleagues to be physically present in the office, believing that long hours and visibility equate to commitment. By contrast, Millennials and Gen Zs are more than comfortable with the technology that enables remote work and flexible schedules, making them more likely to push for hybrid or fully remote arrangements.

Firms that refuse to accommodate alternative work arrangements risk alienating younger employees, leading to high turnover rates. Conversely, firms that move too aggressively toward remote work without maintaining a strong firm culture may struggle with mentoring and essential time invested in knowledge transfer.

Communication barriers

Each generation has distinct communication preferences, which can create friction in daily interactions. Baby Boomers and older Gen Xers tend to prefer phone calls and face-to-face meetings, while Millennials and Gen Z favor instant messaging, emails, and collaborative digital tools such as Microsoft Teams, Google Meet, or Zoom.

Baby Boomers can find instant messaging too informal for business communication, whereas Millennials and Gen Z employees believe that instant messaging enhances workplace efficiency.

This gap can lead to misunderstandings and inefficiencies, particularly in fast-paced legal environments where clear and prompt communication is critical. Younger professionals may feel frustrated by delays in responses, while senior team members may perceive instant messaging as disruptive or lacking professional decorum. In truth, both have their pros and cons and the answer lies in creating a workable process maximizing the benefits whilst mitigating the risk. For example, using WhatsApp for team discussion can be very useful and immediate; however, it can be misused when colleagues become too familiar and exchanges become personal and lacking professionalism. Referencing colleagues not in the "Group" in a negative way can lead to a grievance and claim for harassment / bullying in the workplace.

Attitudes toward career progression and loyalty

Another challenge law firms face is the generational divide in career expectations, advancement, and job loyalty. Baby Boomers and Gen Xers generally subscribe to a traditional, hierarchical career path such as working up to associate level and then it still taking many years before being considered for partner. Millennials and Gen Z, however, are far less likely to wait decades for promotion and are more open to lateral moves or alternative career paths.

The average tenure by generation reflects these differing attitudes. A Career Builder survey in 2021[6] identified the following average time spent with an organization by generation.

- Baby Boomers – eight years, three months.
- Generation X – five years, two months.
- Millennials – two years, nine months.
- Gen Z – two years, two months.

Millennials and Gen Zs are more likely to prioritize skills development, work–life balance, and purpose-driven work over long-term job security. If firms fail to provide clear career progression paths, they risk losing younger talent to more agile and proactive firms, in-house legal departments, legal tech firms, or non-traditional legal roles that offer faster growth and greater flexibility.

Technology adoption and resistance

Technology is rapidly transforming the legal industry, with AI-powered research tools, automation, and virtual collaboration platforms becoming standard. The risk is that the tech takes over our thinking when it comes to managing staff and client relationships and there lies a significant fear for Boomer and Gen X owner managers. Millennial law firm leaders may be less concerned and open to these innovative developments. A balance needs to be struck. While Gen Z and Millennials are digital natives who readily embrace AI-assisted legal research, document automation, and e-discovery tools, Baby Boomers and older Gen X professionals may be reluctant to rely on automation, fearing that technology could replace traditional legal skills. To overcome the disparity between generational approaches, law firms must find ways to bridge the digital gap by providing tailored training, fostering mentorship programs, e.g. younger team members engaged to teach senior staff, and integrating technology in ways that enhance, rather than replace, traditional legal expertise.

Workplace culture and inclusion

Diversity, equity, and inclusion (DEI) initiatives are more important than ever, but distinct generations can have very different perspectives on what they may consider priorities when it comes to workplace culture.

Gen Z and Millennials expect law firms to take clear stances on social issues, actively promote diversity in hiring, and foster inclusive work environments. Boomer leaders traditionally presided over clearly mapped hierarchical structures, serving to reinforce the line of command and culture. Typically, the ethos and personality of the Boomer-led business would be driven by a few, often just one, large personality. Generation X began the move toward an improved work–life balance; however, they often find themselves conflicted by a belief in self-reliance and a strong work ethic.

This generational divide means that firms must be intentional and consistent in their approach to building inclusive cultures that appeal to younger employees while ensuring that older employees are encouraged to adapt and embrace the changing workplace norms.

Addressing these challenges will require proactive and mindful leadership that's firmly in listening mode, offering open dialogue to produce policies that accommodate the diverse expectations of a multigenerational workforce. Rather than viewing these differences as obstacles, forward-thinking law firms can leverage the strengths of each generation, ensuring long-term success in an evolving legal landscape.

Strategies for multigenerational management

To be successful in managing a diverse workforce, law firms need a clearly articulated strategy. Leaders must use their plans to help engage with teams and to ensure that policies that support collaboration and inclusion are appropriate and consistent. Rather than allowing generational differences to become a source of tension, firms that proactively implement effective management strategies can turn diversity into a competitive advantage.

This section outlines key strategies that law firms can use to foster a productive, inclusive, and adaptable workforce, ensuring that each generation is able to contribute its strengths while benefiting from the experience and knowledge of others.

Creating a culture of inclusion and respect

Law firms that succeed in managing generational diversity will be those that focus on a culture of trust, respect, and inclusivity at every level of the organization. This will require the recognition of each generation's unique perspectives, skills, and work preferences, rather than conforming to a single standard.

Key actions:

- Implement cross-generational mentorship programs; for example, senior members of staff sharing institutional knowledge while younger employees provide tech insights.
- Promote psychological safety by encouraging open discussions about generational expectations and potential biases. Understand the need to protect and support the mental health of all workers, noting that Gen Zs are more likely to be proactive in this area and Baby Boomers less forthcoming.
- Use multi-channel communication approaches to accommodate different preferences (e.g., in-person meetings for Boomers, digital collaboration tools for Millennials and Gen Z).

Implementing flexible work models

Workplace flexibility is no longer a Millennial or Gen Z demand – it has become a defining feature of the modern law firm. Regardless of this, understanding the balancing of flexibility with the needs of a structured, client-driven industry still remains a challenge for many firms.

Key actions:

- Offer hybrid work models that allow staff to work remotely part of the week while maintaining regular in-office collaboration.
- Implement outcome-based performance metrics rather than focusing purely on hours worked, aligning with younger generations' expectations for autonomy.

- Provide options for alternative career paths, such as part-time partnerships, project-based roles, or legal consulting positions.

Firms that resist flexibility risk high turnover rates among Millennials and Gen Z employees, the generations that tend to be more willing to switch firms or explore non-traditional legal roles if they feel their work–life balance needs are not met.

Leveraging technology as a unifying force

Technology adoption varies significantly across generations, but rather than being a divisive factor, technology can serve as a bridge between different work styles and preferences when implemented thoughtfully.

Key actions:

- Provide ongoing technology training for senior staff to increase comfort with AI-driven legal research, document automation, and collaboration tools.
- Implement reverse mentoring programs, where younger attorneys help senior colleagues navigate digital tools.
- Select user-friendly, intuitive legal software that works across different generational comfort levels.

Rethinking career progression and succession planning

Traditional law firm career paths, where solicitors slowly ascend to partner over 15-20 years, no longer align with younger generations' expectations. Gen Z and Millennials seek a more accommodating career trajectory that encompasses meaningful personal development alongside work–life balance considerations. To attract and retain top talent, firms must rethink their approach to career progression.

Key actions:

- Introduce non-traditional career paths, such as legal operations, legal technology roles, and alternative leadership positions.
- Create structured mentorship and sponsorship programs to support Millennial and Gen Z staff in developing management and leadership skills.
- Have a clearly mapped career progression plan. Ensure the plan can flex to accommodate those who show initiative and capability, above and beyond expectations, recognizing talent regardless of age and length of service.

Strengthening intergenerational collaboration

Rather than isolating different generations into silos, the most successful law firms intentionally foster collaboration between generations, ensuring that institutional knowledge is preserved while new ideas and innovation are encouraged.

Key actions:

- Implement cross-functional, intergenerational teams to solve complex client issues.
- Use team-building exercises that focus on shared learning and problem-solving.
- Encourage leadership to actively support an inclusive firm culture that values diverse perspectives.

By embracing these strategies, law firms can turn generational diversity from a management challenge into a strategic advantage.

Case studies and best practices – managing generational diversity in law firms

Theory and discussions are all well and good, but there's no substitute for the evidence of practical applications where the value of effective multigenerational management becomes evident. Several leading law firms have successfully implemented policies and cultural shifts to embrace generational diversity and improve workforce retention. Here, we look at case studies of firms that have successfully implemented their plans, offering examples of best practices for firms looking to follow suit.

Clifford Chance – reverse mentorship and tech integration

Clifford Chance recognized almost five years ago that younger lawyers increasingly demonstrated an agility with technology that surpassed that of the senior partners who relied on traditional legal workflows. To bridge the digital divide, the firm introduced a reverse mentorship program, pairing junior associates with senior partners to exchange knowledge.

Younger lawyers trained senior solicitors on AI-powered legal research, case management software, and digital client engagement. But it wasn't all one-way traffic. Senior lawyers mentored junior associates in negotiation tactics, client relations, and case strategy.

The result was a more "tech-savvy" leadership team that could engage effectively with clients, while junior associates benefited from mentorship that accelerated their professional development. The program has proven to be hugely successful across the firm's offices, winning a prestigious inclusivity and diversity award in Germany.

Baker McKenzie – flexible work models and DEI initiatives

Baker McKenzie took a proactive approach to generational diversity by restructuring its work policies to accommodate flexible schedules and advancing diversity, equity, and inclusion (DEI).

The firm introduced hybrid work models that allowed lawyers to balance remote work with in-office collaboration. Billable hour expectations were revised, allowing Millennials and Gen Z lawyers to meet their targets in more flexible ways. A diversity and inclusion council was established to promote generational equity in leadership succession planning.

These efforts significantly reduced churn rates among younger lawyers, many of whom had previously left large firms due to rigid billable hour requirements and limited career flexibility. Firms struggling with talent retention should consider adopting similar flexible policies that prioritize both efficiency and employee wellbeing.

Allen & Overy – AI and automation adoption

Allen & Overy implemented an AI-powered document automation initiative aimed at improving efficiency in contract drafting and due diligence. The firm took great care in the way it introduced this initiative considering generational diversity by:

- Training all generations of lawyers to understand AI's benefits without fearing job displacement.
- Assigning Millennial and Gen Z "Tech Ambassadors" to help senior lawyers integrate AI tools into daily workflows.
- Using AI to eliminate low-value administrative work, allowing senior staff to focus on high-impact case strategy.

As a result of this successful launch, the firm realized a 25 percent reduction in time spent on routine tasks, boosting productivity and enhancing intergenerational collaboration in the process. Firms looking to adopt new technologies and improve working practices can avoid negativity, pushback, and fear of change by adopting a collaborative cross-generation approach.

Best practices for managing generational diversity

Based on the insights gained from these case studies, the following best practices can help firms create a more inclusive and efficient workforce:

- *Implement structured knowledge-sharing programs* – reverse mentorship, cross-generational teams, and firm-wide training initiatives help prevent generational silos.
- *Adopt hybrid and flexible work* – law firms should balance client demands with employee wellbeing by offering hybrid schedules and results-oriented performance metrics.
- *Modernize career progression paths* – recognizing that Millennials and Gen Z may not be interested in traditional partnership tracks; firms should offer alternative leadership roles.
- *Encourage generational inclusivity in leadership* – firms should ensure that generationally diverse lawyers are represented in decision-making committees.
- *Invest in legal tech adoption strategies* – training programs for all generations should be integrated with technology rollouts to avoid resistance from older generations.
- *Prioritize DEI initiatives that include generational awareness* – age-based diversity should be incorporated into broader inclusion efforts.

Firms that integrate these best practices will be better positioned to navigate generational shifts, retain top talent, and enhance workplace satisfaction.

Future generational diversity

As we approach 2030, law firms must recognize that managing generational diversity is not just a "tick box" human resources initiative – it's an effective business strategy. Firms that embrace the strengths of each generation will be the ones that stand better prospects of attracting talent, fostering collaboration, and maintaining a competitive edge. This chapter has explored the defining characteristics of each generation, the key challenges that arise in a multigenerational workplace, and the best practices that successful law firms are implementing to turn generational diversity into an asset rather than a liability.

Managing generational diversity requires a proactive and structured approach. Looking at the core strategies discussed throughout this chapter, firms should consider prioritizing the following key actions:

- *Foster a culture of mutual trust and respect.* Every generation has unique strengths, and law firms must create an environment where senior lawyers' institutional knowledge is valued as much as younger lawyers' technological and ethical approaches to work.

- *Implement reverse mentorship programs.* Junior lawyers can train senior attorneys on AI-driven legal tools and modern client engagement, while senior lawyers can provide mentorship on legal strategy and case management.
- *Redefine leadership and succession planning.* Since Millennials and Gen Z may not follow traditional partnership tracks, firms should consider alternative leadership opportunities to help retain top talent.
- *Modernize work models and performance metrics.* Traditional rigid billable hour expectations may alienate younger lawyers. Hybrid work arrangements and outcome-based evaluations can support retention goals.
- *Prioritize technology training across all generations.* Firms should ensure that legal tech rollouts are inclusive and accessible to prevent resistance from senior staff.
- *Encourage cross-generational collaboration.* Assign mixed-age teams to casework and client relationship management, allowing different perspectives to enhance legal problem-solving and engagement.

The future of the multigenerational law firm

Looking ahead, the legal industry will continue to evolve, with younger generations taking on more leadership roles and new technologies reshaping the profession. As Generation Z enters law firms in greater numbers, they will challenge existing structures and demand greater inclusivity, efficiency, and innovation.

Additionally, firms must prepare for Generation Alpha (born after 2012), who will enter the workforce in 2030 as apprentices. This generation, raised in an AI-powered world, will have even higher expectations for technological integration and work–life balance than their predecessors. Forward-thinking law firms should begin laying the groundwork now for long-term adaptability.

Ultimately, the firms that thrive in 2030 and beyond will be the ones that break down generational silos, prioritize continuous learning, and adapt to new workforce expectations.

The law firm of the future should not be defined by a single generation's preferences but rather by how well it integrates the strengths of all generations. By embracing generational diversity as a strategic opportunity and positive competitive differentiator, law firms can build a more dynamic, inclusive, and resilient workforce – one that not only meets the needs of today but is fully prepared for the challenges of tomorrow.

References

1 www.pewresearch.org/short-reads/2018/04/11/millennials-largest-generation-us-labor-force/
2 www.protectedincome.org/news/peakofpeak65/
3 www.deloitte.com/global/en/about/press-room/deloitte-2024-gen-z-and-millennial-survey.html
4 By 2030 we will see the likelihood of five generations at work. The first members of Generation Alpha, born 2013, will be 17 and seeking work experience and apprentice roles whilst the youngest members of the Baby Boomer generation will be 66 and potentially considering "What next?" with regards to retirement, part-time work, or consultancy.
5 https://tallo.com/blog/genz-demands-diversity-inclusion-strategy/
6 https://web.archive.org/web/20230319020429/ https://www.careerbuilder.com/advice/blog/how-long-should-you-stay-in-a-job

Chapter 8:
Building capabilities for the tech-driven law firm – strategies for 2030 and beyond

By Martin Martinoff, innovation lead – Next Generation Professional and Financial Services, Innovate UK

The shifting sands of legal practice

As the innovation lead for the Next Generation professional and financial services program of Innovate UK, in this chapter I attempt to synthesize reflections and observations regarding the transformative forces shaping the legal profession. Through direct engagement with innovative projects, industry leaders, regulatory bodies, and technology pioneers, I have identified critical strategic considerations for senior leaders aiming to position their firms successfully towards 2030.

Adapting to a new competitive reality

In my role at Innovate UK, I have observed firsthand the profound shifts occurring in how clients procure legal services. Clients, increasingly sophisticated and informed, demand greater value, transparent pricing, and heightened efficiency. The rise of technologically enabled in-house legal departments has intensified pressure on external law firms to innovate their service models significantly. Leaders must now prioritize agility, innovation, and entrepreneurial thinking, strategically aligning their offerings closely with evolving client expectations.

It has become evident how alternative legal service providers, Big Four consultancy firms, and tech-driven start-ups have fundamentally disrupted traditional competitive structures. These entrants employ advanced technology, optimized processes, and flexible organizational models, challenging legacy business structures. The importance of embracing strategic innovation and developing robust partnerships to maintain competitiveness and drive sustainable growth is paramount.

Navigating regulatory shifts

Regulatory frameworks have consistently emerged as catalysts for innovation within the legal sector. Our engagement with regulatory bodies, including initiatives like the SRA's Innovate program, has highlighted significant opportunities created by regulatory developments – the facilitation of multidisciplinary practices, external investments, and flexible operational models – all significantly reshaping the industry's operational landscape.

There are growing societal and governmental pressures on firms to leverage technology ethically to enhance access to justice. It has become clear that future-ready firms must strategically prioritize ethical innovation and regulatory compliance to ensure technology is harnessed responsibly rather than reactively. Such a proactive approach to regulation not only ensures compliance but strategically positions firms for sustained success.

Furthermore, there is a growing emphasis on sustainability and ESG factors within the legal profession. Firms are not only advising clients on ESG compliance but also integrating these principles into their own operations, from reducing carbon footprints to ensuring ethical supply chains in their procurement processes. This alignment with societal values enhances a firm's reputation and meets the expectations of socially conscious clients.

Meeting the demands of global clients

Client expectations have evolved rapidly, a trend that is particularly noticeable in the interactions facilitated by Innovate UK's industry engagements such as our National Showcase and legal match-making events. Clients increasingly demand technologically sophisticated, efficient, and transparent services, accentuated by globalization. International business clients expect seamless cross-border service delivery, necessitating robust digital infrastructures and competencies in virtual collaboration.

There are clear advantages to firms adopting integrated digital platforms that enhance client engagement through consistent communication and transparency, regardless of geographical boundaries. Senior leaders must embed digital transformation deeply within their strategic priorities, equipping their firms with the digital fluency necessary for competitive differentiation.

The future legal workforce

A crucial insight derived from my leadership at Innovate UK relates to the rapidly shifting composition and expectations of the legal workforce. The newer generation of legal professionals notably prioritizes flexibility, meaningful work, and technological integration above traditional career paths. This generational shift, compounded by an ageing legal workforce and heightened competition for tech-savvy talent, necessitates significant recalibration of talent management strategies.

The pandemic accelerated the transition towards hybrid and remote working models. Leaders must now master new competencies in managing remote teams, cybersecurity, and virtual collaboration tools. Promoting a culture that supports continuous professional development and adaptability has become imperative to attract and retain the best talent in this new environment.

Embracing disruptive technologies

My interactions with leading technology initiatives through Innovate UK's program have continually reinforced the pivotal role technology plays in shaping the legal profession. AI and automation have swiftly transitioned from peripheral innovations to essential operational tools. Despite widespread adoption among larger firms, a notable technological gap remains evident among smaller firms, presenting both a challenge and an opportunity for strategic leadership.

Recent technological advancements, particularly in generative AI since 2023, have radically altered how legal processes are conducted. Mastering tools such as generative AI – including competencies in prompt engineering and validating AI-generated outputs – is rapidly becoming essential for legal professionals. Additionally, emerging technologies like blockchain and quantum computing could further revolutionize contract management, dispute resolution, and secure data practices by 2030. These innovations represent forward-looking technological capabilities senior leaders must cultivate proactively.

Generative AI tools, such as large language models, are revolutionizing legal research and drafting by enabling lawyers to generate first drafts of documents and conduct complex legal analyses in a fraction of the time previously required. However, the adoption of these tools also raises critical questions about the accuracy of AI-generated content and the need for human oversight. Firms must invest in training lawyers to effectively use these tools while maintaining the highest standards of legal rigor and ethical responsibility.

Overcoming challenges, building capabilities

It is evident that navigating the convergence of market shifts, regulatory developments, evolving client demands, workforce dynamics, and technological disruption poses distinct challenges. Leaders must strategically cultivate new capabilities to address these.

- *Technological literacy.* Effectively harnessing technologies such as AI, blockchain, and quantum computing.
- *Innovation management.* Actively engaging with and leveraging the lawtech ecosystem.
- *Strategic agility.* Rapidly adapting to evolving market conditions and regulatory environments.
- *Advanced talent management.* Attracting, developing, and retaining a digitally proficient and adaptive workforce.
- *Ethical data governance.* Ensuring responsible, transparent, and compliant use of client data and technological tools.
- *Client-centric service design.* Embedding transparency, flexibility, and responsiveness into all aspects of service delivery.

The capability of senior leaders to anticipate and proactively manage change, strategically invest in capability development, and foster innovation-driven cultures will decisively shape their firms' future success. Firms that embrace these insights will not merely survive the evolving landscape – they will thrive and actively influence the future direction of the legal profession.

Developing individual capabilities for future practice

As the legal landscape evolves, the capabilities required from legal professionals are undergoing a significant transformation. Senior leaders must proactively foster these capabilities within their teams, ensuring lawyers remain effective, innovative, and competitive in the future. This section outlines the critical individual capabilities lawyers must develop to thrive in the changing legal environment, strategically guiding law firms toward sustained relevance and excellence by 2030.

Technical and digital competencies

The rapid integration of technology in legal practice mandates that lawyers possess not merely familiarity but mastery of digital tools. This technical competence is increasingly viewed as a core professional responsibility, with jurisdictions globally embedding technology literacy into ethical and professional standards.

Every lawyer must develop foundational digital literacy in basic tools that are central to modern legal practice, including case management software, digital document collaboration platforms, and virtual meeting technologies. Mastering these foundational digital tools enhances productivity, facilitates seamless client interaction, and supports flexible work environments, crucial in a post-pandemic world. Leaders must ensure structured training programs are in place to maintain this baseline digital literacy across all practice areas.

As lawyers' roles are rapidly changing, with advanced technology increasingly managing routine legal tasks, mastery of AI-driven tools such as generative AI, automated document drafting, and predictive analytics is becoming imperative. Developing capabilities in prompt engineering, validating AI-generated outputs, and understanding limitations and biases inherent in AI systems are crucial.

Legal analytics, powered by big data and machine learning, is becoming an essential tool for informed decision-making in legal practice. By analyzing vast amounts of case law, judicial behavior, and litigation trends, lawyers can provide clients with data-driven insights and more accurate predictions of legal outcomes. Firms that invest in legal analytics capabilities will be better positioned to offer strategic advice and gain a competitive edge in complex litigation and advisory work

Many consider blockchain to be on the back burner, but lawyers must also familiarize themselves with blockchain applications for secure contracts and intellectual property management, as these technologies gain regulatory support and broader adoption. By 2030, quantum computing could further revolutionize secure data handling and complex litigation analytics, placing a premium on forward-thinking technical skills. Leaders should proactively encourage their teams to embrace continuous technical learning and experimentation with emerging technologies.

Cognitive and creative skills

As routine tasks are increasingly automated, lawyers' value will be defined by their cognitive and creative contributions. This shift demands fostering strategic thinking, creative problem-solving, and innovation capabilities among legal professionals.

Therefore, lawyers must develop creative problem-solving techniques, such as design thinking and agile methodologies, to address complex and novel legal issues. Cultivating a culture that encourages curiosity, experimentation, and challenging traditional assumptions is essential. Leaders can support this by hosting innovation workshops, internal hackathons, and cross-departmental collaborations to develop and apply creative solutions to practical legal problems.

Legal design thinking, which applies design principles to legal services, is gaining traction as a method for creating more user-friendly and accessible legal solutions. By focusing on the end-user experience, lawyers can develop innovative products and services that better meet client needs, such as simplified contract templates or interactive legal guides. This approach not only enhances client satisfaction but also positions firms as leaders in client-centric innovation. Employing client journey mapping and legal service design methodologies allows firms to proactively identify friction points and innovation opportunities across client interactions. This approach not only enhances client satisfaction and loyalty but also streamlines internal processes, improving overall service delivery and operational efficiency.

With automation increasingly handling routine tasks, the legal profession will value strategic and critical thinking. Lawyers must synthesize legal, technical, and business insights into strategic recommendations. Leaders should encourage their teams to develop lateral thinking and systems thinking skills, ensuring they can anticipate broader implications and create innovative solutions proactively. Training programs that emphasize scenario planning, future-casting exercises, and strategic risk assessments are crucial for developing these cognitive skills.

Interpersonal and collaborative skills

The future legal professional must excel at interdisciplinary collaboration, emotional intelligence, and sophisticated communication – particularly in hybrid and globalized working environments.

Lawyers increasingly work in teams with technologists, data analysts, and project managers, necessitating effective multidisciplinary collaboration across professional boundaries. By 2030, integrated multidisciplinary teams will be commonplace, requiring leaders to foster cross-disciplinary knowledge-sharing and teamwork skills through rotational programs, joint training, and collaborative project initiatives.

It is generally accepted that enhanced emotional intelligence, encompassing active listening, empathy, influencing, and conflict resolution skills, will distinguish future leaders. Given the growing prevalence of virtual and cross-cultural interactions, law firms must ensure lawyers are proficient in managing relationships and communications effectively across diverse, geographically dispersed teams. Leaders must model these skills, signaling their critical importance to the firm's success.

Professional development and adaptability

Continuous learning and adaptability have become non-negotiable traits for lawyers. Of course, the rapid evolution of technology and regulation mandate continuous professional development. However, lawyers must be more flexible and creative and engage in lifelong learning through micro-credentials, certifications, and self-directed training. Firm leadership should institutionalize this through structured learning programs, innovation sabbaticals, and strategic partnerships with tech providers to continually update lawyers' skills in cybersecurity, digital ethics, and emerging legal technologies.

Within the professional context, adaptability, coupled with resilience, is crucial to enable legal professionals to pivot quickly as market demands and technologies evolve. Leaders must create environments that reward adaptability, encouraging lawyers to proactively seek diverse and challenging experiences that build agility. Promoting a growth mindset throughout the organization is fundamental to maintaining lawyers' effectiveness amid continuous change.

Resilience training is becoming critical as lawyers navigate constant technological advancements and rapidly evolving market conditions. Law firms should incorporate resilience-building programs, equipping legal professionals with psychological strategies to sustain high performance and adaptability under continuous change and uncertainty.

Business acumen and entrepreneurial thinking

Where I have seen tensions between worldviews is when lawyers try to increasingly view legal practice through a business lens, understanding clients' commercial drivers, exploring innovative service models, and contributing actively to firm growth. Understanding law as a business is important. Developing financial literacy, understanding pricing strategies, and gaining insights into clients' industries and business models are critical competencies. Senior leaders should facilitate practical business training such as mini-MBAs, secondments, and client-focused workshops, aligning legal advice directly with commercial realities.

Encouraging lawyers to think entrepreneurially, identifying opportunities for innovation, and developing scalable legal solutions or products can significantly differentiate firms. Leadership can foster internal "intrapreneurship" through structured innovation challenges, business development training, and incentives for lawyers who actively contribute to the firm's strategic growth and diversification.

Ethical and professional responsibilities

Maintaining rigorous ethical standards remains crucial as technology reshapes legal practice, presenting new dilemmas around data privacy, AI accountability, and transparency with clients. Lawyers must uphold ethics and integrate traditional ethical principles with modern technological competence, ensuring responsible and ethical use of digital tools and client data. Leaders should establish clear guidelines, provide continuous ethics training tailored to technology use, and conduct regular compliance audits to maintain high ethical standards and safeguard the firm's reputation.

Within both low-tech start-ups and law firms, it is widely accepted that as AI tools become commonplace, lawyers must cultivate the judgment to critically assess their outputs, maintaining professional skepticism and rigorously addressing biases or inaccuracies. Transparency with clients regarding AI use will be increasingly vital for maintaining trust and compliance. Firm leaders should provide practical training to empower lawyers in making ethically sound decisions involving AI and technology.

As legal professionals increasingly rely on digital tools and platforms, the importance of cybersecurity and data privacy cannot be overstated. Lawyers must be well-versed in data protection regulations, such as GDPR and CCPA, and understand how to safeguard sensitive client information in a digital environment. Firms should prioritize cybersecurity training and establish robust protocols to mitigate the risk of data breaches, which can have severe reputational and legal consequences.

There are more than enough competency frameworks but, ultimately, developing these individual capabilities strategically positions lawyers to effectively navigate and lead within the transforming legal environment. Such proactive investment by senior leaders in these competencies not only enhances individual performance but significantly strengthens organizational resilience and competitive advantage in the evolving legal market.

Building the firm's organizational capabilities

In engaging with senior leaders, we often discuss approaches to investing proactively in building organizational strengths, ensuring their firms remain agile, innovative, and competitive in an increasingly complex and technology-driven environment. Distilled to a handful few, here are the key areas where firm-level capabilities must be developed strategically for sustainable future success.

Cultivating genuine innovation cultures

Innovation isn't merely about adopting new technologies – it involves embedding a mindset of continuous exploration and intelligent risk-taking throughout the firm. Effective innovation cultures require active leadership endorsement – not just rhetoric, but tangible support such as allocating dedicated resources for experimentation, creating internal innovation incubators, and instituting regular innovation challenges. It's clear that the most successful leaders encourage calculated risk-taking, viewing failures not as setbacks but as critical learning opportunities. Real innovation comes from intentionally designed ecosystems where creativity is nurtured, and where the imperative to evolve supersedes attachment to the status quo.

Firms can significantly enhance innovation by actively promoting intrapreneurship through structured innovation challenges, internal incubators, and dedicated accelerator programs. Recognizing and rewarding entrepreneurial efforts internally fosters a vibrant culture of continuous innovation and proactive service development.

Strategic leadership development beyond traditional boundaries

Leadership capabilities in legal firms are evolving rapidly. The traditional hierarchical approach is increasingly giving way to more distributed leadership models, reflecting broader business trends towards agility and responsiveness. Today's leaders require competencies in digital strategy, agile team management, and cross-cultural communication, especially as firms embrace hybrid and remote working environments. Structured leadership development programs focused explicitly on these emerging areas equip leaders to guide their organizations through disruption effectively. The firms that thrive tomorrow will be those actively investing in developing diverse leadership talent at all organizational levels, creating resilient and flexible leadership structures.

Integrating new professional roles and agile structures

A significant shift underway in innovative legal firms is the deliberate integration of non-traditional roles – such as legal technologists, data scientists, project managers, and innovation specialists – into multidisciplinary teams. This approach enriches service delivery by blending deep legal expertise with critical complementary skills. Firms pioneering these integrated teams gain agility, responsiveness, and enhanced capacity for innovation. Importantly, clearly defined career pathways for these emerging roles are essential for attracting and retaining top talent from diverse professional backgrounds.

Transformative knowledge management and continuous improvement

Through extensive engagement with UKRI projects, I've seen that effective knowledge management, enhanced by sophisticated AI-driven tools, is indispensable for delivering superior legal services. Firms that leverage collective knowledge systematically and embed continuous improvement methodologies, such as Agile and Lean, significantly enhance their client offerings. Senior leaders must champion modern knowledge management practices, provide continuous upskilling for their teams, and institutionalize feedback loops and regular process reviews. The ultimate goal is an adaptive organization that continuously refines its methods based on real-time insights and client feedback.

Legal Project Management (LPM) is increasingly recognized as a vital capability for managing complex legal matters efficiently. By applying project management principles – such as scoping, budgeting, and resource allocation – firms can improve the predictability and transparency of their services. LPM not only enhances client satisfaction but also helps firms manage costs and risks more effectively, making it a key differentiator in the market.

Proactive process optimization and AI integration

One particularly innovative insight from our program has been the necessity of proactively addressing organizational debt – the legacy processes and structures hindering technological and operational advancement. Forward-thinking firms systematically identify and eliminate these inefficiencies to pave the way for seamless AI and automation integration. Leaders who prioritize modernization create an environment conducive to technological experimentation, rapid deployment, and iterative learning. Robust data governance frameworks and cybersecurity practices further ensure ethical and compliant technology deployment.

Legal operations, as a discipline, has emerged as a critical function for driving efficiency and innovation within law firms. By adopting best practices from other industries, such as Lean Six Sigma and process mapping, firms can systematically identify bottlenecks and redundancies in their workflows. This structured approach to process improvement not only enhances service delivery but also frees up lawyers to focus on higher-value, strategic work.

Client-centricity as a strategic imperative

Leading firms differentiate themselves through deep, institutionalized client-centricity. This means proactively anticipating client needs, systematically soliciting client feedback, and integrating these insights into agile, technology-enhanced service models. Techniques like client journey mapping and legal project management enhance service transparency and predictability, significantly boosting client satisfaction. Client-centric firms build meaningful partnerships with their clients, becoming trusted advisors rather than transactional service providers.

Clients are increasingly seeking outcome-based legal services, where the focus is on achieving specific business goals rather than traditional billable hours. This shift requires firms to adopt more flexible pricing models, such as fixed fees or success-based arrangements, and to align their services more closely with clients' strategic objectives. By embracing this approach, firms can differentiate themselves in a competitive market and build stronger, long-term client relationships.

Visionary, influential leadership for future success

Finally, leadership in the future legal landscape must be visionary, adaptable, influential, and ethically robust. Tomorrow's leaders must excel at anticipating market shifts, leveraging technological opportunities, and fostering resilient, adaptable organizational cultures. Building strategic coalitions beyond traditional industry boundaries, particularly with technology firms and academia, will be crucial. The ethical implications of technological adoption, especially concerning data privacy and AI ethics, will demand vigilant oversight and proactive leadership.

Final call to action

In conclusion, senior leaders are uniquely positioned not merely to anticipate or adapt to the evolving landscape of the legal profession, but to actively shape and influence its trajectory. Strategic investment in capability development – at both the individual and organizational levels – is paramount, requiring a comprehensive approach that blends technological mastery, innovative mindsets, strategic agility, and unwavering ethical responsibility.

Drawing on insights from our Next Generation Professional and Financial Services Program, I've observed directly the transformative potential when firms proactively engage with these emerging capabilities. The opportunities outlined in this chapter reflect areas I am particularly passionate about developing and exploring further. Therefore, I warmly invite collaboration with forward-thinking senior leaders, innovative firms, technology pioneers, and industry experts committed to driving this future-forward agenda.

Together, we can not only navigate but define the future of legal services, setting new benchmarks for excellence, innovation, and client-centric value. The firms that embrace these collaborative opportunities today will stand out tomorrow – not just as survivors, but as influential leaders reshaping the very fabric of the legal profession.

Chapter 9:
The socially responsible legal practice

By Aoife Greally, people business partner, Clio – Cloud-based Legal Technology

Introduction

The legal profession has long been associated with high stress, long hours, and intense competition – factors that have contributed to widespread burnout, anxiety, and attrition. This deeply ingrained culture has made these challenges a reality for many in the industry. Recent research by the *ABA Journal* on lawyer mental health[1] reveals that 83 percent of lawyers experience stress[2] at least some of the time, while 71 percent struggle with anxiety.[3]

In response, the legal profession is shifting towards more flexible and sustainable career structures and workplace practices. The move away from rigid, high-pressure environments – evidenced by the rise in alternative employment models and flexible work arrangements – reflects a growing demand for a healthier, more balanced approach to legal work.

However, changes to such deeply entrenched norms don't come from nowhere. What's behind this growing demand?

Two major forces are reshaping how the legal profession approaches well-being:

1. *Cultural change*. Society is placing greater emphasis on wellbeing – understood as a holistic combination of mental, physical, and emotional health – and how it impacts job performance.
2. *Technological advancements*. Innovations in legal technology are streamlining workflows and making flexible work arrangements more viable than ever before.

Working together, these forces are creating new opportunities for law firms to redefine their cultures, improve individual wellbeing, and enhance overall organizational performance – now and in the near future.

The primary driving force is the increasing recognition of wellbeing as a crucial factor in the workplace. As awareness grows, discussions about mental health – once overlooked or even taboo – are now acknowledged as essential for productivity and employee satisfaction.

Across industries, wellbeing-focused initiatives such as Mental Health First Aid[4] and workplace wellness programs are becoming standard practice. The UK corporate wellness market reflects this shift, with a projected compound annual growth rate (CAGR) of 4.72 percent from 2024 to 2029.[5] This growing emphasis on workplace wellbeing is set to reshape even traditionally rigid professions, like law, by 2030.

The second driving force is the rapid advancement of legal technology, which has transformed lawyers' workflows – enhancing efficiency and flexibility. Innovations such as artificial intelligence (AI), automation, and cloud-based platforms have streamlined essential tasks like document review, contract drafting, and client communication, allowing legal professionals to work smarter and more effectively.

Insights from Clio's *Legal Trends Report*[6] show that 96 percent of UK law firms already use AI, with 62 percent planning to increase adoption over the next year. These innovations free lawyers from many time-consuming and mundane tasks, offering them increased opportunities to focus more on meaningful work and overall wellbeing.

What does this all mean for the legal profession in the next five years and beyond? Prioritizing wellbeing is essential for law firms, both for business outcomes and employee wellness. By 2030, we predict that law firms that invest in a culture of wellbeing will not only be better positioned to attract top talent and improve retention but also to deliver better client outcomes.

This chapter explores how law firms can build these environments by redefining what success means, leveraging technology, and embracing leadership accountability.

The business case for wellbeing

For law firms in today's competitive landscape, a foundation of workplace wellbeing isn't just an employee perk or talking point, it's a business strategy that can deliver measurable results. Firms that actively invest in wellbeing initiatives – such as leveraging technology to streamline workloads or offering flexible work schedules – don't just support their teams; they see improved engagement, reduced turnover, and stronger client relationships.

As we've discussed, the legal industry has long been known for demanding long hours and generating stress. But, in today's legal talent market, these conditions are increasingly viewed as a retention risk rather than a mark of distinction. Workplace culture is more and more a deciding factor for in-demand employees, especially in a competitive industry like law.

Lessons from the Great Resignation

Take the post-pandemic Great Resignation,[7] for example. In 2021 and 2022, amid the uncertainty of the COVID-19 pandemic, record numbers of professionals across industries quit their jobs – often citing reasons like inflexible work arrangements, burnout, and unsustainable workloads. This shift signaled a new focus on employment priorities for modern workers where work–life balance and mental health are often equally important to financial compensation, status, and career growth.

For law firms going forward, a core lesson learned from the Great Resignation is clear – prioritizing employee wellbeing is a competitive advantage. Firms that embrace work flexibility, mental health initiatives, and balanced workloads are better positioned to attract top talent and keep their best employees happy and engaged.

Building a business case for increased productivity and lower stress

Beyond hiring and retention, the business benefits of a focus on wellbeing extend even further.

Research from the University of Oxford[8] indicates that happier employees are up to 13 percent more productive, while lower stress levels can enhance cognitive function and ethical decision-making – which are critical in high-stakes legal work.

Numerous studies related to lawyer mental health and wellness have shown that firms with strong wellbeing policies tend to experience better decision-making,[9] improved workplace dynamics,[10] and improved performance.[11] In fact, Clio's *Legal Trends Report*[12] found that firms using cloud-based legal practice management software – technology that supports lawyer flexibility and efficiency – are 43 percent more likely (86 percent compared to 60 percent) to have satisfied clients.

Additionally, emotionally resilient lawyers with balanced workloads are often better equipped to manage high-pressure cases, communicate effectively, and build long-term client relationships.

To put it another way, while happy, engaged lawyers are more likely to stay in their roles, they're also well-positioned to deliver higher-quality service to clients. By making wellbeing central to law firm policies and workflows, firms can foster a more engaged and resilient workforce while also strengthening their bottom line.

However, from a business perspective, investing in wellbeing is about more than just keeping lawyers engaged. It's also about creating a high-performing workforce that delivers better client outcomes – which ultimately drives firm success.

Redefining success in legal practice

To meaningfully integrate wellbeing into legal practice, law firms need to rethink long-standing industry habits and norms – starting with how they define success. At its core, this means shifting key performance indicators[13] (KPIs) beyond traditional measures to reflect a more balanced, sustainable, and people-first approach.

The human cost of traditional success metrics

Law firms have long centered their success around the billable hour, prioritizing hours billed and hitting challenging revenue targets. However, when billable hours are a firm's predominant measure of success, the human impact on lawyers and staff can be significant – driving burnout,[14] mental health struggles, and, for law firms, retention issues.

The rise of wellbeing as a performance indicator

Recognizing the challenge of traditional law firm success metrics, forward-thinking firms are increasingly moving beyond the billable hour. Instead, they are embracing broader performance metrics that prioritize wellbeing and sustainable legal careers.

Examples of key wellbeing metrics for law firms include:

- Employee satisfaction scores (such as job satisfaction surveys).
- Employee turnover rates (such as tracking rates of retention and voluntary departures).
- Access to mental health resources (such as utilization rates of therapy or wellness programs offered by the firm).
- Workload balance metrics (such as tracking overtime hours and time spent on non-billable tasks).
- Annual leave usage rates (that is, ensuring employees are taking their full holiday entitlement).

However, this isn't to say that this shift towards wellbeing is only about improving employee satisfaction. A focus on wellbeing can also enhance a law firm's success from a business perspective.

Embracing new approaches to success

To actively improve wellbeing, many law firms are adopting innovative approaches to legal work, such as:

- Client-centric performance metrics that reward client satisfaction and value-driven legal work – instead of just hours billed.
- Flexible work models, such as hybrid and remote work arrangements, which support flexibility and work–life balance.
- Alternative employment structures that give lawyers greater autonomy over their careers and daily tasks.

One alternative employment model that aligns with a major shift challenging the traditional UK law firm model is the rise of consultant lawyers[15] – self-employed legal professionals who serve clients without being tied to a conventional law firm structure. Research by LexisNexis[16] estimates that one in three lawyers could be working as consultant lawyers by 2026, which aligns with the growing demand for flexibility in the profession.

Why is this employment model so attractive in today's industry? Consultant lawyers have control over their workload, clients, and working hours, often operating remotely and managing their own practice – all of which aligns with the modern era of prioritizing flexibility and wellbeing.

Striking the right balance – productivity, profitability, and wellbeing

Looking ahead, it's apparent that the most successful law firms of 2030 will be those that can effectively and consistently balance financial performance with wellbeing-focused success metrics. This balance will be crucial not just for ensuring profitability in a competitive, technology-driven legal industry, but also for fostering a work environment that supports the wellbeing and satisfaction of employees – ultimately paving the way for a more sustainable and successful future.

Firms that can integrate initiatives focused on employee satisfaction, mental health, and wellbeing alongside traditional productivity and profitability measures will be better positioned to attract top talent, retain experienced lawyers and staff, and drive long-term business growth.

Leadership and wellbeing

For a law firm to successfully embrace a culture of wellbeing, leadership teams and managing partners must champion transformation. Workplace culture and policy start at the top, and when leaders actively prioritize wellbeing, they create an environment where employees feel empowered to do the same.

Setting the tone for lasting change

As Clio CEO and founder Jack Newton discusses in his book, *The Client-Centered Law Firm*,[17] lawyers are often resistant to change – especially when it comes to shifting long-standing industry norms towards new processes or mindsets. That's why leadership must lead by example to ensure wellbeing initiatives are embraced by everyone.

"Most lawyers do not like change," Jack Newton writes. *"I can't tell you how many stories I've heard of lawyers outright refusing to accept a new process, a new tool, or a new mindset without even considering the potential benefits to be had. There are many reasons for this, of course. Lawyers are famously risk averse, and being risk averse often translates to being change averse. But unfortunately, this deeply ingrained resistance to change could hold entire firms back – even if it only comes from a few staff or lawyers."*

Leading by example – key areas for wellbeing

In addition to implementing policies aimed at driving improvements in wellbeing, law firm leaders should take the time to understand the value of wellbeing at work and actively demonstrate it. Some key areas where leadership can make a significant impact include:

- *Personal care.* Leaders can prioritize their own physical and mental health to set a positive example. This may mean openly discussing the use of firm-provided wellness resources, engaging in wellness and exercise activities, and showing vulnerability around wellbeing struggles.
- *Open communication.* Fostering a workplace culture where discussing wellbeing and seeking help is encouraged, and not seen as a weakness, can make a big impact. Leaders can strive to create safe spaces for staff to discuss challenges related to work–life balance and wellbeing.
- *Work–life balance.* Leaders should advocate for sustainable workloads and model healthy boundaries. This could involve taking regular breaks, using annual leave and personal days as entitled, and respecting time away from work by not sending non-urgent emails late at night.

Newton has also highlighted the importance of prioritizing wellness for law firms. As he wrote in a post discussing the future of law,[18] there is a clear connection between driving innovation and success in the legal industry and remembering that lawyers are human beings first.

"To effectively provide legal services, keep improving the profession, and uphold the laws that govern our society, lawyers both need and deserve the space to take care of themselves," he writes. *"You cannot serve others from an empty cup, and treating yourself as a human being should not be opposed to career and/or law firm success."*

He also emphasizes that wellbeing is more than just an individual concern – it can directly impact a law firm's success.

"Remember, a client-centered approach is not a client-first one – it's also a firm-focused mindset. Your ability to effectively meet client needs is central to the success of your law firm. However, this should not come before the health of your business, your personal health, or you as a human being. Putting clients first unreservedly while putting your law firm and yourself second is not a recipe for personal or firm success."

The future of leadership in law firms

As the legal industry moves away from more rigid, profit-driven models towards a people-first approach, law firm leadership styles will need to evolve in kind. The firms that thrive in the future will be those whose leaders embrace wellbeing focused, empathetic, and flexible leadership.

This shift will require rethinking leadership priorities, placing greater emphasis on:

- People-centric leadership, where employee wellbeing is prioritized as a key driver of firm success.
- Trust-based management, focusing on outcomes rather than tracking hours worked, fostering greater employee autonomy.
- Mentorship and professional development, ensuring that lawyers receive guidance, growth opportunities, and support.

By cultivating a firm culture that prioritizes wellbeing, law firm leaders can unlock long-term benefits – from increased employee engagement and motivation to higher productivity, improved client service, and even greater firm resilience.

Leveraging technology for wellbeing

One of the most effective ways to improve wellbeing is to create more time – and today's legal technology is increasingly making this not only possible, but achievable, for legal professionals.

The role of technology in reducing mundane tasks

Another long-accepted norm in the legal industry is that there's simply a lot of tedious, repetitive work that must be completed – no matter how long it takes to trudge through it. Tasks such as manually searching through case law, reviewing contracts, tracking time, and preparing invoices can consume significant time and energy, contributing to stress, burnout, and a lack of work–life balance.

By adopting legal technology tools that use automation[19] and AI,[20] law firms can streamline many of these tasks, freeing up valuable hours and reducing workload pressure.

How AI can boost efficiency and reduce lawyer stress

Legal AI tools offer an unprecedented opportunity for law firms to leverage technology to free up time and reduce workloads, which can lead to improved wellbeing.

Research in Clio's *Legal Trends Report*[21] found that the UK legal industry is rapidly embracing AI.[22] Of the law firms surveyed, 97 percent have adopted AI in some way, and more than half (56 percent) of those firms report widespread or universal AI adoption.

Law firms are using AI to automate many of their most time-consuming tasks, with the *Legal Trends Report*[23] noting that UK firms are using AI to assist with tasks related to:

- Document drafting and automation (36 percent);
- Contract review and analysis (29 percent);
- E-discovery (20 percent); and
- Legal research (17 percent).

The *Legal Trends Report*[24] highlights some of the numerous benefits of AI adoption, including improved work quality and productivity (43 percent), business growth (41 percent), and cost savings (29 percent).

The time savings generated from using technology to streamline processes benefit the individual lawyer, of course, but they can also have a positive impact on client service. For example, by reducing the time spent on mundane tasks, lawyers have more time and mental energy to focus on complex cases, build stronger client relationships, and provide better strategic advice – which ultimately leads to client satisfaction.

How technology can help lawyers improve wellbeing

When lawyers can use technology – securely and responsibly – to reduce the time spent on mundane tasks and improve efficiency, they gain greater flexibility to focus on meaningful legal work. By reducing the time dedicated to routine administrative tasks, technology like AI and automation can have a significant positive impact on work–life balance and overall wellbeing.

Additionally, by automating repetitive work tasks, AI can help reduce overall cognitive load. Reducing cognitive load allows lawyers to focus on intellectually stimulating and fulfilling tasks, which can contribute to greater job satisfaction and better mental wellbeing.

Notably, when it comes to wellbeing, 21 percent of UK respondents in the *Legal Trends Report*[25] said that AI helps reduce late nights and weekend work and 20 percent said that AI enhances their mental wellbeing at work.

This highlights how adopting legal technology today is not merely a measure for efficiency. It's also a key tactic for cultivating a modern, sustainable culture of wellbeing that will shape the future of law firms.

Building a culture of wellbeing

Embracing wellbeing at your law firm is not just a nebulous future aspiration – it's essential for long-term success in today's competitive legal market. As we've discussed, cultivating a law firm culture that prioritizes wellbeing can lead to numerous additional benefits, such as improved employee recruitment and engagement, higher productivity, and better overall law firm performance.

However, building a culture of wellbeing can feel overwhelming, and law firm leaders may be unsure of where to begin. To help navigate this challenge, here are some practical strategies to help foster a law firm workplace culture centered on physical health, mental health, and wellbeing.

Implementing mandatory wellness training

Wellness training initiatives – such as workshops covering topics like mindfulness and time management – can help educate staff on the importance of mental and physical health. Taking the time to focus on these topics and learn tools and strategies can go a long way towards helping employees better manage stress and avoid burnout.

While offering these training initiatives is beneficial, making them a core part of professional development sends a clear message that wellbeing is important and helps ensure employees will prioritize wellbeing and gain maximum value from them.

Offering access to mental health resources

Providing employees with accessible mental health resources, such as counselling services or stress relief workshops, helps create a supportive and psychologically safe workplace. This is particularly important in the legal industry, where mental health challenges have historically carried a stigma. By actively promoting mental health support and fostering an open, accepting culture, law firms can help break down these barriers.

When employees feel safe discussing their wellbeing and are equipped with access to the right resources, they are more likely to become more resilient, engaged, and productive.

Creating flexible work policies

Rigid working nine-to-five (and beyond) hours in the office have traditionally been the norm in law firms, but offering flexible work arrangements can significantly improve wellbeing.

From remote work options to flexible hours or compressed workweeks, offering flexible work arrangements signals trust and respect while allowing lawyers and staff to manage their work–life balance in a way that works best for their individual situation. In turn, this flexibility can help reduce stress, improve employee satisfaction, and lead to a more engaged and happy workforce.

Fostering a psychologically safe work environment

A psychologically safe work environment is one where employees feel safe to voice their opinions, take risks, and make mistakes. In law firms, leadership can embrace open communication and make it clear that lawyers should feel empowered and safe to speak up – particularly around concerns about workloads or wellbeing challenges – without facing negative consequences.

Initiatives such as regular check-ins, anonymous feedback channels, and visible leadership commitment to mental health and workload balance are all useful tactics for achieving this in a law firm culture.

Conclusion

By 2030, establishing a culture of wellbeing will not be a luxury or a superficial branding effort – it will be a fundamental necessity for firms that want to thrive. Societal shifts, evolving employee expectations, and rapid technological advancements are reshaping the legal industry. As such, firms that fail to prioritize wellbeing risk falling behind the competition in key areas ranging from talent retention to innovation to overall firm success.

However, law firms that haven't previously focused on wellbeing shouldn't see this as a reason to panic. Instead, now is the time for law firm leaders to proactively integrate wellbeing into their core organizational strategy.

To build a future-ready, well-being-focused workplace, law firms should:

- Leverage legal technology like automation and AI to reduce workload pressures.
- Embed wellbeing into the firm culture through training, access to mental health resources, and flexible work policies.
- Foster a psychologically safe work environment where employees feel empowered to voice concerns and maintain a healthy work–life balance.

Keep in mind that building a wellbeing-focused law firm doesn't require an all-or-nothing approach – the steps outlined here are simply strategies to help start or refine the process. Starting with small changes and shifts – even as simple as leadership openly discussing wellbeing on a regular basis or encouraging breaks – can lay the groundwork for larger initiatives.

With that said, that doesn't mean that building a culture of wellbeing should stem solely from the efforts of law firm leaders. While leaders are ultimately responsible for driving the changes, involving employees in shaping wellbeing policies is a good way to ensure that initiatives are truly impactful and relevant to their needs.

It's also important to note that shifting the legal industry's traditional mindset around wellbeing won't happen overnight, and implementing these changes at a law firm will require intention and persistence. However, the rewards from building a culture of wellbeing at a law firm can be substantial.

Law firms that act now will gain a significant competitive edge and will stay competitive in the years to come. Forward-thinking firms that embrace a wellbeing-focused culture are more likely to attract and retain top legal talent, operate more efficiently, and build stronger client relationships. On the other hand, firms that resist change and stick to rigid norms despite shifting lawyer and client expectations are more likely to face higher turnover, lower morale, and an outdated reputation in a rapidly evolving industry.

Firms that embrace this transformation will not only build more resilient, motivated, and engaged teams, they will also position themselves at the forefront of a new generation of legal practice. By making wellbeing a priority today, law firms can shape a future that is not just more sustainable for their employees, but also more agile, innovative, and socially responsible.

References

1 Braithwaite, C. (15 August 2024) Mental health in the legal profession, Clio. www.clio.com/uk/blog/mental-health-in-the-legal-profession/

2 Cassens Weiss, D. (12 April 2023) Lawyers report high level of satisfaction with their jobs, but stress remains an issue, survey finds. *ABA Journal.* www.abajournal.com/news/article/lawyers-report-high-level-of-satisfaction-with-their-jobs-but-stress-remains-an-issue-survey-finds

3 Robert, A. (19 May 2023) Mental health initiatives aren't curbing lawyer stress and anxiety, new study shows. *ABA Journal.* www.abajournal.com/news/article/mental-health-initiatives-arent-curbing-lawyer-stress-and-anxiety-new-study-shows

4 Mental Health First Aid England, https://mhfaengland.org/

5 GLOBE NEWSWIRE (22 April 2024). United Kingdom corporate wellness report 2024-2029, featuring Zevo, ComPsych, Elevate Health, Mantra Care, Healthy Performance, Joyful Living, Reinvent Lifestyle, SuperWellness and Workplace Options. Yahoo Finance. https://finance.yahoo.com/news/united-kingdom-corporate-wellness-report-101400864.html

6 Clio (2024). *The latest Legal Trends Report: AI adoption in UK law firms.* www.clio.com/uk/resources/legal-trends/2024-report/ai-adoption-uk-infographic/

7 Gratton, L. and Cable, D. (22 June 2022) What's driving the Great Resignation? London Business School. www.london.edu/think/whats-driving-the-great-resignation

8 University of Oxford (24 October 2019) Happy workers are 13 percent more productive. University of Oxford. www.ox.ac.uk/news/2019-10-24-happy-workers-are-13-more-productive

9 Krill, P. R., Degeneffe, N., Ochocki, K., and Anker, J. J. (3 June 2022) People, professionals, and profit centers: The connection between lawyer wellbeing and employer values. *Behavioral Sciences* (Basel), 12(6), 177. https://pmc.ncbi.nlm.nih.gov/articles/PMC9219783/

10 Sloan, K. (1 October 2024) Workplace bullying affects one in four lawyers, study finds. Reuters. www.reuters.com/legal/litigation/workplace-bullying-affects-1-4-lawyers-study-finds-2024-10-01/

11 Lucking, N. (14 April 2024). Beyond billable hours: A study of mental health in the legal sector. Unmind. https://unmind.com/blog/beyond-billable-hours-a-study-of-mental-health-in-the-legal-sector

12 Clio (2022) 2022 Legal Trends Report. www.clio.com/uk/guides/legal-trends-report-2022/

13 Matich, T. (3 April 2024) *62 law firm KPIs for evaluating your firm's success*. Clio. www.clio.com/uk/blog/law-firm-kpis/

14 Miki, S. (15 August 2024) Work-related stress: avoiding solicitor burnout. Clio. www.clio.com/uk/blog/work-related-stress-solicitor-burnout/

15 Donnery, L. and O'Neill, B. (14 February 2025) The rise of the consultant lawyer: Why 33 percent of lawyers could join the model by 2026. Clio. www.clio.com/uk/blog/consultant-lawyer/

16 Brown, D. (5 April 2022) Will a third of lawyers really be legal consultants by 2026? LexisNexis. www.lexisnexis.co.uk/blog/future-of-law/will-a-third-of-lawyers-really-be-legal-consultants-by-2026

17 Clio. *The Client-Centered Law Firm*. www.clio.com/resources/client-centered-law-firm/

18 Newton, J. (10 November 2021) The future of law: thriving as a legal practitioner and a person. Clio. www.clio.com/blog/thriving-practitioner-and-person/

19 Braithwaite, C. (23 February 2023) How legal workflow automation increases law firm revenue and efficiency. Clio. www.clio.com/uk/blog/legal-workflow-automation-law-firm-revenue-lawyer-efficiency/

20 Clio. A lawyer's guide for artificial intelligence. www.clio.com/uk/guides/ai-guide-for-lawyers/

21 Clio (2024) *The latest Legal Trends Report: AI adoption in UK law firms*. www.clio.com/uk/resources/legal-trends/2024-report/ai-adoption-uk-infographic/

22 Donnery, L. (18 November 2024) How UK law firms are adapting to AI and technology: key insights from the Legal Trends Report. www.clio.com/uk/blog/ai-technology-trends/

23 Clio (2024) 2024 Legal Trends Report. www.clio.com/uk/resources/legal-trends/2024-report/

24 Clio (2024) The latest Legal Trends Report: AI adoption in UK law firms. www.clio.com/uk/resources/legal-trends/2024-report/ai-adoption-uk-infographic/

25 Clio (2024) The latest Legal Trends Report: AI adoption in UK law firms. www.clio.com/uk/resources/legal-trends/2024-report/ai-adoption-uk-infographic/

Part 3:
Finance and Operations

Chapter 10: Pricing strategy and profitability in an AI-enabled future

By Chantal McNaught, manager of client success, LEAP AI

The law firm of 2030 will have practical complexities to navigate, including profitability, pricing, and capacity due to advances in artificial intelligence (AI) technologies. This chapter outlines how profitability and pricing intersect, and why it is of equal importance to consider law firm capacity when setting pricing and measuring for profitability. This chapter first addresses pricing methodology, noting that whilst in some cases time-based billing will have its place, this will ultimately be usurped by more client-centered billing models. Then, profitability is addressed as billing modes shift, and measures of profit-per-equity-partner are likely to adapt. Finally, I look at how AI's impact on capacity will influence both pricing and profitability, which is an important aspect of the law firm of 2030 not to be ignored.

To begin with, let us explore the terms used in this chapter and expand on what is meant by profitability, pricing, and capacity, and why they matter to the law firm of 2030.

Profitability is existential for law firms. To provide legal services and deliver access to justice, there must be law firms to distribute those services. As law firms are businesses in a capitalist market, profit becomes one of the very few ways in which law firms can continue to provide legal services. Even as pro bono services become more essential, profitability is the foundation on which law firms can start to consider providing some legal services without charge.

The rapid adoption of AI technologies in law firms has inflamed the time-based billing debate. This debate is ultimately about pricing models. Legal services are classified by economists as "credence goods" – meaning an inherent knowledge asymmetry exists between lawyers and their clients.[1] This knowledge asymmetry means that clients cannot accurately assess the quality or necessity of the received legal services. This makes it difficult for lawyers to transparently price the value of their legal services. Some have reasoned that this is why the billable hour has lasted so long.[2]

Now with AI technologies disrupting this knowledge asymmetry, new challenges arise for law firms:

- Increased efficiency means less time spent on legal tasks;
- Less time spent equates to fewer billable hours charged; and
- Fewer billable hours leads to reduced profitability.

This disruption in profitability means that new pricing models will be adopted by firms eager to remain profitable.

At the center of profitability and responding to the pricing challenges posed by AI technologies is law firm human resources. Law firm human resources require active management and scheduling to ensure the right capacity for profitable legal services delivery. David Maister's wisdom explains that a good scheduling system considers profitability, client service, skill building, and motivation and morale.[3] The challenges posed by AI technologies in the law firm impact all four of these areas.

Traditionally, profitability considerations to scheduling have been about utilization. Making sure all human resources are kept busy on legal work is, indeed, fundamental to the firm's profitability and continued existence in business. But, as Maister puts it, this is "far from the whole story". Client service can have a profound influence on the strategic decisions to place law firm human resources on particular matters. This has been a trend in the legal profession, with larger law firms servicing multiple areas of law allocating client work to expert teams. AI technologies shift the power to the client, making personality and approach much more important than knowledge and expertise.

Building the skills of those in the law firm is also a strategic decision that is made at each capacity assignment. Maister identifies three outcomes in skill building – area of practice specialists, industry experts, and generalists. It is arguable that AI technologies will result in a fourth outcome – empathetic specialists. As functional and industry expertise falls in demand due to client access to AI technologies, clients will demand more emotional skills from their lawyers.

This is where clients will see the value of their lawyers. The only way law firms can support increasing emotional skills is through actively considering how they assign the human resources to matters to develop this skill alongside practice and industry knowledge.

Motivation and morale in the legal profession is a crucial issue generally, not just in the law firm context. A mental health crisis in lawyers has been reported globally.[4] Law firms have some responsibility for this through the assignment of legal work. Maister identifies a myriad of criteria within the motivation and morale consideration, including interests and professional development. It is these two that are most likely to be influenced by AI technologies, as more lawyers graduating with computer science degrees look to grow their ambitious careers. Only the law firms considering how best to grow their human resources motivation and morale can seek to have a well-rounded scheduling system to adequately manage capacity and support profitability.

How profitability and pricing intersect

As explained above, profitability is existential for law firms in the capitalist market. Law firms trade in legal services and legal services are credence goods, which by their nature have a knowledge asymmetry causing clients not to know the value of the legal services received. This is fundamentally why both profitability and pricing intersect, and why the law firm of 2030 will have to contend with how AI technologies are disrupting the incumbent hourly-billing model.

Law firms have traditionally priced legal services as a rough estimate determined by the number of hours and who in the team would be completing the work. This estimation process is inaccurate and at times adjusted so that the prospective client agrees for the firm to commence the instructed legal work.

As the work is completed, sophisticated time keeping software tracks and calculates the time spent by everyone in the legal team, often calculated in the infamous six-minute unit. This ultimately means the matter is "front loaded" so when it comes to billing, the senior lawyer responsible for the client's relationship or the firm's billing team (or both) adjusts the time entries down to a more "suitable" billable amount to be charged to the client.

Over the course of a year, this approach can result in hundreds of thousands of unbilled, written-off time recordings in a small law firm (for example, five to 20 fee earners). That is if the firm has disciplined processes to ensure all work completed was time tracked accurately against the matter to begin with. Often, it is not.

In many instances, law firms do not have disciplined time-keeping, resulting in only a fraction of the time spent completing the work for the client being entered into the timekeeping software. Then, when it comes to billing, the sophisticated discounting process proceeds, slicing off time recordings to suit a number that appears reasonable to charge the client. What this ultimately results in is firms lacking the complete data to know how much time in monetary value is spent on an item of legal work (see Figure 1).

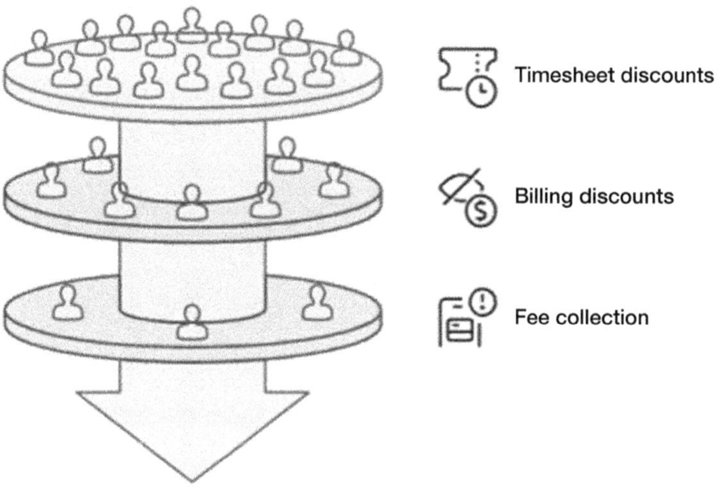

Figure 1: Types of revenue leakage.[5]

According to industry research conducted by legal technology provider, Clio, the average 2024 United States lawyer misses 5.1 hours in time recording per eight-hour day. Upon billing, a further 5.4 hours are deducted. Collections are short by 5.7 hours.[6] Plugging this into a calculator created with the assistance of Claude.AI, the ratios of billed and collected are 89.7 percent and 79.3 percent respectively. This means that the time recordings entered in the system make a profound difference to the ultimately collected value at the end.

Prompt for AI to create a calculator based on the Clio data:
Can you please create a calculator that shows the correct proportional differences between three categories of legal work: Hours worked, hours billed, and hours collected? Setting hours worked to be 2.9, this is proportioned to 2.6 hours billed, which is further proportioned to 2.3 hours collected. I want to be able to calculate hours billed and hours collected by adjusting how many hours worked. Can you build this for me?

In law firms where time records are not accurately maintained and discounting becomes a routine part of billing, the profitability of each matter recedes. The firm itself becomes less profitable and therefore not sustainable.

The AI technology threat to the time-based billing model is acute and devastating to firms reliant on their human resources recording 2,600 billable hours per year.

When the only product produced is a service, the pricing of that product becomes a critical feature in the law firm's profitability picture. Going back to how a piece of legal work is priced, there is very little reference to how long things took last time. When there is, lawyers often turn to what they have billed. This is a critical issue as only 89.7 percent of recorded hours are in fact billed on average. The practice of inaccurate or undisciplined time keeping, undercut further by routine discounting, makes it impossible to provide an accurate upfront price for legal services based on the time model.

This is how profitability and pricing are inextricably linked. Without a robust pricing model from which law firms can bill, AI technologies and all the productivity benefits that come with them will continue to tear strips out of the law firm's profits, leaving them exposed to collapse.

The role of capacity

The third corner of this triangle is how law firms deal with scheduling their human resources. Without adequately, appropriately, and strategically assigning work to the right lawyers, law firms risk the very resources they rely on to deliver the legal services they provide in the market.

Lawyer conduct codes require lawyers to be competent in their legal service delivery. This is consistent across the world. Competency can only be developed through on-the-job training. Law school graduates are proficient in legal reasoning but not in the practice of law. This is where the tradition of lockstep came in; the rationale is that for each year of legal practice, the lawyer commands more competency and thus is a more valued asset to the firm, commanding a higher charge-out rate.

This hourly charge-out rate is how the traditional firm prices legal services. Pricing the matter upfront is a conservative estimate based on what was previously billed and is related to who would be conducting the work on the matter. Only in rare cases do traditional law firms take into account Maister's considerations of:

- Client service;
- Skill building; and
- Motivation and morale.

In those rare cases, it is generally in complex and expensive litigation where firms can justify the time and energy spent preparing such estimates. In cases of transactional work, prices are set from what was previously billed, and the firm allocates whoever is available to work on the transaction. Utilization is king. Only the most sophisticated and moderately large firms can afford to consider other aspects to capacity. Or so many have thought.

By ignoring capacity when pricing the legal service, traditional law firms pay a handsome opportunity price. This is a price the law firm of 2030 can no longer afford. The law firm of 2030 has a menu of pricing methodologies available, with the selection made appropriate for each type of work. These are now considered in turn.

Pricing strategies

As AI technologies are now becoming ubiquitous in law firms, the challenge to traditional pricing and billing modes has reached fever pitch. Whilst time-based billing (and therefore pricing) was never favored, discussions on improving the process have become more prevalent. Just as horse-centered transportation reached its peak right at the advent of automobile transportation, so too has time-based billing reached its peak in 2025.

More modern pricing methodologies have steadily been developed over the course of decades. The legal profession is primed to undertake a revolution. In much the same way as the automobile transformed transit, AI technologies transform the way law firms of 2030 undertake pricing strategy.

Here is a selection of ten pricing strategies that have emerged and gained prevalence.

Value-based pricing

Value-based pricing outdates the billable hour. It is a pricing model suited to some legal services better than others. Family law, commercial transactional work, and immigration all spring to mind. Here are three steps to apply a value-based pricing strategy:

- Focus on the importance of the matter to the client.
- Emphasize the outcome or results rather than the time spent.
- Consider the complexity and novelty (to the client) of the questions involved.

Test the efficacy of this pricing strategy with market research and benchmark against the time spent on those types of matters (as a check for profitability) to make sure the levels are set correctly.

AI technologies can be of assistance here, providing analysis of previous similar matters and how much clients actually paid. If this data is not available, the 79.3 percent collection value from the Clio research can be used.

Value-based pricing works well with work that is well automated with defined processes. As the pricing strategy is repeatable, it is best suited to repeatable work.

Novel and complex matters are not appropriate for value-based pricing strategies unless that work is something that is completed often and the law firm has substantial data on which to base the price.

Outcome-based pricing or stage-based pricing

As the name suggests, this pricing strategy model is about staging out specific outcomes of legal work. This can be done for a range of practice areas, including family law, immigration, commercial, and criminal.

In practice, the outcome-based pricing model works by setting out the agreed amount in payments for key milestones. The agreed amount can be established in a similar way to the value-based pricing strategy, with the key difference being the client will pay in instalments at agreed intervals. Often with value-based pricing, the total amount is billed, or billed at a monthly cadence.

The outcome-based pricing strategy works well for clients who demand certainty and appreciate updates to the legal services at the same time. The value of the work can be delivered (and the asymmetry of the credence goods managed) at the same time the work is due to be paid for.

Matters should not progress until the money for the next milestone is held in trust. Outcome-based pricing is inappropriate for speculative or research matters where the milestones are uncertain at the time of disclosure.

Hybrid pricing

Hybrid pricing strategies combine elements of value-based, outcome-based, and time-based strategies as required. Many New Zealand law firms apply hybrid pricing strategies by setting the price at the beginning (usually an estimate based on the sparce information available at the time) and then adding additional coverage for uncertainty. Coverage can be an extra fee or an hourly rate. This type of pricing works well for transactional work and where clients might not have a full understanding of what their needs are.

Tiered service packages

Tiered service packages are also known as unbundling pricing models. This pricing strategy is to offer different levels of services to suit clients' needs and budgets. It can look similar to outcome-based pricing or value-based pricing but with more options.

Pricing options will be higher or lower for factors such as urgency, time limitations, and risk. This approach works well for legal work that contains discrete tasks, such as legal aid and debt recovery. Those employing tiered service packages should consider how many update emails the client may expect and explain to clients how more communication will attract a higher-tier level (due to the higher demand in effort).

Allowing the client to select what is important to them and price themselves accordingly is a sound approach employed by other industries, such as airlines and insurance.

Productized legal services

Productized legal services are the most standardized of the pricing strategies available. With this standardization in pricing, this strategy is best suited for the most automated and standardized legal services in the firm.

This pricing strategy works well for the types of firms fully prepared to embrace technology to provide the data and process needs necessary to give clients the certainty of standardized fees.

Productized legal services should be thought of like a "McDonalds menu" where clients can select what they need a la carte. This approach is actively used by Janey Haringa of JH Legal in New Zealand. It works well with document-production work such as shareholder agreements, wills, and basic commercial agreements.

The client should also be a consideration when reviewing the appropriateness of the productized legal services pricing strategy. Clients requiring a highly routinised legal service and certainty of costs are more likely to purchase a legal service priced with this strategy than one with a speculative and fee estimate time-based billing strategy.

Transparent pricing calculators

Some firms have compiled pricing calculators that are used internally to calculate the fees to be billed. Law firms can make this process transparent by building a calculator into their webpage or going through the calculator with the client, so the client can control the costs involved in their matter.

The calculator allows the client to take comfort from the transparency and addresses the professional requirements for estimates. Firms can use the calculator logics to create a bot to provide the information in a user-friendly way. They can stick with the pricing selected by the client at the time of billing for streamlined billing and client satisfaction.

Collaborative pricing

Whilst not common, the collaborative pricing strategy is about assessing the client's fee and service expectations at the beginning of pricing the service. Newly established law firms often engage in a collaborative pricing strategy without conscious thought, if previous experience is not helpful when pricing a new service the firm wishes to provide.

Collaborative pricing draws on the agreement factor and establishes confidence in those engaged in the work as they are not having to watch the clock for pricing issues.

This option can be great for sole practitioners or small law firms looking to establish market data on new legal services. Collaborative pricing can also be a good fit for those on-occasion type matters that either will contain a pro bono element or where pricing data is not readily available.

Collaborative pricing can also be used on an interesting research question or to aid a vulnerable client. Whatever it may be, collaborative pricing can give both the lawyer and the client confidence to get the job done without the specter of the billable hour.

A collaborative pricing strategy can be coupled with data analysis to create more certainty for a more appropriate billing method, if this is in relation to an emerging legal service market.

Dynamic pricing

Whilst potentially more difficult than other pricing strategies, dynamic pricing can factor in the firm's lawyers' capacities and market demands. When the firm is experiencing high demand in one area (such as residential conveyancing), the pricing of those legal services will increase to cater for the demand and protect the firm's capacity.

Leveraging the firm's technology to predict the seasonality of various work to anticipate peak demand can be a highly profitable pricing strategy. This pricing strategy does require understanding both the clientele and the work well. It would not be appropriate to deploy dynamic pricing for long-standing clients or "evergreen" work that does not have a significant seasonal impact on the firm.

A word of caution: use dynamic pricing sparingly and only to protect the firm's quality as no one enjoys a "pricing surge".

Experience-based pricing tiers

Experience-based pricing tiers is a pricing strategy recognized as the "partner premium". Pricing is determined by the level of experience and seniority of the listed lawyer in the engagement. Milestones or outputs completed by more junior staff will be cheaper than those completed by senior ones.

This pricing strategy allows clients to choose their experience and sets their expectations come billing time. This strategy can be coupled with others in this list and is already part of the time-based billing pricing strategy.

Reviewing historical data to see the types of tasks or actions completed by junior versus senior staff can be helpful to provide more buying information to the client for them to decide. This pricing strategy should not include required supervision, as that would be a firm cost and professional obligation.

Market-adjusted pricing

This is not a standalone pricing strategy but one that should be deployed frequently as part of the process in becoming the law firm of 2030. Sustainable and profitable law firms regularly review and adjust their pricing strategies for their legal services offerings. Throughout the 2020s, it might have been necessary to do this quarterly, but it should be done at least annually.

By assessing the pricing of all legal services, firms cover their reasonable costs. Reviewing the firm's competitiveness and engaging in important conversations with clients about price expectations are essential to completing the firm's pricing data.

Therefore, profitability can be increased through appropriately deploying suitable tools that positively impact productivity, pricing, and the firm's capacity to deliver legal services.

The law firm of 2030 has all these options at its disposal. Instead of sticking to one method as the firms of the past did, the law firm of 2030 utilizes all pricing strategies. This has several benefits:

- Experiments mean rich datasets to analyze what works well and what to discard.
- Human-centered pricing due to client preferences in accurate up-front pricing.
- Balancing capacity with client pricing preferences provides more

options for clients to select from a menu of services ranged at different price points, rather than a "take it or leave it" pricing approach.
- More available data to understand which methods result in the smallest and largest profit margin for work conducted. This means that lawyers can more appropriately balance commitments to access to justice and maintain profitable law firm businesses.

Law firm profitability

As has been established, multiple pricing strategies can be deployed to help law firms remain sustainable and profitable. In addition to the changes in pricing, the law firm of 2030 will face significant disruption to traditional metrics of law firm profitability. This will fundamentally alter the profit-per-equity-partner (PPEP) model. The confluence of AI technologies being rapidly adopted in law and evolving client expectations is fundamentally reshaping how legal services are valued and delivered, necessitating a reimagining of profitability models.

The ability of AI technologies to handle increasingly complex legal tasks is creating a legal services value redistribution. Tasks that firms could price at a premium – such as document review, basic drafting, and preliminary research – are experiencing significant downward pressure on pricing. Technology-driven efficiency is compelling law firms to reassess their value proposition and pricing strategies.

The legal services market is differentiating between AI-augmented legal work and uniquely human legal services. By 2030, this bifurcation will be more pronounced, with routine legal tasks becoming commoditized through AI automation. It will be unsurprising if some of these are offered without cost. This shift challenges the traditional correlation between expertise and profitability, as the credence goods nature of legal services dissipates. Expert technical legal knowledge is becoming increasingly automated and therefore less valued by the market.

As technical legal knowledge becomes more accessible through AI technologies, clients place greater value on lawyers' emotional and interpersonal capabilities. This emotional expertise encompasses:

- Strategic counselling and judgment;
- Complex stakeholder management;
- Crisis leadership and emotional intelligence;
- Creative problem-solving in novel situations; and
- Cross-cultural competence and emotional resonance.

This emotional expertise (which AI technologies cannot easily replicate) is central to the law firm value proposition. However, this shift towards emotional expertise presents challenges for traditional profitability metrics, as these soft skills are often more difficult to quantify and price than technical legal work.

The PPEP metric, long considered the gold standard measurement for law firm success, may become less relevant or require significant reconceptualization by 2030. Four factors contribute to this evolution:

- The democratization of legal expertise through AI technologies is flattening traditional value hierarchies based on technical expertise alone.
- The increasing importance of emotional expertise may lead to new partnership selection criteria and law firm operational models.
- Client demands for alternative pricing strategies are replacing time-based billing or hybridizing them.
- The need for significant technology investments is affecting capital structures and profit distribution.

To maintain profitability, the law firm of 2030 must embrace discontinuous innovation – fundamental changes that break from traditional business models. Some potential ways this can happen include:

- Developing new pricing strategies that better reflect the value of emotional expertise;
- Creating hybrid service offerings that more effectively combine AI technologies with human insights;
- Investing in professional development programs that enhance lawyers' emotional and interpersonal capabilities;
- Restructuring partnership models to recognize and reward newly established expertise; and
- Building technology platforms that enable scalable legal service delivery whilst maintaining premium pricing for high-value human interaction.

The law firm of 2030 will need to balance the efficiency gains of AI technologies with strategic investments in human capital and technological infrastructure. Success will depend not on resisting change but on fundamentally reimagining how legal services create and capture value in an AI-augmented world.

AI technologies' impact on capacity

AI technologies are transformative and will fundamentally recalibrate how legal work is conceptualized, performed, and valued. It represents more than mere incremental improvements to workflow. As highlighted, the PEPP metric is at risk of modification due to the profound change to legal services delivery and impacts on firm profitability.

Decades of law firm underinvestment in technology is starting to show in the remarkable upswing in capital investments many firms are making in technology. This suggests that law firm leaders understand that change is required to meet the challenges posed by the impacts of AI technologies.

The greatest impact that AI technologies will likely have on law firm capacity is in changing how lawyers obtain their practice skills. Just as manual discovery that was typically delegated to the most recent law graduate to undertake in a room full of document boxes has been replaced with complex e-discovery software, a digital replacement is likely for other routine and discrete tasks. This evolution does not cease the requirement for law firms to imbue junior staff with experiential learning – it just changes what this will look like.

The law firm of 2030 will have significantly invested in the professional development of all legal professionals to redistribute technical specialization to emotional expertise. Leadership and mentorship skills are likely to be the prime focus for those seeking leadership positions.

Previously high-valued technical work will be commoditized, meaning that the value of relationships and industry expertise will grow. The law firm of 2030 recognizes this and strategically schedules human resources to further develop these capabilities.

As legal practice continues to change with AI and other emerging technologies, discontinuous innovations are likely to disrupt the profession further. Whilst the nature and type of disruption is not predicable, preparing and anticipating for the disruption (or to disrupt) is of strategic importance.

Concluding questions

The 2020s have already seen seismic change for the legal profession. New technologies require new ways to operate and deliver valuable legal services to society. The five years from 2025 to 2030 will see more of this, with the most successful law firms adapting and responding to this changing environment.

It has been argued that profitability is impacted by pricing and the capacity of human resources delivering the legal services within the law firm. Profitability is, of course, essential for law firms to maintain the capability to provide legal services in the first place. This means that to respond to disruptions in traditional profitability and pricing strategies, law firms will need to adapt.

The law firm of 2030 will consider how it provides new skills to its emerging expertise – with less focus on technical and knowledge-based expertise and more focus on human-centered capabilities. In the end, the best way to shape the future is to make it, and that is what the law firm of 2030 will do.

References

1 Dulleck, U. and Kerschbamer, R., "On Doctor, Mechanics, and Computer Specialists: The Economics of Credence Goods", *Journal of Economic Literature*, volume 44, 2006.
2 Bell, F., and Rogers, J., "'Fit and Proper' Coders? How Might Legal Service Delivery by Non-Lawyers Be Regulated?", *Legal Ethics*, volume 24, 2021.
3 Maister, D., *Managing the Professional Services Firm*, Simon & Schuster, 2003.
4 Stack, S., and Bowman, B. A., "Suicide among Lawyers: Role of Job Problems", *Suicide and Life-Threatening Behavior*, volume 53, 2023.
5 Figure adapted by the author from Cotterman, J. D., "Calculating Profitability", 2019. www.altmanweil.com/wp-content/uploads/2022/04/Calculating-Profitability.pdf.
6 Clio, "Legal Trends Report", 2024. www.clio.com/wp-content/uploads/2024/10/NA-2024-Legal-Trends-Report-Full-Publication.pdf

Chapter 11:
The rising role of the legal operations professional

By Richard Brzakala, senior director, Global External Legal Services

Background

The legal marketplace has undergone dramatic changes over the past decade, reshaping how legal services are delivered. Law firms and corporate legal departments (CLDs) have been increasingly challenged to find new ways to create operational effectiveness and efficiencies at their companies to either save money or to grow market share and profitability.

Traditionally at a law firm, it was the accounting, finance, technology, or marketing teams that managed such areas as receivables, overhead costs, finances, technology initiatives, external clients, and anything unrelated to the actual practice of law. But as firms evolve into more complex, business-oriented enterprises, these functions are increasingly being integrated under the strategic guidance of legal operations professionals (LOPs), who will serve as architects of the next-generation law firm.

In-house legal teams have also seen a shift. Internal costs that were once managed by either departmental administrative managers, accounting, or a company's procurement department are now part of the broader "business of law," which has steadily become the domain of the LOP. This role is poised to grow even more critical as CLDs modernize and adapt to future business demands, including increasing automation, global regulatory complexity, and the demand for real-time legal analytics.

The LOP typically has a unique and eclectic background and skill set. More often than not, these are business professionals with established experience in finance and accounting, banking, legal, technology, and project management. They are also highly disciplined multi-taskers, leading and delivering on complex business, operational and technological strategies, while possessing excellent organizational and communicative skills in managing a variety of subject matter experts (SMEs). LOPs focus on optimizing the delivery of legal services to add value and maximizing a firm's or CLD's effectiveness and efficiencies through improved business processes or leveraging technology tools. Junior lawyers have increasingly been drawn into the legal operations (legal ops) space, especially when working within a law firm, but legal ops continues to be dominated by non-lawyer professionals with strong business and project management acumen.

How corporate legal departments are leveraging LOPs

CLDs and their general counsel have increasingly inherited responsibilities that extend beyond the day-to-day mandate of providing legal advice and managing risk for their organizations. Managing external counsel, legal costs, e-billing, matter and document management systems, and e-discovery software are just some of the areas that are today managed by LOPs.

LOPs are also increasingly responsible for monitoring outside counsel compliance, negotiating pricing arrangements, implementing cost control and savings strategies, management of panel firms and alternative legal service providers (ALSPs), compliance with regulatory requirements around third party governance, and information security. Given such a comprehensive list of priorities that fall outside the practice of law, it's not surprising to see why many CLDs are adopting a legal operations strategy and hiring an LOP to help them manage the multitude of projects and responsibilities that face them today. By focusing exclusively on the business of law, an LOP enables the CLD to become more efficient and liberates in-house counsel from routine administrative tasks. This helps them become more productive by focusing on the practice of law and strategic or critical matters that impact their organizations.

Given the multitude of non-legal tasks, oversight, and special projects that today fall within the scope of a legal department's responsibilities, many of those accountabilities often require additional "non-lawyer" support. Depending on the level of operational maturity and priorities within a legal department, a single LOP may quickly grow into a small team of multiple individuals, each of whom are an SME and responsible for their individual area of expertise within the legal operations space. As an example, sophisticated CLDs may have an SME dedicated exclusively to managing their company's legal e-billing and financial reporting responsibilities and another SME responsible for taking e-discovery or matter management responsibilities with the legal department.

It is also not uncommon to find LOPs in a CLD that are solely focused on cost reduction, pricing, benchmarking analytics, and negotiating pricing arrangements with external legal service providers. These team members work closely with a company's finance and accounts payable team and may overlap with their legal e-billing team where there is an abundance of billing data to leverage for spend management and forecasting purposes. All of these different SMEs are considered part of the legal operations space and may end up reporting into a senior or chief LOP. Their value and contribution to CLDs has grown exponentially over the years, so much so that they are now considered a critical component to how in-house legal teams function and manage the business of law. Hiring the right person in a legal operations role will ultimately help a CLD run like an efficient and cost conscious business. This is extremely important in an economic climate where many GCs are now tasked by their boards to manage, control, and reduce legal costs as much as they can. The oversight and contribution that LOPs bring to any organization is extremely valuable.

How legal operation professionals add value to a law firm

In a rapidly transforming and competitive marketplace, law firms are increasingly looking to LOPs to help them navigate future challenges. The legal marketplace has become extremely challenging and competitive for law firms. Dynamic economic factors and inflationary pressures, resource retention challenges, market demand, higher infrastructure, technology, and overhead costs have all in some way impacted profitability margins, competitiveness, and market share of firms in various markets and practice groups.

Faced with these economic challenges, the future law firm will increasingly invest in legal operations professionals to help them overcome and manage the challenging legal marketplace. Leveraging an LOP who can implement a legal operations strategy will help a firm optimize its internal business processes, better leverage its internal resources, and ensure that a firm's strategic goals are lined up to meet the latest market pressures.

To be successful in a competitive legal marketplace, it is critical that a firm understands its structure, processes, resources, objectives, clients, and strategy. An LOP can assist a firm's leadership with valuable analysis and measurable data to help them make strategic plans or execute tactical decisions.

Similar to CLDs, law firms have also traditionally relied on external consultants to assist on special projects, firm reviews, pricing, or to develop strategies that would help the law firm become more competitive.

Investing in an in-house "captive" LOP, as opposed to an external consultant, and creating specialized teams around the LOP's functional role, will give firms a strategic advantage to focus on finding ways to better leverage processes, time, people, and technology more efficiently in order to save money and become more competitive.

Firms may still have a need to utilize external consultants on highly specialized work, but to a lesser extent, as much of what used to be outsourced now stays internally and is undertaken by the law firm's LOPs. Project management, implementing process change, and monitoring the progress of cost savings initiatives are best done by LOPs internally and their teams of agile SMEs who are well suited to deliver on projects from within. Over time, as LOPs learn internal business processes, establish buy-in with crucial stakeholders, build familiarity with internal approval flows, and understand where optimal efficiency opportunities lie, their value grows even more as they become agents and champions for change and drive critical value for a firm.

Delivering on efficiency and cost control initiatives has been front of mind for many GCs. For years, institutional clients and their CLDs have been looking to become more efficient and are now demanding the same from their panel law firms. It is for this reason that clients are increasingly attracted to those law firms that reflect the client's core values when it comes to efficiency and practicing fiscal prudence. CLDs want to know that the firm that they hire has an operational mindset and are conscious of wanting to save money, as operating costs are typically passed onto the client in the form of rate increases. If a firm is working diligently towards saving money and making itself more profitable, then clients are more comfortable with engaging a legal partner who is ultimately looking out for their best interest in delivering legal services as efficiently as possible.

LOPs can help a law firm's leadership team by providing valuable operational data and insights into how change can help firms become more efficient and effective in how they deliver services to their clients. This type of strategic awareness can have a lasting impact on existing relationships and client retention and ultimately law firm profitability. LOPs know how to make informed decisions that align with short- and long-term goals as many LOPs hired by firms understand the legal marketplace and bespoke law firm practices.

Moreover, LOPs can further assist firms in strategically understanding business operations, how resources are leveraged, and how technology can help a law firm to achieve maximum profitability in the most efficient way. LOPs work closely with a law firm's executive board and managing partners to understand how a firm can increase its realization rate and minimize waste by focusing on value outcomes, rather than low level administrative tasks or needless work that gets written off by the firm.

LOPs help the firm's leadership understand and improve productivity by identifying areas and opportunities where it can reduce highly repetitive time-consuming tasks, liberate lawyers from administration, and better leverage clerical staff where needed with technology and AI tools.

Reviewing and/or replacing legacy technology tools can present an assortment of challenges, regardless of who is spearheading a project. However, transformational change has started to take place in the legal marketplace with the utilization of AI, which is reshaping how lawyers work. Alongside law firm technology partners, LOPs are undertaking projects to understand and deploy AI tools around use cases that can help automate routine tasks such as legal research and analysis, document review and document management, as well as billing. It's an exciting time for LOPs who are clearly having an impact on helping firms maximize productivity and improve on the delivery of legal services to their clients in sometimes difficult and challenging economic conditions.

Law firms not only face economic challenges, but also the challenges of having to adhere to legal and regulatory requirements that are increasing in frequency across geographical jurisdictions and industries. In addition, there is an increased need for regulatory and reporting around third party relationships. The confidentiality and security of the client data that those third parties maintain presents increased responsibilities at any firm. LOPs are increasingly being called upon to assume accountability for these areas and to ensure that law firms meet their regulatory requirements and obligations in a timely manner.

Law firm marketability, building a brand, growing market share, client retention and loyalty, interfacing with and managing client relationships are other critical areas of importance where the LOP may assist law firm partners and their leadership team.

Managing partners (MPs) at a firm who may be responsible for a specific client relationship will almost certainly rely on their legal operation professionals and SMEs to assist with whatever client matters or enquiries that arise. LOPs are crucial in providing back-office support by coordinating timely and comprehensive responses to whatever impacts a client. This may come in the form of providing responses to subject areas such as billing issues, third party governance questions, data management and records storage queries, DEI surveys, information security questions (including breach notifications), and competitive bid responses as well as pricing and cost estimate proposals. If a law firm is fortunate to be on a client's panel of pre-approved firms, then expectations of service delivery are exceptionally high. Clients expect timely, accurate, and reliable information to be returned to them. LOPs play a vital role in helping to pull information together from the appropriate law firm stakeholders and deliver that information either to the MP or directly to the client.

How legal operation professionals add value to a corporate legal department

CLDs have always been considered an expensive but vital functional group for many large companies. Over the years, the GC's role at many large corporations has expanded beyond transactional legal advice to include administrative and infrastructure areas such as resources, technology, infrastructure, and premises. GCs have also been challenged by their boards to manage and control external legal costs that are typically associated with external law firms, contingent workers, and alternative legal service providers (e.g., e-discovery, document management companies, cloud providers, data safe rooms, e-billing software, matter management companies etc.). When a GC needed assistance with a special project or technology implementation in the past, they would typically leverage internal departmental administrative resources or other intra-company resources from another functional group or look to external (expensive) consultants to assist with the management and oversight of those projects.

As the legal marketplace has matured and legal expenses have increased, many CLDs have turned to the adoption of an in-house legal operations strategy and hiring LOPs to assist the GC with the business and operational responsibilities that have befallen them in managing a modern-day CLD.

As has happened at law firms, the LOP has quickly become the go-to operations resource, replacing expensive and often sub-optimal consultants who may not always be readily available or require training on a company's processes, all of which may impact a CLD's project timelines, budget, and/or success.

Whether that professional or team of professionals resides in-house or at a law firm, the value that LOPs bring to an organization cannot be understated. Listed below are just a few high-level advantages to utilizing a LOP:

- Less costly than external consultants.
- Captive internal, dedicated, and 100 percent accessible resource.

- Over time, the LOP develops and builds in-house project expertise.
- Acts as a bespoke legal project manager for all strategic initiatives.
- Acts as an agent of change, driving and leading strategic initiatives.
- Manages and oversees the delivery of cost saving initiatives.
- Tracks, monitors, and manages an organization's legal spend, accounts receivables, profit margins, realization rates, and spend reporting.
- Negotiates optimal pricing for the organization.
- Develops and implements governance and control processes to satisfy regulators or to help monitor compliance with outside counsel guidelines and third-party regulatory requirements.
- Negotiates with third-party legal vendors when purchasing and implementing new legal technology.
- Manages legal software tools (e-billing, DMS, matter management, AI tools).
- Measures and monitors law firm performance against established guidelines.
- Manages contingent worker engagements and relationships.
- Manages panel law firm relationships and/or relationships with CLD and their LOP counterpart.
- Implements and optimizes cost cutting, cost control, and cost avoidance initiatives.
- Recommends changes to legal service delivery models.
- Collaborates with internal/external stakeholders on behalf of GC's office on legal service delivery matters.

How legal operation professionals help the client relationship

Although internal LOPs and external law firm counterparts may share similar responsibilities, law firm LOPs find themselves in a mainly supportive and responsive position when it comes to dealing with external client requests from their CLDs. Timely and professional responses to client enquiries help foster a stronger and lasting client relationship. As we look towards 2030, a law firm LOP would be responsible for such things as:

- Preparing and responding to client pricing proposals (e.g. AFA, hourly rate caps, billing policies, and pricing issues).
- Responding to client request for proposals.
- Preparing and responding to cost estimates and budget requests.
- Preparing e-discovery strategies, budgets, and requests for information.

- Responding to third party inquiries.
- Managing responses for information security requests and artifacts.
- Managing oversight regarding cyber security incidents.
- Managing client conflict clearances and requests for waivers.
- Managing client access to firm safe rooms.
- Managing and ensuring law firm professionals are in compliance with CLD guidelines.
- Managing technology onboarding processes and licenses.
- Client information governance, storage, and safe keeping of confidential data, including data destruction of physical and digital client records.
- Acting as the primary liaison point for clients and/or CLD LOPs.

In addition, LOPs at a firm will almost always be involved in projects focused on creating operational efficiencies and looking for ways to optimize their lawyers' time for the practice of law. LOPs will typically work with a project team to analyze and understand current state workflows, looking for ways to streamline, change, eliminate, transfer, or re-engineer those processes to minimize the burden of non-essential tasks on law firm lawyers who can then shift their attention to practice high value, substantive legal work. One of the LOP's most critical skills is project management and ensuring that the right people are included on the right projects and then managing those projects for successful and timely delivery. By doing this, the LOP can help a law firm deliver greater value to its clients more frequently without having its high valued legal professionals encumbered by non-value tasks.

The future for legal operation professionals in the legal marketplace

Legal operations professionals that manage the business of law for both law firms and CLDs will continue to play a significant role in the legal marketplace for many years to come.

In an increasingly challenging regulatory environment, coupled with continuing economic pressures and greater utilization of AI and changing technology, LOPs will continue to be involved in a multitude of dynamic projects that require their skills and expertise.

Efficiency opportunities abound in areas such as contract lifecycle management, data management, information security, legal spend management, AI use cases and generative AI, enterprise risk management programs and risk mediation, continual compliance monitoring, and automation and digitization. All these areas will offer up continuous opportunities for LOPs at CLDs and at law firms to help them achieve their goals and to help foster a culture of greater effectiveness and efficiencies.

Richard Brzakala contributed this chapter in his personal capacity. The views expressed are his own.

Part 4:

Risks and Opportunities

Chapter 12:
ESG unraveled

By Jenifer Swallow, lawyer and strategic advisor

Introduction

ESG is all but dead. The process may take some time, but in the form of its past, ESG has no future. ESG being the global phenomenon of the environment, social, or better said societal, and governance movement, which represented one in every three dollars of major market investment[1] and generated entire departments in corporations.

The principles of responsible business will be as important as ever in the coming decades, where financial resilience and integrity will be paramount amidst a shifting world order, geopolitical volatility, and the practicalities of modern business in an accelerated phase of technological development.

Climate-focused and broader ideological narratives and investment will give way to surgical focus on growth and security worldwide. Corruption will be under sustained attack, and we will be leaning on innovation in systems of governance to deliver trust and transparency. The policy agenda is moving and with it public sentiment, as well as the other way round. This will precipitate into all areas of business, society, and the state.

For any law firm still using the phrase ESG, phase it out now. Encourage the same in your client base, in all but specific contexts, such as investment, where describing a class of assets retains factual relevance. The language of "ESG" carries packages of the past that won't belong in the future. Namely the misuse of purpose in the interests of profit, versus the opposite originally claimed it was about. Whether justified or not, the association with greenwashing, "woke" ideals, and wasted money undermine societal advancement and the many priorities we need to tackle now and next. It is time to move on – to new language and specificity of focus.

More than ever, law firms need to note the impacts of geopolitics and the force of technology on their businesses and their client work. What happens in the world comes ever closer to home and what happens at home impacts the world. Deregulation, fractured globalization, and AI have implications for all clients in all industries, affecting decision-making, operations, and stakeholder expectations. What is important is the core work to be done relevant to each individual business, and removing any distractions and complications that get in the way of that.

The elements of integrity that survive the death of ESG will live on in specific ways, aligned with core priorities. This includes responsibility across supply chains, taking care of staff, fair treatment of customers and communities, risk and harm mitigation, and having the systems and evidential base to assure and prove it. These things do not go away. They make great business sense, as they always have. It will take some time to unravel, but to 2030 and beyond, these elements that were previously bucketed together under ESG will no longer travel in a pack. They will become simply part of doing business in a way that endures. New language will emerge to represent that. The same focus of responsibility and transparency applies for lawyers and the ethical standards and independence they are called to uphold as well as – increasingly – to evidence.

It is this coming context for which law firms can prepare now and which is the purpose of this chapter. We provide some framing thoughts below and then tackle each topic of environmental, societal, and governance and the future for each of them.

Context

For the coming decade there are two policy priorities worldwide – growth and security. These priorities will seep into every area of business and society, shaping everything from corporate strategies and investment decisions to technological advancements and international relations.

As economies seek financial stability and expansion, businesses will double down on revenue and innovation, while governments invest in national security to address geopolitical instability – some for the first time in decades. Amid shifting power dynamics, nations are needing to move mountains for economic growth – competing to attract investment, secure supply chains, and drive innovation. Pro-business priorities are trending, to be folded into industrial strategy. This is shaping alliances as countries and industries seek to secure technology, manufacturing capabilities, and energy and economic independence.

With the US cutting defense and other support abroad, government plans in the UK and around the world had to go in the bin. Every country now needs a defense strategy that does not rely on the US. Countries proximate to war zones have to activate peacekeeping capabilities and the responsibilities that go alongside them. For infrastructure like NATO to survive, defense spending has to multiply. New frontiers of war are opening up. Discretionary contribution elsewhere is no longer viable.

Everything has had to be reprioritized. And so it will remain for the foreseeable future.

Through this lens, difficult choices become simpler and "second order" impacts come into sight. Costs have to be cut, armies have to be built, and financial return is at a premium. Money and attention have to be rerouted away from other things. Industries long languishing get dusted down to get going again. In the re-prioritization, social and environmental causes will be the collateral damage. We already see this happening, with the US and UK ceasing or repurposing foreign aid budgets, reviewing spending on social welfare, and shaking up systems of administration.

With a focus on growth comes a shift in regulation, acknowledging the overhead it causes for business and therefore economies. Policy makers in the US, UK, and parts of Asia are signaling a deregulatory agenda, to streamline bureaucracy, strip out cost, and encourage investment and R&D. Despite past emphasis, even the EU has signaled the need for reform and simplification.[2] The call in the US is for a withdrawal of the "deep state" and reduction in influence of regulatory and other agencies. Sectors like technology, finance, and energy have long argued that excessive rules stifle growth and global competition. The irony is this comes at a time of ever greater acknowledgement of the risk of harms in society – from technological developments, imbalances of power, corruption, and exploitation of consumer vulnerabilities. Nonetheless, we already see the changes coming through, with the UK already announcing the abolition of the payment systems regulator, and the US committing to cut ten outdated regulations for every new one it introduces.

This is not across every market evenly, but those for whom the re-prioritization imperative is the greatest are moving first. We will see a polarization emerge, between those countries that choose or need to make the change and those that do not. Policy positions are already fragmenting and will continue to do so, which of course has a knock-on effect on public sentiment, election outcomes, and business decision-making. No longer will we see singular domination by the US, but a multipolar order where power is distributed between major players like China, India, and country alliances.

It has taken more than two decades for the climate agenda to gain momentum, as governments, businesses, and global institutions prioritized sustainability, driven by scientific consensus and public pressure. Landmark initiatives like the Paris Agreement set ambitious targets, pushing nations toward decarbonization and green commitments involving largescale investment. For the UK alone, achieving "net-zero" emissions by 2050 is estimated to cost £1.4 trillion.[3] As conflicts reshape global priorities and focus attention on energy security and economic growth and resilience, governments are likely to soften climate commitments in favor of investor-friendly environments, securing stable energy supplies, and maintaining military readiness.

The same goes for the societal dimensions of the ESG movement. Vast sums have been spent on social-driven initiatives over the past decades and many claims have been made as to contribution. Yet poverty, injustice, and societal harm remain prevalent worldwide, including in the most "advanced" jurisdictions. The initiatives of the past are not working and money spent is not solving the problem.

Only with growth and security can we afford and tackle other things. When that reality bites, the focus turns to the practicalities of current priorities. Anything else is seen in the light of idealism. The next five to ten years will be a tumultuous time with many things thrown up in the air and many surprises. Grasping this context and the first and second order impacts it involves will be critical for law firms figuring out where to place their attention to 2030 and understanding the future of the ESG agenda for their services, clients, and own operations.

Environmental

The climate agenda gained momentum in the early 2000s through a combination of scientific consensus, global activism, and international cooperation, leading to major agreements like the Kyoto Protocol and later the Paris Agreement in 2015. Particular personalities initiated and drove the cause, including Al Gore, Barack Obama, and Greta Thunberg. The United Nations played a key role, such as through the Intergovernmental Panel on Climate Change. Governments, businesses, and institutions increasingly recognized climate change as an economic and security threat, driving policies, initiatives, and swathes of legislation. Laws continue to track through to implementation at various stages all around the world.

The early agenda focused on reducing carbon emissions, tackling air and water pollution, and transitioning to renewable energy and cleaner technologies. This extended to include issues like biodiversity loss, soil health, climate justice, sustainable supply chains, and the social impacts of climate change, recognizing that environmental challenges are interconnected with economic and social systems.

Legal requirements and best practice frameworks on sustainability reporting alone are prolific across industry. To illustrate the point, these include Streamlined Energy and Carbon Reporting (SECR) in the UK, European Sustainability Reporting Standards (ESRS) under the EU Corporate Sustainability Reporting Directive (CSRD), Corporate Sustainability Due Diligence Directive (CSDDD) for supply chain impacts, the IFRS Sustainability Disclosure Standards for investor disclosures, the Task Forces on Climate-related Financial Disclosures (TCFD) and Nature-related Financial Disclosures (TNFD), and the voluntary frameworks of the Global Reporting Initiative (GRI) and Integrated Reporting Framework (IIRC).

Political decision-making in the US has jolted the environmental agenda worldwide. Prioritizing domestic energy independence and economic growth, the US withdrew from the Paris Agreement and rolled back a raft of environmental regulations, particularly those related to emissions standards for vehicles and power plants, restrictions on coal and gas mining, and infrastructure projects. The narrative around scarcity of "fossil fuels" has shifted, with adjustments in language such as towards "clean coal" and "fact checking" oil as a mineral not from fossils and gas formed through geological processes. We may see this precipitate into a shift away from the language and embedded implications of "renewable energy" versus "non-renewable" resources. Certainly, we already see the impact on electric vehicles, with stock market corrections reflecting what was already noticeable through reducing sales and concerns about safety, running costs, and inability to recycle EV parts. With the shift in investment, we may also see funding for scientific research result in developments such as questioning current findings on the harms of carbon dioxide, with knock-on effects for policy and regulation.[4]

These changes have introduced uncertainty and weakened international momentum on environmental issues. Reality has shifted in a number of ways. However, we are unlikely to see the progress of environmental laws halted to 2030. Many countries, particularly the EU, Canada, and India are committed to advancing climate goals, with a raft of renewable energy targets baked into law and public profile. Reliable, affordable electricity will remain a key power source, the costs of which will eventually drop. The wheels of industry have already been set in motion on emissions reporting in particular, with changes in operations and governance mechanisms already in place to meet requirements. Even with U-turns in policy that may come, 20 plus years of momentum does not stop overnight. There remain many people in society who are concerned about climate change and committed to environmental issues.

Lawyers can expect the following over a five- to ten-year horizon:

- Direct impacts from legal changes and shifts in industrial strategy for industries such as automotive, construction, agriculture, manufacturing, defense, technology, investment, and obviously energy. All sectors will experience indirect impacts.
- Greater divergence will emerge in legal requirements between different jurisdictions as some countries pull away from established standards or liberalize markets for economic and other advancement.
- Demand will increase for risk, cost and benefit analyses of current activities, and compliance, seeing best practice giving way to cost savings from moving to compliance-only regimes and rolling back past commitments.
- Extra-territoriality of regulations will be challenged, arguing compliance and disclosure are limited to organizations within a relevant jurisdiction, not across wider value chains spanning other markets. Such legalities may be drawn on in international trade positions between governments, e.g. tariffs.
- Environmental compliance will fold into operational teams with wider ESG initiatives being run as a normal part of strategy under the most relevant executive sponsor, rather than being owned by a discrete ESG team. For example, AI ethics run by the CTO and supply chain responsibility by procurement or legal.
- Risk appetite will be adjusted upwards, with a more pragmatic approach taken to compliance, interpreting requirements in a more business-friendly way, and/or anticipating lower likelihood of enforcement activity and sanctions.
- Unless climate science changes, emissions reporting will remain a requirement. Core reporting will sustain, whereas voluntary reporting will decrease.
- After a period of protest and operational adjustment for legislative change, climate related issues and stakeholder activism will fall down the board and general counsel agenda.
- Language will shift significantly in how we label things.
- Public policy interventions will re-focus on targeted issues for which impact can be achieved in the shorter term with lower public investment, such as waterway pollution or the health impacts of pesticides.

With all this comes a re-evaluation of what "sustainability" means in a modern era focused on growth and security.

Proponents of responsible business have long articulated the importance of companies operating ethically, considering the impact of their actions on people, the environments in which they operate, and society more broadly. Environment in this context goes way wider than "the environment" in a climate context. Sustainability through this lens is about conducting business in a way that meets present needs, but also sustains over the long term, and that does not pass on harms down the chain or to future generations. This includes limiting pollution and waste management, yes, but it goes beyond that to fair sourcing, taking care of people and relationships, and, crucially, remaining profitable while adapting to changing market conditions, such that you can make a contribution to the future.

Future-forward organizations have already made these shifts and will continue to commit to them. We will find people speaking less about what they do and it being simply normal. Environmental compliance will fold into usual operational practices and be part of business as usual risk management. Language will change accordingly, for example towards operational and financial resilience. Organizations differentiating based on responsible business and care for people will find ways to communicate that without talking about sustainability, or will do so in a broader context.

The law firm "E"

Law firms obviously need to track and advise on legislation and understand the policy and legal environment that surrounds their clients. With the historic rise in climate related legislation, law firms, particularly at the "big law" end of the scale and those with regulatory practices or advising clients in certain industries like energy, mining, and investing, have built ESG or "responsible business" teams and threaded ESG principles through their working practices. Some firms and consultancy practices exist entirely to advise in this space. Others will be on the receiving end of requirements in deal documents and supplier agreements.

All such advisors need to be mindful of the impact of global shifts on their work and where they will be needed and not needed next. Due diligence processes, contractual language, and advice will all take on a different flavor. For firms that act for clients across borders, navigating fragmenting regimes and delivering operationally across them will be a rich seam of work, necessitating multi-disciplinary people and methodologies, across government relations and public policy, compliance, data analytics, and risk management expertise. After initial work on transition to new regimes, workflow will change and may scale back as workloads move between internal stakeholders and get overtaken by different priorities. Dedicated practices will need to pivot to new service offerings. Horizon scanning and being able to respond to changes as they arise will be more important than ever.

To retain relevance, law firms will need to review websites and RFPs to make sure language matches the demands of clients as part of the new reality. That work is for some already hastily underway. For those who have undertaken the internal strategy work on what responsible business means for their practice over the coming decade, very little work will be needed to ensure their commitment, initiatives, and framing are congruent with the changing external environment. For those who have not, chapter six of Globe Law and Business' *What Clients Want From Law Firms*[5] includes suggestions on how to approach this important internal work. Initiatives that are more for show are the ones that will fail in this climate. The ones that hold integrity with an organization's vision, purpose, and strategy will work in any climate.

A note of caution also, with regards to law firms working with in-house counsel in client organizations. A number of general counsels have taken a leadership role in ESG and that has been a positive force. The trend has also had a positive impact on the status and influence of general counsels inside their employer client organizations, where they have been "at the top table" on ESG and taking a coordination role across the organization. One challenge has been in categorizing the areas of work that sit in the ESG "bucket". All areas of operations can be argued to have a responsible business angle, even cyber security. Without going into the different structures and approaches to corporate ESG and the alternative options now, general counsels may be disincentivized from recommending different structures and/or "giving up" leadership of ESG. Law firms can support with both these aspects. First, helping to review and refresh priorities in light of the changes relevant to each client organization. Second, helping in-house counsel to advise clients on how to respond to the changing landscape, independent of their own interests as employees. While the dynamics between in-house lawyers and their employer-clients can be dysfunctional, with general counsel not feeling valued for all they bring, they do not need ESG to have standing. Their value is enormous with or without that responsibility.

Societal (social)

A number of trains have been set in motion with impacts across "Social", or better said "Societal", dimensions for the next decade.

The "S" pillar of ESG has gained prominence over the last few decades as businesses faced pressure to demonstrate their impact on workers, communities, and society. High-profile events like the #metoo movement, black lives matter, and the COVID-19 pandemic generated public outrage at inequalities. ESG was used by investors and activists to influence organizations in the boardroom and, collectively, government and global affairs. Social dimensions burst to the fore along with climate concerns, prompting companies to adopt stronger policies on diversity, equity, and inclusion (DEI), labor rights, and ethical sourcing. Attention turned to what businesses – law firms included – were doing (or more commonly not) to take care of their people and make a broader contribution societally.

The adage "silence is violence" became common, with staff and stakeholders expecting organizations to take stands on issues ranging from LGBTQ+, conflict, racial justice, gender equality, modern slavery, vaccines, immigration, politics and more. Social outcry has prompted law-making throughout history, and this time of concentrated activity was no exception. Social impact reporting became codified in law and extended into best practice. Reporting on diversity and pay, employment practices, wellbeing initiatives, social mobility, human rights, and community engagement variously emerged – some voluntary and some through legislation such as the Equalities Act, Modern Slavery Act, and the EU's Corporate Sustainability Reporting Directive (CSRD) and Corporate Sustainability Due Diligence Directive (CSDDD).

Companies have dedicated millions in investment to social initiatives. Microsoft committed $1.5 billion to its DEI efforts, Unilever millions to sustainable sourcing and workers' rights, and Apple heavily invested in employee mental health. The rise of the B Corp further demonstrates the movement, where 8,000 certified companies operate in 93 countries employing over 700,000 workers globally at the time of writing.[6] The global impact investing market grew by 21 percent in five years to reach $1.6 trillion in assets under management.[7]

The shift

With the recent shift in global priorities towards growth and security, much is set to change. Led from the US, companies will have more autonomy in how they address social issues, with profitability and shareholder value taking precedence over stakeholder activism.

As the UK government looks for deregulation opportunities, employment practices may be adjusted in a business-friendly direction, despite the ideological basis of the prevailing government. It is hard to see disclosure around long fought for workforce diversity and labor rights being rolled back, but this is possible, for example around union rights that inhibit the speed and efficacy of government implementation, or issues such as trans rights that previously attracted a lot of attention and dissent.

It will become acceptable or politically favored not to comment on social or geopolitical issues, staying focused on core business and producing shareholder return. Bosses won't feel so obliged to put out press releases about alignment with social issues or spend as much resource demonstrating they are doing good in the world. Activism will not disappear but will cool off in intensity. Press attention will begin to tally with new social and political agendas, taking pressure off previously hot topics such as mental health and DEI, more of which on the latter below. We will see less investment in generalized issues and more on initiatives that can be seen directly to impact delivery and the bottom line – note to self for all those wishing to continue to drive programs of change. We may also see this impact charitable donations and pro bono schemes, although tax offsets remain strategic.

This will impact the approach to materiality, in what determines the significance of an issue in influencing decision-making. In the ESG context, materiality evolved into two key concepts – financial materiality, focusing on risks and opportunities affecting a company's bottom line, and double materiality, which considers the company's broader impact on people and the environment. Each were to provide correlation through to shareholder value, whether by creating it through business opportunities, or avoiding its erosion through managing ESG risks. Despite both concepts being embedded in regulatory frameworks like the EU's CSRD, the trajectory is for the focus to drop away from double materiality, leaving the emphasis on financial materiality only. Law firms should keep their eyes peeled for business practice and regulatory signaling or adjustments along such lines.

This will not all happen overnight and as things get thrown up in the air, so gravity has them falling and settling into a new place. There will remain legal requirements in the category of societal advancement through the coming decade, including the UN Guiding Principles on Business and Human Rights (UNGPs), where human rights continue to underpin legal frameworks and obligations, such as we see with the UNGP principles being incorporated into the EU's CSDDD, requiring human rights oversight and mitigation across supply chains.

On DEI, we will see two themes. The first is a move away from gender as the focus, to socioeconomic mobility. This shift will prioritize creating ways for individuals from disadvantaged socioeconomic backgrounds to access opportunities, particularly in industries such as professional and financial services, traditionally dominated by higher-income groups. The second will be a focus on equality of opportunity rather than equality of outcomes. This means that organizations will focus on demonstrating they have provided equal opportunities and made decisions based on merit, rather than ticking boxes to achieve outcomes.

Under this regime we can expect use of quotas to decline and capability to be evaluated on measures other than years of experience. Board diversity will remain a key topic through the 2030s, across additional dimensions to the number of women at the table. This will be through a different lens on diversity to the past, focused on strength in decision making more than minority characteristics. In fact, we are seeing in the US use of the law to work against positive discrimination, arguing it is illegal to advance certain groups over others, even for the purposes of more equal representation. Long-held hiring practices in fintechs and other tech scale up businesses will become popular across the wider business community, such as training or promoting people from more junior levels, de-emphasizing university degrees, and seeking talent in untapped communities to find the best person for the job based on capability.

Deploying technology to training and development aims will also be a key shift, both levelling up junior and in fact all staff with access to expert-trained language models, use of AI agents to remove the need for them to know how to navigate processes, and using technology such as AI and augmented reality to monitor for and deliver training and support needs.

While organizations may choose to play politics, with regards to social issues it could be said that things are to become much simpler than in past decades. Take care of your house; take care of everyone and everything in your sphere of influence. When all those spheres combine, we will have responsibility and holistic caretaking in society. For some organizations that will mean recruitment and training – for others, that will mean consumer protection, health and safety, community engagement, supply chain audits, and/or paying SME vendors on time. For all, it will mean fair treatment and pay. But it will be from the inside out, not the outside in.

Focusing on employee base, supply chain, and direct stakeholder communities is a future proof strategy, with human rights principles as the baseline, ensuring safe and supportive conditions, open communication, and correct compliance, oversight, and reporting.

Scrutiny and corruption

Nonetheless, organizations will remain under public scrutiny. In fact, corruption will be under sustained attack. Public demand is accelerating for transparency and accountability, alongside shifting political landscapes that default to open data and real-time public insight. Restrictions on free speech bed in on social media, bringing more and more topics out of the woodwork and making it harder to suppress discourse and information sharing. Governments release documents long locked away, exposing lies and secrets of the past. Data files like the Pandora Papers and FinCEN Files expose financial wrongdoing that impacts society at all levels, not just the top echelons.

Corporate misconduct stirs the populous and their politicians. We can expect political and regulator action in such cases at increasing certainty, speed, and scale, where regulators are under state instructions to send a strong message and "be seen to be doing something". As we saw with government intervention in the UK on compensation for sub-post masters in the Post Office Horizon Scandal, and as we can expect with the enforcement action that will follow in that case for its lawyers and executives, truth finds a way through and leadership emerges in unexpected places.

Advancements in technology will also play a key role on the topic of societal factors and eliminating corruption. As data becomes more accessible, accountability will be built into systems at every level through technology such as distributed ledger and AI. From public institutions to private companies, this integration and capability means corrupt practices or attempted criminality can be more easily detected and evidential trails become immutable and hard to conceal or destroy.

Lawyers will need to be mindful of this reality and the heightened risks it contains, both for their clients and also in respect of their own conduct as advisors. In the past, it might have been possible for "the lawyers" to fly below the radar in corruption cases, but that is no longer the case. The consequences of being caught up in corporate capture are significant. This is also relevant to how lawyers validate facts, and document and govern their work, more on which is mentioned in the governance section below.

Whatever the geopolitical landscape, the legal work needs doing and it needs doing well. More than ever, clients need support to prevent issues, rapid, multi-disciplinary response teams when those issues arise, and technically capable advisors who can help them navigate the landscape, as well as the horizon.

The law firm "S"

Law firms not thinking about the 2030 horizon for their own businesses will want to get started on that evaluation. The biggest "S" topic is people and it requires a strategic approach to navigating the evolving profession.

Firms must rethink how they attract, train, and retain talent in a profession increasingly shaped by technology and changing client expectations. The traditional path – from junior associate to partner – is fading. Technology vendors, alternative service providers, and in-sourcing of work by sophisticated in-house teams cast a long shadow over the law firm business model and ability to re-invest in its future and its people. AI-powered document and data work, online dispute resolution, self-service models, and agentic tools will reduce both legal work overall and the traditional training path for lawyers. Yet use of these tools is also exciting for generations coming through and to not adapt to them will be to hamper hiring. Digitization of state infrastructure will have a further impact, as working practices change around legal system changes with open access to data feeds, automated processes, and tech pioneers disrupting the market.

Clients will demand faster, cheaper, and innovative products and services that match the way they work and get ahead of their needs. Firms will need to rethink their business model as well as their resourcing model. Legal engineers, project managers, behavioral scientists, data analytics, and AI specialists will become as critical as legal experts, requiring investment in digital skills, multidisciplinary teams, and the infrastructure and environments to support them.

Alongside this technology-focused trend is the strong reaction in US public policy to DEI, where law firms specifically are under attack for diversity and inclusion commitments. Several have been withdrawing such commitments and removing content from their websites and involvement in DEI initiatives. By 2030, this force will have settled down. Equality laws as regards fair treatment are not changing and firms will be able to hold steady with programs to support equal opportunities, including retaining female, minority ethnic, and other leaders through to partnership. As referred to above, positive discrimination will be more difficult, with firms needing to ensure advancement based on merit.

Law firms will need to evaluate their internal social context to be ready for 2030. This will involve understanding the future role and activities of their staff, mapped to client demand and tech capabilities, then finding and developing the right staff in line with that role and those activities, and supporting them through accelerated change. Add to this much greater attention to and support with enabling staff to identify, navigate, and report on ethically charged issues that arise in and around their work.

The culture of the legal profession will itself evolve as the sector re-shapes. More tech-enabled working practices will change the dynamics of excessive workloads over time. New generations coming through will continue to test the boundaries of presenteeism, but across a shorter timeline we can expect remote working in traditional law firm environments to become rare and salaries to continue to match productivity requirements.

Over the longer term, there are more fundamental questions to consider, like the implications for businesses, staff, and society of technology doing 90 percent of the work lawyers do today, and the laws and mechanisms we need to prevent and address harms caused by capabilities and uses of advanced technologies.

Governance

As we look to the future, it is clear a shift is coming on the topic of governance.

On the one hand are the pressures of investor security, heightened stakeholder expectations, the pace of change, geopolitical uncertainty, and the increasingly complex regulatory and risk environment. On the other are the imperatives for growth and the immense frustration of all else that gets in the way of achieving it, bureaucracy often number one. The ability to make decisions quickly and make them consistently well is at a premium, as is the ability to hold an entire organization in alignment and ensure information flows with stakeholders are effective, accurate, timely, transparent, and complete.

How does an organization direct, control, and hold itself accountable in a volatile and complex world? How does its leadership achieve that without grinding down its dynamism and the empowerment of its people? How does it tackle the ever-growing data deluge, harness the opportunities of technology, and mitigate the risks? These are matters of both competitive advantage and existential importance for law firm clients today. As they are those too for law firms themselves.

Governance is at the heart of these questions, as it too is at the heart of the policy agenda towards deregulation as outlined above. The acknowledgement is of the need for greater simplicity; less bureaucracy.

More regulation or less regulation, harmony of regulation or divergence – governance practices have become critical for sustained success, speed of response, and risk management. The law firm that builds strength and flexibility in governance will be the one maintaining relevance and offering critical value to its client base.

Of the many considerations for law firms on the subject of governance, there are three particular trends to attend to over the next five to ten years – personal liability, technology and data, and ethics and independence. Ethics and independence are covered in the next chapter, along with a range of suggestions on the measures relevant to governance more broadly. Personal liability and technology and data are covered below.

Personal liability

From a client point of view, personal liability for corporate actions is a trend that is on the rise across regulatory regimes and industries. Legislators and regulators are moving beyond organizational penalties as their levers of control, and targeting decision-makers directly. We can see this across finance, technology, healthcare, construction, cyber security, environmental protection and more.

NIS 2[8] in cyber security for "critical infrastructure" such as energy, transport, and banking, and DORA[9] in finance are two cases in point. Add to that building safety regulations in response to disasters like the Grenfell fire in the UK and new rules for companies polluting waterways. Anti-bribery legislation and the senior managers regime in financial services carry the same principles. There are similar examples around the world.

As policy makers need to demonstrate effective action to address the strength of public sentiment and as regulators see the positive impact of personal liability regimes on behavior, the focus on personal liability in business is set to continue. The impact on banks and other financial services organizations during implementation of the SM&CR[10] regime was immediate. Those going through the certification process had to sign for their responsibilities. From one day to the next they became keenly interested in the risks to them personally, how they would fulfil their duties, the support the organization would provide to enable them to do that, and the existence and efficacy of wider mitigations and controls. Demand for corporate indemnities and insurance increased and questions were asked at levels rarely previously seen. In the case of the building industry, where corporate manslaughter is a real risk on construction sites and in high rise buildings, personal liability is causing great concern and a high degree of focus. In water regulations, we see additional financial levers such as banning performance-related bonuses for those failing to meet statutory obligations, e.g. implementing pollution incident reduction plans.

Even in a de-regulatory environment, regulation that does sustain will continue to trend in this direction.

Of further relevance is the increasing anti-corruption sentiment in society. Corporate misconduct hits our news feeds, TVs, and the big screen. In the UK we saw public outrage at the Post Office Horizon Scandal reach unprecedented levels after the nation collectively watched a TV series.[11] Vitriol was targeted at executives who took the stand and had nothing to stand upon. This was worsened by the clear lack of institutional governance and their attempts to blame that. Social media is full of commentary about conspiracy theories that turned out not to be theories at all. Evidence finds a way to get out. Executives are keenly aware of this and do not want to be on the wrong side of the reputation cycle.

Add to this the trend towards bringing litigation against not just companies but their directors and officers. We have seen ClientEarth[12] suing Shell's directors in the UK and the trend towards CEOs, CFOs and general counsels being named defendants in actions alongside their employer-clients, whether by disgruntled ex-employees, M&A partners, or activist shareholders.

This trend towards personal liability has significant implications for the governance agenda and the needs of executives, boards, and the legal and operational teams that support them. The stakes have gone up. Directors are required to have a handle on what is going on and the "internal systems of control" to direct and oversee them. In the UK they now have to certify that publicly according to the latest update to the UK Corporate Governance Code.[13] Governance is under review by the Institute of Directors, in the UK, with a new code in place[14] and insurers are taking a keen interest in standards of reasonable care in relation to pay outs. As a result, we can expect to see increased demand for the following practicalities:

- Clear lines of responsibility and accountability.
- Robust risk management frameworks and internal controls.
- Diligence in decision-making.

- Oversight and monitoring mechanisms.
- Comprehensive information, reporting, and record keeping.
- Resourcing and efficacy of risk related teams.
- Horizon scanning.
- Culture and its impact on risk and growth.
- Training at the executive and board level.
- Board effectiveness and expertise.

These practicalities are not new, but the methodologies and level of attention to achieving them will be. The trend towards personal liability is altering the governance landscape. It is compelling executives and boards to require more rigor and transparency, with a stronger focus on responsibility, risk, and compliance.

Law firms have traditionally been more distant from corporate governance and risk management within their clients, focusing on providing specific advice then leaving the rest to internal teams. For the future, such an approach would be to miss the significant context in which the advice is being given, and to miss the opportunity to help clients get ahead of the demand curve in a more integrated way. Legal advice on regulatory regimes, liability, and horizon trends can lead to and mesh with deeper, more operational and governance-related work to bring boards, executives, legal, and risk teams into not only compliance but into a state of confidence. More on the opportunity of operational advice and more integrated delivery frameworks can be found in chapter six of *What Clients Want From Law Firms*.[15]

Technology and data

Clients more than ever need data for governance and governance for data. Just as they need technology for governance and governance for technology. The reason for this is two huge waves colliding as we look to 2030 – operational complexity and technological advancement, both of which reach high and wide.

Taking operational complexity, the contributing factors are extensive. The regulatory landscape is increasingly intricate across industries, negatively impacting growth across a number of dimensions.[16] Data volumes have been growing at pace and are projected to double in the coming few years,[17] plus complexity of data across diverse sources. Hybrid working models and remote working complicate operational procedures and workflows. Geopolitics impacts supply chain strategies and networks. Customer and stakeholder expectations have moved towards more personalized, proximate experiences. Sustainability initiatives have put pressure on operational efficiency and decision-making.

In terms of technological development, we are all experiencing in real-time the rapid advancements in artificial intelligence, particularly LLMs, generative AI, and the development and use of AI agents to come. We can expect to see AI move beyond our user interfaces and increasingly into the background of all our tools and systems. Just as we can use a chat interface or search our photos by name today, so can our platforms summarize our emails without us asking for that. Soon enough our virtual PA will have taken over our cursor to get things done on our behalf, and shopped around for our insurance renewal without us asking. On the enterprise side, "agentic" functionality will have our systems talking to each other behind the scenes and running operational workflows without us having to know how.

Beyond AI, we are seeing an increasing cadence of announcements about developments in quantum technologies. Trials are live in London on quantum secure communications, whereby data transmission between sites is undertaken using quantum states to make attacks and eavesdropping impossible. Quantum computing is a challenging frontier, but with the scale of investment, it is realistic to expect significant breakthroughs over the next five years that will have an impact across security and the performance of our systems. Blended technologies offer a combination of them all, with distributed ledger (blockchain) technology used with AI, quantum, augmented reality, internet of things, 6G connectivity and more, to enhance security, streamline operations, and provide new revenue models, from supply chain management to financial services.

On the consumer side, we are seeing advancements in brain-to-machine interfaces, virtual reality, and predictive analytics impacting healthcare, law enforcement, finance, and retail. The tech we will see and use in 2030 will bear resemblance to what we see emerging today, but its capability will be an order of magnitude more advanced and it will sit alongside developments and applications we have not yet even heard of.

The complexity of the modern operational environment is necessitating new methodologies of governance at the same time that advances in technology are providing the capacity for such innovation. The costs of certain technologies are also trending down.

Forward-looking organizations are already leveraging advanced analytics, AI, and big data to enhance decision-making and operations. Tech capabilities and applications are reshaping how boards and executives operate. Board oversight and governance, and risk and compliance tools streamline methodologies and improve transparency, accountability, plus speed and confidence in decision-making. Real-time insights will become par for the course, demanded by boards, leadership teams, shareholders, regulators, and others as they seek an observation window into company performance, risk management, and compliance issues.

The blended technology referenced above is of particular interest in the reporting context, for example with emissions reporting under environmental related regulation. No longer will reports require re-keying of information or even data gathering from different systems. The integrity of that data will be able to be tracked and validated from source. Contracts will be coded upstream to generate data automatically. They will interact with other contracts, policies, and data from a range of internal and external sources "agentically", for example calculating emissions across supply chains, applying exchange rates and taxes at prevailing rates, and flagging or correcting anomalies and errors. Systems will be coded to initiate steps normally taken by people, to gather, summarize, cross check, and visualize information into required forms and notify relevant people, or require actions from them such as approvals. Data will be tracked in audit-ready frameworks and held in an immutable form on distributed ledgers to be tamper-proof. External access can be provided under secure controls so that each stakeholder gets what they need (and only what they need) when they need it.

Law firms that embrace, develop, or integrate with such tools and methodologies deliver their advice in ways that match those technology enabled methodologies, and make their information available by API for ingestion by and from such tools, will be at a premium to those who do not.

Add to this two further phenomena – embedded governance and distributed governance.

Embedded governance

Governance will become embedded into systems in a way that takes on a broader remit. Leaders, lawyers, and compliance professionals will be able to code a system directly from their decision or advice into operational processes and organizational conduct. Much like cruise control on your car, you will not be able to break the speed limit or adjust the data to lie about the speed at which you were travelling. You could call this coded compliance or embedded governance, but in the longer term it will not require a name. It will simply be how things are. This has been around for a long time, for example in contract approval flows, where your Docusign or Salesforce flow requires a certain order of signature and ensures signatories have correct signing authority in line with board approvals. Or where you can't export or delete files out of a business repository to protect confidentiality, IP, and evidence for audit. This will extend across all manner of dimensions.

Over time this means the number of decisions and internal variables for staff will shrink down, systematizing workflows and business environments. There are social implications of these changes, where they can have a negative or positive impact on staff empowerment and culture, depending how and the extent to which they are implemented. For example, all emails could be automatically screened and blocked if they contain disparaging content or language that indicates price fixing. The current recommended approach is to use embedded governance for high risk, high friction issues only, such as we are seeing in the AML space in the legal sector. However, their deployment will depend on a range of factors including the level of automation an organization is motivated to deploy. Within law firms themselves, client onboarding is an example of a currently expensive and high risk, high effort area of work where coded compliance and use of agentic tools would be a great fit.

Whether for their own operations or in supporting clients as they adjust to and adopt these new methodologies of governance, law firms will need to be familiar with the state of the art and be able to interrogate, navigate, and direct systems and tech-integrated ways of working if they are to advise clients on the legal issues and opportunities relevant to their work.

When it comes to agentic tools, lawyers will play the role of system designers and auditors, making sure the correct risk profiles are built into programs and that they are performing in line with legal advice, risk appetite, and regulation. They will need to think through issues like enforcement and liability in the context of agents performing actions on behalf of people and businesses, and practical measures such as coding in kill switches.

This also raises the critical subject of AI governance.

As AI becomes integrated into our systems and decision-making processes, AI governance is emerging as a critical area for businesses and for the law firms that advise them. These systems will span all aspects, from employment decisions to financial risk assessments. Law firms will play a pivotal role in guiding businesses on algorithmic accountability, bias mitigation, privacy and liability structures, ensuring that AI deployment aligns with both regulatory requirements and ethical best practices – the latter of which is covered in the next chapter. Law firms will need to ensure their own use of AI does the same. They will need to be familiar with the frameworks, policies, and regulations that ensure artificial intelligence systems are ethical, transparent, accountable, and compliant with legal and societal standards.

Such frameworks combine human oversight, regulatory compliance, and technological standards. For example, the NIST AI Risk Management Framework and ISO/IEC 42001 AI Management System Standard are common frameworks that offer tools for identifying, mitigating, and monitoring AI-related risks. Legal compliance with the EU AI Act will be necessary for certain clients, with country segmentation for those seeking to ringfence its jurisdiction. The OECD AI Principles, the Singapore Model AI Governance Framework, Australia's AI Ethics Principles, and the upcoming IAPP AI governance textbook chapter on legal practice are also helpful reference points in the implementation of ethical AI practices, while balancing innovation with legal and societal responsibilities. Law firms will need to develop expertise in these areas or work with external specialists.

In the context of embedded governance for AI, technical governance has long been used to manage risk and support decision-making within organizations. Access controls and audit logs are examples of technical governance. Tools are entering the market that automate AI governance, including AI-powered audit platforms, automated bias detection tools, and compliance management software, which streamline tasks like monitoring algorithmic fairness, ensuring regulatory adherence, and providing real-time transparency into AI decision-making processes. These tools[18] can be set to chosen frameworks and internal policies.

The key is to ensure AI enhances corporate responsibility rather than undermining it and that governance is proportionate and adaptive to a technologically-enabled and fast changing environment. For law firms, this means advising on compliance, ensuring their own compliance as a firm, and also helping clients design AI governance frameworks that proactively address liability, security risks, and ethical concerns before legal challenges arise.

Distributed governance

The second phenomenon is the distribution of power within and around organizations to 2030 and beyond. Technologies such as distributed ledger and smart contracts are enabling new forms of stakeholder engagement and voting, shifting the balance of decision-making from traditional board-centric models, where these serve the needs of the organization and its societal context.

For efficiency, voting processes can be moved "on chain" allowing real-time, secure, and transparent voting, enabling shareholders to participate actively in corporate-decision making. This may be as simple as digitizing the currently unwieldy AGM, as is underway for many organizations. Or it may mean moving beyond that, allowing for more decentralized and frequent or continuous decision-making, which can also facilitate the inclusion of broader stakeholder groups or assignment of specific advisory roles to experts or groups of experts, whether via a digital twin, AI avatar, or in person. An analogy here is the "direct democracy" referendum model in Switzerland where cantons vote regularly on the spectrum of local issues. For example, you could access technical expertise on a cyber issue or an evaluation of what is a standard term or position across the market on a deal negotiation. You could include employee voting on allocation of profit sharing and workplace policies, integrate community voting on a green or brownfield construction project, or shareholder voting on prioritization of sustainability projects or capital allocation.

Taking the distribution of power to the next level, technology can also be used to redesign the core organizational structure of an organization. Decentralized Autonomous Organizations or DAOs use distributed ledger technology, smart contracts, and token-based voting systems to distribute decision-making, creating what some argue is a more transparent and democratic structure of governance. DAOs already control billions of dollars in assets worldwide.

A DAO is deployed via a self-executing digital agreement called a "smart contract" on a form of digital infrastructure that is "decentralized", called a "distributed ledger" or "blockchain". This means it is held across a range of "nodes" rather than centralized in one place. It exists as a legal entity in this form – something on which the Law Commission has opined in the UK.[19] Governance tokens are distributed to members representing ownership stakes and voting powers. Members submit proposals for action by the group and votes are automatically weighted according to token ownership. If a proposal reaches a required threshold, set as part of the organization programming, it is automatically executed via smart contacts, along with day-to-day operations, reporting, data gathering, payments and the like.

Transactions and governance decisions are recorded "on chain" with transparency to all members.

We may see these community-driven structures rising in popularity for a range of reasons from cost, efficiency, decentralization of decision making, transparency, ease of collaboration, mistrust of state infrastructure, and geopolitics. Self-executing rules also have the benefit of reducing legal disputes. Blockchain based systems offer "decentralized finance" or DeFi alternatives to intermediaries like banks and brokers, enabling people to access capital and trading or other transactions through smart contracts. "Real world assets" or RWA tokenization is bringing traditional assets like real estate, commodities, and bonds onto blockchain systems, opening up liquidity, fractional ownership, and global participation in asset markets. These structures and methodologies change traditional legal dynamics such as how property rights are recorded, transferred, and enforced.

As the "crypto economy" gains strength worldwide as a result of the US presidency's support for digital assets, we can expect to see demand and confidence increase over time for such structures, with the regulatory landscape evolving to surmount current uncertainties. Such uncertainties include legal status, potential vulnerabilities in smart contract code, difficulties assigning liability, constraints in the ability to enforce rights globally when members can be in any jurisdiction, and the inability to switch off persistent scripts in software code. The UK Jurisdiction Taskforce confirmed digital assets can be property at law and for insolvency purposes and that smart contracts can constitute legally binding agreements.[20] The Digital Assets Bill is currently passing through the UK parliament to establish digital assets in a new category of personal property, which would strengthen legal certainty.[21]

An even more novel construct to the DAO is the concept of "algocracies". These are governance systems where decisions are primarily made by algorithms or automated processes, rather than human leaders. In an algocracy, AI systems analyze data, predict outcomes, and make policy or operational decisions based on pre-set rules or learned patterns. The point being that decisions are taken – or at least proposed – by algorithms based on data, rather than by appointed human representatives. We can expect to see increased demand for such arrangements and adjustments in legal practice to accommodate them.

This technocratic or data-driven model of governance we can expect to see more of in society, business, and systems of the state. There are many examples of potential use, such as in civil or criminal justice, where algorithms determine sentencing or case outcome recommendations based on legislation analysis or past data. In the corporate world, uses are already in play or under development, such as dynamic pricing models or automated recruitment and talent management and supply chain and inventory management. Such systems obviously promise efficiency, speed, scalability, and consistency, but also present concerns about transparency, fairness, bias, and error.

As organizations navigate digital transformation in governance and seek to harness data and technology as core strategic assets, they are also grappling with new challenges, including data integrity, access and security, privacy concerns, and the need for digital literacy among leaders. These challenges are equally for the advisors as well as the clients. Some anticipate law firms will run as DAOs with AI partners and associates in the mid-term future.[22] Keeping up with these developments and governing an organization across all such dimensions will be a significant undertaking. Yet this is what law firms as well as their clients must do to 2030.

What will become increasingly obvious over the mid-term future is the difference between organizations that make governance seamless and easy, and that have advisors that help them do that, and those that do not innovate in this space.

Those that embrace technology and data and know how to work with it and mitigate the risks across critical dimensions of decision-making, operational efficiency, and the ability to innovate at scale, will pull ahead in competitive advantage.

The law firm "G"

As indicated, there is both an impending compliance necessity and competitive advantage for law firms in reviewing and upgrading their governance needs and practices. A new "baseline" is emerging for legal practitioners across all types of employment contexts, in proving compliance with professional, regulatory, and ethical duties. Add to which the needs of clients are changing in terms of the state of their technological art, and the basis on which they evaluate and work with external advisors.

Law firms, in-house lawyers, and other practitioners that have mapped the risks and applied mitigations that are efficient, effective, and measurable will be those that maintain relevance, market share, and client trust over a longer timeline. This requires a range of "systems and controls", applied at a professionalized level not previously seen scaled in the legal community outside of anti-money laundering measures.

This includes meeting increasingly well-resourced and data-savvy regulator expectations and practices, and tracking to technological developments over time, for example developing frameworks for governing AI and the direction of travel towards use of increasingly capable and autonomous tools in the workplace. Figuring out and securing your own "governance stack" as a legal practice or practitioner, in a similar way to how organizations develop, right-size, and maintain their "technology stack"[23] will be both critical and normal over the next five plus years.

There is a further, critical dimension for legal practice and that is ethics, as a professional and regulatory requirement. This dimension is covered in the following chapter, titled Ethics infrastructure, which also covers suggestions on "governance stack" for law firms that apply more broadly.

Conclusion

To 2030, the unwieldy nature and ideological narratives of ESG give way to a new set of priorities. The future agenda is for growth and security, where countries and companies look to financial and structural resilience, operational independence, and expansion through innovation. The international order is re-shaping, bringing with it a new set of challenges to address and opportunities to embrace. Frameworks of the past will not meet these new market conditions and the accelerated change they will bring.

ESG as a movement will not survive. The elements previously categorized under the E, the S, and the G that continue to serve a practical purpose within the new world order will sustain, moving into the background without need of a label. These will include the basics of responsible business in compliance and care through a supply chain, fair treatment in the workplace, and preventing contamination for communities. The activated de-regulatory agenda will stay away from such things. But we can expect to see a roll back in other areas, to make way for the production of energy at unprecedented levels, and manufacturing to support defense, technology, and economic development. There will be many surprises, including breakthroughs in technology, U-turns and the wildly unexpected in policy, international alliances, and the possibility of research findings that go to the very heart of climate science.

Organizations on the front foot will be getting ahead of this now, reviewing compliance versus voluntary, upward reviewing risk appetite, future-proofing supply chain resilience and governance infrastructure, and doubling down on business. Governance rises up the ranks in importance, as a way for businesses to control costs, strengthen decision-making, and ensure they are focusing on the highest impact areas. Operating in an era of ever greater transparency, business leaders need the ability to capture, analyze, and use data, provide evidential certainty, and understand what is happening across their ecosystem. Automated reporting and agentic functionality will ease overheads and increase accuracy. Data volumes and adoption of AI and other technologies have their own drivers and challenges, prompting the need for capability in technical and embedded (automated) governance.

As per the adage often used in the venture capital world, *"The future is already here – it's just not yet evenly distributed"*,[24] ESG will fade at differing rates in different countries and contexts. Markets following suit with the US are moving fast and seeking closer alignment. Countries and leaders with more embedded commitments and mandates will hold with ESG for longer. In the investment space, ESG assets such as green and social bonds and ESG-linked equities remain a relevant categorization, though they may be rebranded along with other initiatives to reflect evolving investor preferences. More broadly, we will see the approach of "bucketing" different issues together under a single label fall away, and organizations and administrations speak in more specific terms about their priorities and performance.

For law firms to retain relevance through the coming decade, they will need to get ahead of this curve and the increased scrutiny they themselves will come under. The anti-corruption sentiment in society and trend towards personal accountability is not going away. More than ever, lawyers need to ensure their decision-making and internal governance provides strength in a coming storm, both in respect of who they choose to act for, in the lines they draw, and how they themselves behave. They will find themselves at once both under less pressure to align themselves with ideological standpoints, while also under increased regulatory pressure to demonstrate integrity and independence in legal practice.

As the legal sector is disrupted by market forces, AI and new entrants, technically adept law firms, those who can read the tea leaves of geopolitics, responding quickly to policy changes for their clients, and who understand how to get the best out their multi-disciplinary teams, will be the ones who lead and get to shape the market for the next cycle, independent of prevailing narratives.

References

1 www.linkedin.com/pulse/short-history-esg-richard-hardyment-vmouc/
2 https://commission.europa.eu/document/download/10017eb1-4722-4333-add2-e0ed18105a34_en
3 https://lordslibrary.parliament.uk/government-climate-policy-economic-impact/
4 www.epa.gov/climate-change/endangerment-and-cause-or-contribute-findings-greenhouse-gases-under-section-202a
5 www.globelawandbusiness.com/books/what-clients-want-from-law-firms
6 www.bcorporation.net/en-us/news/blog/reflecting-on-our-impact-in-2023/?utm_source
7 https://thegiin.org/publication/research/sizing-the-impact-investing-market-2024/?utm_source
8 https://digital-strategy.ec.europa.eu/en/policies/nis2-directive
9 https://eur-lex.europa.eu/legal-content/EN/TXT/PDF/?uri=CELEX:52020PC0595&rid=10
10 www.fca.org.uk/firms/senior-managers-certification-regime
11 www.itv.com/watch/mr-bates-vs-the-post-office/10a0469
12 www.clientearth.org/latest/press-office/press-releases/clientearth-files-climate-risk-lawsuit-against-shell-s-board-with-support-from-institutional-investors/
13 www.frc.org.uk/library/standards-codes-policy/corporate-governance/uk-corporate-governance-code/
14 www.iod.com/events/business_as_a_force_for_good_and_growth68731621/
15 www.globelawandbusiness.com/books/what-clients-want-from-law-firms
16 www.pwc.com/gx/en/issues/risk-regulation/global-compliance-survey.html
17 www.statista.com/statistics/871513/worldwide-data-created/
18 Such as https://vanta.com/
19 https://lawcom.gov.uk/project/decentralised-autonomous-organisations-daos/
20 https://27221500.fs1.hubspotusercontent-eu1.net/hubfs/27221500/LawtechUK%20archive%20reports/UKJT%20Legal%20Statement%20on%20Digital%20Assets%20and%20English%20Insolvency%20Law.pdf?
21 www.gov.uk/government/publications/property-digital-assets-etc-bill/property-digital-assets-etc-bill-factsheet
22 https://joetechnologist.com/the-legal-landscape-of-2030-what-no-one-is-saying-but-everyone-should-hear/
23 www.forbes.com/councils/forbestechcouncil/2024/01/22/the-proper-tech-stack-for-your-growth-stage/
24 Often credited to author William Gibson, www.nytimes.com/2012/01/15/books/review/distrust-that-particular-flavor-by-william-gibson-book-review.html

Chapter 13: **Ethics infrastructure**

By Jenifer Swallow, lawyer and strategic advisor

Introduction

The principles and requirements of legal practice are expressed by leading legal services regulators to be ethical duties as well as regulatory ones. For example, as the Solicitors Regulation Authority expresses it, *"Our Principles embody the fundamental ethical behaviours that we expect all those we regulate to uphold".*[1] Ethics is placed at the core of legal practice, integral with regulatory duties, requiring lawyers of any qualification to uphold high standards of integrity, professionalism, and public trust. Regulators require those they authorize to act with honesty, independence, and in the best interests of their clients, while promoting the rule of law, administration of justice, and equality. These duties apply in all types of employment contexts from in-house lawyers to freelance, to private practice, chambers and alternative legal business structures. They apply both within and outside professional settings.

There is currently no such equivalent in business, certainly in the UK. There are laws that must be followed, such as employment, health and safety, consumer protection, and corporate governance, and those laws may overlap with ethics. However, there is no legal or operating requirement to act ethically in a general sense. Public, investor, and stakeholder pressure can strongly incentivize ethical conduct and there is a requirement in section 172 of the UK Companies Act[2] to consider stakeholders like employees, suppliers, and local communities. However, the primary duty owed by directors is to the company and towards its success.

It is a fact that the license to operate as a business is a contract with the state under companies laws, which requires high standards to be upheld. However, the wider practical reality does not reflect that. This is why the Institute of Directors issued a code of conduct for directors in the wake of the Post Office Horizon Scandal[3] and is advocating for the professionalization of the role of director. The gap is also part of why the B Corp movement[4] and other "better business" initiatives have arisen.[5] We may see further developments in this space, for example the introduction of a duty of candor, at least in the public sector,[6] and changes to regulatory requirements and oversight in corporate governance.[7]

To 2030 and beyond, the ethical dimensions of legal practice and the developing landscape of business ethics should be a priority focus area for lawyers and legal services businesses, both as an opportunity and a risk. This is not as an ideological approach, but as a practicality of responsible business. The focus of this chapter is that practicality – considering the infrastructure necessary to meet ethical duties in legal practice and support clients with the same in decision-making and deployment to the future.

Ethics dimensions

There are three areas on the subject of ethics to draw out that are pertinent to the law firm landscape over the next five to ten years, and the governance required in response to that. These are ethics for lawyers, ethics for clients, and ethics in technology.

Lawyers

Ethics are a requirement of legal practice, set out in the rules and codes that bind lawyers and upon which their livelihood relies. These rules and codes reflect the role of lawyers in society and the imperative that we are able to trust them not to rip us off or act in a way that would undermine the very fabric of the legal system. A lawyer abusing their privilege and power can cause outsize harm. Business ethics sits within the "S" and the "G" dimensions of the historic ESG model (see chapter 12).

Through the ages there have been lawyers who have not met standards that support society. Lawyer jokes exist for a reason, back to Shakespeare's time and beyond. This is a pertinent topic for the era we are living in now and the headwinds faced by the legal profession over the coming decade. Law firms have been caught up in all number of ethical issues, from weaponizing litigation and using "lawfare", use of NDAs to cover up physical abuse and other forms of client wrongdoing, misleading the court, use of strategic lawsuits against public participation (SLAPPs), involvement in money laundering, working for kleptocrats, facilitating tax evasion, and fraud. In the US, free speech laws are used to block application of all number of regulations, for example to defend false certification of securities on the basis that to make misleading statements is part of free speech.[8] Such actions would be defended as "zealous advocacy" by some and for others it brings the profession into disrepute, degrading the integrity of every lawyer in the mind of the public.

Once confined to academic journals and legal circles, the role of lawyers, who they choose to work with, and their involvement in misconduct are increasingly common subjects in the press. This is for both private practice lawyers and in-house counsel, across litigation, regulatory activity, civil, criminal, and commercial contexts. We have seen lawyers take center stage in public inquiries and media outlets and target those who are seen to cross ethics boundaries in their representation.

These dynamics are on the rise. They affect not only reputation, but can trigger public outrage, regulatory investigations, and financial losses. The trajectory for lawyers is for greater scrutiny, greater public profile, and attention to conduct beyond legal technicalities. This, too, in the context of the very significant issues and risks we can see coming in the 2030s, such as the increase in defense manufacturing, activities of war, high risk uses of technology, development of nuclear power, space exploration, and more.

The tension at the heart of these issues is the incentive structures that sit behind legal practice and the frameworks that regulate it. On the one hand, the lawyer must act in the best interests of their client and on the other they must give primacy to the interests of society in upholding the rule of law and administration of justice. But society is not paying them. In the "big law" context at least, the client is.

These matters will reach a crescendo over the coming years, as regulators – certainly in the UK – lean into a number of high-profile scandals and the public outrage that surrounds them. The Legal Services Board, the UK oversight regulator, has initiated a series of work on ethics in response to evidence of a decline in ethical standards across the profession. This includes considering new regulatory measures. In the in-house legal space, regulators such as the UK's largest legal services regulator, the Solicitors Regulation Authority, has acknowledged the intense pressure[9] in-house counsel come under to compromise their regulatory and professional duties in favor of commercial drivers. They are stepping up engagement, guidance,[10] and supervision, as well as considering further measures to strengthen ethical practice. Professor Richard Moorhead's excellent Hamlyn Lectures provide further context and direction.[11] There are also a number of wider ethics initiatives, including the IBE Taskforce on Business Ethics in the Legal Profession,[12] the Post Office Project,[13] and ethics work being undertaken by the Law Society and the International Bar Association.

Historically, governance in legal practice has been focused on client conflicts, AML checks, and handling client money. What is precipitating now is a wholescale re-evaluation of what governance necessitates in and of the legal sector. On top of basic compliance, the focus turns to the primary duties of lawyers to (1) act with integrity, and (2) maintain professional independence. Law firms will need to be able to evidence the practice of these principles in all they do, regardless of the context in which they work. They will increasingly be called upon to provide such evidence, and to support in-house lawyers within client environments to do the same. It will no longer be enough to certify ethics training, ethical practice, and compliance once a year or perhaps never, or to see ethics as a separate "thing on the side" that may or may not be about morality. Nor will independence be assumed or accepted when asserted. It will need to be demonstrated.

To assure these duties and be able to evidence they are being upheld, law firms will need to build out their governance infrastructure via systems and controls. These will integrate ethics into all areas of practice and decision-making. Areas of focus will include the following.

Commitments	Ethical codes of conduct, training, and logging ethical risks.
Decision making	Decision making around client representation with record keeping and transparency as to decision factors, weighting of such factors and ongoing monitoring and alerts. We may see independent advisory committees established, staffed with experts across different disciplines, including ethics, technology, behavioral science and governance, to input on decision-making for sensitive and challenging topics.
Conflicts	Digitizing client due diligence and conflicts checks to strengthen accuracy, completeness and ongoing monitoring, mindful of emerging standards.[14]

continued on next page

Independence review	Independence risk reviews and automated monitoring, based on factors such as proportion of client instructions by revenue, volume and fee earner utilization, plus "trophy client" brand reliance.
Fact checking	Policy and processes for fact-checking client information prior to reliance, e.g. a client's tax affairs or 'side of the story'.
Litigation strategy	Litigation strategy evaluation, periodic ethics assessments, and team oversight to ensure proportionality and provide "fire breaks" to assess stakeholder interests.
Spot checks	"Four eyes" reviews and spot checks of advice such as used in financial services compliance.
Team rotation	Client relationship partner and fee earner rotation.
Culture reviews	Ethics culture reviews including "tone from the top", incentive structures, and "informal ethics" (based on workplace norms), undertaken independently.
Reporting	"Speak up" mechanisms enabling staff and clients to report unethical conduct without fear of retaliation, and demonstration of their use across all levels.
Promotions	Governance framework for promotions and leadership decisions including independence and integrity factors.
Board	Board governance and partner ethics reviews.
AI governance	Frameworks for managing ethics in technical systems.

To 2030, it is also likely we will see changes in regulation for the legal profession. Regulators are already issuing detailed guidance on ethical practice and reconsidering regulation of in-house counsel. State action is being taken to curb the influence of lawyers and judges in markets such as the US and Mexico. Regulators may also step in on the ethical use by lawyers of AI, and on AI-led legal products and services that currently sit outside regulatory regimes. Much is likely to move over the coming decade as the market reshapes.

Clients

Corporate and institutional misconduct is one of the biggest risks to society. It is estimated that 28 percent of employees experience pressure to compromise workplace standards or the law, whilst 84 percent say they have witnessed misconduct. They report it in increasing numbers.[15] "Speak up" policies and whistleblowing lines are becoming the norm. In the consumer space, people increasingly opt for products and services from companies that align with their personal values, and boycott brands based on ethical considerations. Public scandals hit hearts as well as minds, strengthening resolve to speak out. "Ethics washing" and "virtue signaling" have been criticized similarly to "greenwashing".

Even with a shift towards a growth-driven agenda and wider deregulation to boost business, organizations need to be mindful of what keeps them afloat and provides both financial and reputational endurance. In self-regulatory environments, organizations need to take a more proactive role in defining and adhering to their own ethical standards, beyond the reach of government mandates. As has been studied in driving conditions in countries such as Sri Lanka and Thailand, fewer rules can result in greater road safety, despite initial perceptions.

The needs of clients will become increasingly polarized based on their stance. Some will want to tip out the focus of the past and distance themselves from a "woke" agenda, which by 2030 will be seen as a fading relic. Others will hold their values either in alignment with their already solid purpose or to an agenda that suits their objectives for other reasons. This latter group may maintain prior ethical practices, but adjust their narrative towards financial resilience and risk mitigation to be more relevant or less conspicuous for the times. Stance will dictate ethos and legal needs, for example polarized between (1) wanting advice on a closely defined legal question and nothing more, even if ethics issues loom large, or (2) being desirous of broader input, including input on ethicall decision-making and wider adjacencies.

These stances track intriguingly with the reshaping of the legal profession around technological advancement. The questions being, what will the role of lawyers and the law firm of the future be? What will a law firm look like and what services will it provide? Will it be about the provision of deep expertise in a specific area, with technology deployed around those experts, or will it be a more full-stack service model along the lines of a specialist business consultancy? The geopolitical landscape and the ethics frameworks that feed into and flow from that will have a role to play in the supply and demand cycles that shape how law firms operate in the future. Those clients that simply want legal information and process versus those that want and value broader support will inform service models and structures.

Lawyers can help coach and will need to be ready for whichever stance their clients wish to take, within the limitations of their own ethics and governance frameworks set out above and as further detailed in chapter 12. Where they can help clients the most is in supporting effective decision-making, for which governance is an important underpinning. It is one thing to provide the legal answer and leave it there. It is quite another to provide a truly valuable service. Clients need processes and record keeping to provide confidence that:

- They are making informed decisions;
- The implications of those decisions are understood, including ethics factors;
- The necessary actions and mitigations arising from them are implemented; and
- They can prove required standards are met, such as taking reasonable care.

Law firms can provide or help ensure such processes are in place, regardless of the types of decisions clients wish to take. There will be moments when lawyers need to cease to act for clients if they step over legal or ethical red lines, but this does not negate – and in fact if anything simply underscores – the need for dynamic governance, systems that enable decisions to be made at speed, with imperfect information, in a consistent way. Being able to flag such red lines up front can itself help raise awareness. Influencing decision-making at this level can have positive impacts on ethical culture and "tone from the top" within businesses, supporting long-term growth and resilience. Ultimately, ethical decision-making is led by the integrity of leadership and care for people, but it can also be developed, bolstered, and institutionalized.

The types of processes that support ethical decision-making and the wider culture on ethics inside client organizations include:

- Decision-making criteria decided up front, which include ethical considerations aligned with the objectives and values of the organization.
- Approval flows, ensuring correct information and approvals are in place and the right people are aware of the considerations.
- Personal accountability or integrity statements to ensure people have considered their responsibilities up front.
- Ethics incident or conflict logs and audits to keep track of challenging circumstances, see emerging trends, and mitigate material risks.
- Ethics oversight boards or named board representatives to provide a point of focus in decision-making and risk evaluation, including AI "sounding board" versions of the same.
- Ethics criteria in investment, employment, and supply chain processes and documentation to provide consistency in business operations.
- Independent ethics reviews and training to provide external input on risks and opportunities, such as during high value litigation or at inflection points in the company.

Lawyers to 2030 will need to be prepared to follow, plug into, or implement systems to support the ethics and governance needs of their clients. This includes data visualization to help prevent ethical lapses before they occur and evaluate remediation options if they do. Firms that integrate such governance considerations into their counsel and deliverables will be closer to board and executive decision-making and better positioned to help clients navigate the various pressures they will face, advising beyond compliance frameworks and more deeply into board responsibilities, risk management strategies, and ethical decision-making at the highest levels.

Tech ethics

With the acceleration of technological development, clients and firms will also need to attend to the responsible use of technology, through ethics frameworks and governance.

By 2030, the technology we use will be vastly advanced to what we are seeing today. We will be creating, capturing, and using data in new ways at unfathomable rates. New AI capabilities will have emerged and we will have seen breakthroughs in innovations such as advanced robotics. Much as we saw with the development of data protection regulation, by 2030 we can expect AI regulation of some form or another to exist in countries all around the world. Quantum technologies will be in live production across a range of categories with exciting and worrying impacts. We may have seen by then such significant developments that crisis regulation or intervention has become required, such as "quantum supremacy" to break encryption, or to control for artificial general intelligence, where machines surpass human oversight and cognitive capability.

Law firms will be using advanced technology systems and will need measures in place to ensure such use and further development is not only compliant with laws but is also ethical. Further, their regulators and clients will require it of them, for example, general counsel folding AI ethics conditions into RFPs, and regulators requiring annual certification as to supervision of machines. The smart law firms will be offering AI ethics and AI governance as value added services alongside risk evaluations and advisory work.

AI ethics is a distinct but related topic to AI governance, which we covered covered in chapter 12. AI ethics focuses on the principles and values that guide the responsible development and use of AI, such as fairness, transparency, accountability, and avoiding harm. It is about ensuring AI respects societal needs and expectations. AI governance refers to the frameworks, policies, and regulations that oversee AI development, deployment, and risk management. It could be said AI ethics is about what should be done, while AI governance is about how it is controlled and managed.

Lawyers will therefore need to be familiar with AI ethics and institute guidelines in their use of AI, as well as other technologies. Law firms that build or use tech-enabled products, or invest in companies that do, will need to make sure they have experts that can oversee these guidelines and apply relevant frameworks. Practically, this includes designing algorithms that avoid bias, ensuring data used is representative, and establishing mechanisms for explaining AI decisions to users and stakeholders. Ethical AI also entails ensuring that AI technologies do not cause harm, for example providing misleading information or impacting people's rights or opportunities based on profiling, or where they have no right of recourse. Practitioners and teams will need to have visibility and confidence in system performance and data outputs, whether those systems are their own or third-party licensed. As firms have incident response specialists on retainer today, so they will have relationships with AI governance professionals and ethicists in the future.

Conclusion

The trajectory for law firms is towards a broader range of governance infrastructure that enables them to be confident in and demonstrate compliance with the ethical requirements of legal practice, and that they can leverage for advantage in the market. As societal and political pressure continues to mount on the subject of ethics, for business and for lawyers, and as regulator scrutiny increases, following informal practices and procedures of the past will not be enough. There will be a movement towards greater clarity over what ethics means, and a greater than ever overlap between ethics, the law, and our interpretation and application of both. Technological developments open up new risks around ethics and a range of possibilities in how to evaluate and manage them. This is an opportunity the most savvy lawyers in a range of contexts will embrace in the evolution of their own practices and businesses, and in how they can support clients to maximize theirs.

References

1 www.sra.org.uk/solicitors/standards-regulations/principles/
2 www.legislation.gov.uk/ukpga/2006/46/section/172
3 www.iod.com/news/governance/iod-press-release-governance-lessons-from-the-post-office-scandal/
4 https://bcorporation.uk
5 https://betterbusinessact.org/, https://unglobalcompact.org/
6 www.gov.uk/government/publications/findings-of-the-call-for-evidence-on-the-statutory-duty-of-candour/findings-of-the-call-for-evidence-on-the-statutory-duty-of-candour#:
7 www.frc.org.uk/
8 www.amacad.org/publication/daedalus/free-speech-clause-deregulatory-tool
9 www.bloomsbury.com/uk/inhouse-lawyers-ethics-9781509944323/
10 www.sra.org.uk/sra/news/press/2024-press-releases/support-in-house-solicitors/
11 https://law.exeter.ac.uk/about/thehamlyntrust/
12 www.ibe.org.uk/knowledge-hub/legal-profession-taskforce.html
13 https://postofficeproject.net/
14 www.ibe.org.uk/resource/legal-profession-must-embed-ethical-decision-making-to-avoid-assisting-kleptocrats-and-to-restore-reputation-says-legal-taskforce.html
15 www.ethics.org/global-business-ethics-survey/

Chapter 14:
Rebranding for the future – the power of trade names and branding in legal practice

By Wayne Hassay, managing partner, Maguire Schneider Hassay

For over a century, law firms have clung to traditional naming conventions. Think Jones, Smith & Smith or the infamous fictional firm, Dewey, Cheatum and Howe. It is time for law firms to rethink their approach to branding and client engagement. To stay competitive, law firms must evolve, crafting relatable and recognizable brands that authentically reflect their mission, values, and the communities they serve, starting with their name and extending to every aspect of their marketing strategy. The question is no longer *whether* firms should change. The question is, *how quickly* can they pivot to remain relevant in an increasingly dynamic marketplace?

Why law firms historically used surnames

Ask a lawyer why their firm is named the way it is, and the likely response is, "Because that is just how it's done. We use our names." This long-standing tradition is rarely questioned.

In the early days of the common law system, a lawyer's reputation, and really every business, was tied solely to the individual, not to an organization. This is unlike modern business practice, where companies build distinct identities separate from individuals. In addition, consider the absence of technology. Without modern communication tools, a lawyer's surname on a sign, reinforced by word-of-mouth, was the only means of marketing services.

Over time, bar associations codified these norms, and the technology of the day, into rigid rules. Even as other industries evolved, the legal profession clung to relics of the past, positioning itself as a prestige-driven institution distinct from commercial enterprises.

The argument was that surname-based firm names preserve accountability, credibility, and ethical integrity. If traditional naming conventions ever were about professional responsibility, they quickly became about prestige and hierarchy. Surnames were used to gain a competitive edge, just as businesses in any industry seek advantages. Generational firms leveraged their names as symbols of exclusivity, much like modern corporations use branding. For decades, law firm names have projected an aura of distinction, subtly sidestepping the ethical prohibition against guaranteeing superior results while still implying superiority. There is nothing pure or ethical about using surnames to name a law firm.

Ego has further entrenched this practice. Many lawyers take pride in seeing their names on the door, viewing it as a marker of status and achievement. More recently, aggressive advertising, fueled by regulatory changes and access to capital, has allowed lawyers to amplify the commercial reach of their surname. Certainly, the goal in doing so was not accountability, credibility, or ethical integrity.

From the client's perspective, legacy-based firm names and word of mouth were their only measures of a law firm's reputation. As a result, both lawyers and clients became bound by outdated traditions, even as firms evolved from downtown solo practitioners and small partnerships into more sophisticated organizations. While surname-based naming was once considered a neutral tradition, it has long served as an advantage for firms that could build prestige over decades – reinforcing hierarchy rather than leveling the playing field.

Despite regulatory shifts easing restrictions on trade names, most law firms still resist change, not out of necessity, but inertia. The legal profession has it backward – the real risk is not in evolving; it is in remaining stagnant.

Beyond tradition – why trade names resonate with today's clients

Unlike previous generations, today's clients do not choose any product based on vaguely familiar surnames or word-of-mouth. They conduct online research, read reviews, and engage with companies that clearly speak directly to them. Trade names allow law firms to present themselves in a client-focused rather than lawyer-centric way. Regardless of how lawyers perceive branding, clients expect firms to prioritize their needs.

A law firm's name plays a critical role in digital visibility because of search engine optimization (SEO). A well-chosen trade name can improve online discoverability and increase client engagement. Short, distinct, and easy-to-search names outperform long, complicated firm names that are difficult to remember. Thus, "Summit Legal" is easier for consumers than Smith, Kowalczewski, Taylor & Associates, LLP.

While the legal profession remains deeply tied to surname-based firm names, other industries have long ago moved forward. Healthcare, accounting, finance, architecture, and engineering have all embraced branding as a strategic tool, connecting with consumers while maintaining professional integrity. These industries invest in branding that reflects their mission, values, and credibility, building recognizable identities that align with modern expectations. Do you know anyone picking a doctor based on the doctor's ancient ancestral surname? Of course not.

So why is law the exception? Does corporate branding in medicine, finance, and other regulated fields somehow undermine ethics while law alone upholds a higher standard? That notion is absurd. Branding has modernized other professions without eroding public trust, and law can and should do the same.

The role of developing non-lawyer competition

The competition is no longer merely other law firms. It is an entirely new class of market players that did not exist when outdated surname-based naming rules were established. The legal profession is undergoing rapid transformation, driven by non-lawyer competitors who are aggressively leveraging branding. If law firms resist modern naming and branding, they risk losing market share to tech-driven competitors, including artificial intelligence.

Lawyers question the quality and motives of this non-lawyer competition. Perhaps that is partially self-interested or robustly well founded. It does not matter. The competition is here to stay. To uphold their commitment to public service, law firms must adapt, ensuring clients receive representation from trained legal professionals rather than being steered toward non-lawyer alternatives.

How current ethical rules assume lawyers and the public cannot be trusted – and why that is a mistake

Some jurisdictions still outright ban trade names. A flawed assumption is that lawyers will misuse trade names to deceive the public. This overlooks a fundamental truth – the vast majority of attorneys enter the profession to serve, not to deceive.

Other jurisdictions permit trade names but there is an exhaustive list of caveats, concerns, and focus on "risk", discouraging lawyers from fully embracing trade names. Ethical rules already prohibit false and misleading claims, principles that govern all aspects of legal practice, including advertising. This should be sufficient to regulate trade names. Instead, there is a slippery slope that discourages trade names.

For instance, in most jurisdictions, a law firm cannot ethically call itself "Winning Law Firm" or "EZ Divorce Services" because such names supposedly imply guaranteed outcomes rather than legal services. Similarly, names like "Public Defenders Legal Group" or "Legal Aid Associates" are prohibited for purportedly suggesting a connection to a government agency or nonprofit organization. The assumption that legal consumers lack the discernment to differentiate branding from deception is not only flawed but also patronizing.

"WeWinEveryCase.com" is undeniably false, and any reasonable person would recognize it as such. Meanwhile, "Winning Law Firm" is arguably nothing more than a statement of confidence. The real issue is that focusing on names as a foundation of ethical compliance is misguided when true accountability lies beyond branding. Bad actors are filtered out by the marketplace and more substantive ethical regulations, not by restrictions on names. A well-chosen trade name and branding, backed by professionalism and quality service, will naturally succeed. For firms choosing a trade name, this is the clear and rational path forward. This stands in stark juxtaposition to the fact that, for decades, lawyers have plastered highways with outlandish billboards, showcasing their surnames while calling themselves things such as "'The Hammer". In fact, strong branding and well-chosen trade names could transform legal advertising itself, shifting it away from gimmicks and toward professionalism, restoring credibility in the process. Yet, it is trade names that have been prohibited and continue to be discouraged; the lack of logic is astonishing.

Troubling is an unspoken reality: resistance to trade names may be less about ethics and more about limiting competition. As noted, a surname-based system reinforces prestige and hierarchy, making it harder for new entrants to gain visibility. Rank and file lawyers merely fall in line.

Trade names, by contrast, level the playing field, allowing innovative, client-focused firms to compete on service, accessibility, and trust rather than inherited reputation. This shift threatens traditional power structures, which may explain why lawyer leadership has been slow to adapt despite branding's clear advantages.

How branding works at a psychological level

Decades of research in consumer psychology[1] show that people make decisions based on familiarity, emotional connection, and perceived credibility. Three key psychological factors explain why branding is so effective in building trust:

- *Cognitive ease – the power of recognition.* People trust what they recognize. A clear, memorable brand name helps potential clients quickly identify and recall a law firm when they need legal services. If a firm's name is confusing, generic, or indistinguishable from others, it creates friction in the decision-making process, causing clients to hesitate or look elsewhere.
- *The halo effect – positive first impressions matter.* A strong brand creates an immediate perception of professionalism and competence. When a firm presents itself with clear messaging, a modern identity, and a client-centered focus, potential clients assume that the legal services will be equally high quality. This is why companies across industries invest heavily in branding, because first impressions shape long-term trust. Law firms that fail to invest in branding appear outdated, impersonal, or inaccessible, even if their lawyers are highly skilled.
- *Emotional connection – why clients choose brands that feel relatable.* The most successful brands create an emotional bond with their audience. Consumers engage with brands that feel approachable, human, and aligned with their needs. Law firm branding should signal empathy, clarity, and accessibility. Qualities that make clients feel safe entrusting their legal matters to a firm. A name like "Family First Legal" feels warm, approachable, and reassuring for someone seeking legal help for estate planning or custody issues, while Jones & Baxter LLP feels distant and, paradoxically, more corporate, despite being a traditionally structured law firm.

Trade names and branding as a tool for expanding access to justice

This psychology directly impacts access to justice. The access to justice crisis affects a broad segment of the population, extending beyond vulnerable communities to include the middle class, upper class, and others. While it goes by many labels, at its core it encompasses anyone who is not accustomed to regularly using legal services and cannot afford hourly rates in the hundreds of dollars. Ultimately, the access to justice crisis is not a niche issue. It affects the vast majority of the public.

Many people do not seek legal help simply because they do not know where to start or whether a lawyer could help solve their problem, leaving many legal needs unmet and unrecognized. Trade names educate the public, making legal assistance more identifiable even before individuals need services.

Even when someone recognizes they have a legal issue, traditional law firm names create barriers rather than pathways. Access to justice depends on accessibility, relatability, and clarity – qualities many firm names fail to provide. A person might see a firm like Johnson & Smith and assume it is not meant for them. What was once a necessity, then ostensibly a sign of high-quality service, now functions as a psychological wall. While projecting prestige, traditional firm names often feel distant and impersonal, reinforcing the perception that lawyers are disconnected from those they serve. Johnson & Smith may be both capable and willing to help, but the connection is never made.

At an even more basic level, traditional law firm names fail to communicate their services, leaving those who seldom access legal services guessing whether a firm can address their legal needs or worse, assuming all lawyers handle every issue. As the public shops for services, a clear trade name immediately signals a firm's focus, ensuring clients know what kind of help is available.

Finally, trade names reinforce a firm's values and mission. For lawyers serving marginalized communities, branding can signal a commitment to advocacy, affordability, and trust. The same principle applies to lawyers seeking to serve clients who cannot afford $300 an hour. A well-crafted trade name not only helps clients find the right lawyer but also reassures them that the firm understands their concerns, strengthening the trust that forms the foundation of the attorney–client relationship.

In consideration of everything above

Given the tangled history of legal naming conventions, convoluted ethics rules, evolving public expectations, the psychology of branding, the progress of other professions, rising non-lawyer competition, and the ongoing access to justice crisis, trade names and branding are not ethical concerns. *They are ethical imperatives.* Embracing trade names and authentic branding is not just a modernization effort, it is a necessary reform to ensure legal services are accessible, transparent, and reflective of the evolving needs of both the public and the lawyers who serve them.

The practical business case for trade names and branding

Beyond marketing and consumer accessibility, trade names offer law firms other tangible business advantages. In fact, trade names provide law firms with the same strategic benefits that have long been leveraged by other professional service industries.

One of the major weaknesses of surname-based firm names is the challenge they create for long-term firm continuity and succession planning. As founding partners retire, pass away, or leave the firm, their names often remain on the masthead, creating a disconnect between the brand and the attorneys currently leading the firm. This not only leads to awkward rebranding dilemmas but also risks diminishing credibility when the firm's leadership no longer reflects the name on the door.

With a trade name, firms can establish a lasting brand identity that is independent of individual attorneys. Whether the firm is transitioning to new leadership, expanding its partnership structure, or expanding into new markets, a trade name provides continuity and stability. Clients and the broader legal community will recognize and trust the firm's brand regardless of internal personnel changes.

A well-crafted trade name creates brand equity – the value associated with a recognizable and respected business identity. Just as national accounting and consulting firms have successfully built multi-billion-dollar enterprises around their brand identities rather than individual partners, even small law firms can do something similar.

Firms that establish strong brand equity enjoy several advantages:

- Higher client retention and referral rates due to increased brand recognition.
- Greater valuation if the firm is ever sold or merged. A recognizable, client-centered trade name is an asset.
- Law firms expanding beyond their original market often struggle with surname-based branding, which may lack recognition in new regions. A trade name like "Midwest Legal Advisors" creates a scalable, wider jurisdictional brand that fosters seamless growth without client confusion.

Just as SEO improves consumer visibility, it also plays a crucial role in attracting top legal talent, ensuring that firms appear in job searches and professional networks. Historically, recruitment was driven by prestigious downtown office space, often with a coveted view of the courthouse.

However, in the modern legal landscape, branding plays a far greater role in attracting top talent.

Trade names will provide a key advantage in recruitment, as they can be strategically crafted to resonate with the firm's mission, culture, and values. That helps attract the right legal professionals. A clear, purpose-driven trade name, combined with strong branding, signals a firm's identity and differentiates it from competitors. Ultimately, law firms do not just compete for clients; they compete for the people and relationships that drive their success.

The race to own a trade name – a new challenge for law firms

Once the decision to adopt a trade name is made, the next challenge is finding one that can be legally secured. Unlike traditional surname-based firm names, which are practically impervious to disputes, trade names must be distinct, protectable, and compliant with intellectual property laws. In some jurisdictions the rush to claim desirable names is already underway, forcing law firms to either act quickly or rethink their approach.

In fact, even the trade name examples suggested in this chapter may be too generic to protect or already in use. This leaves law firms with two choices – secure a strong name early or get creative. As noted, lawyers, as a group, are rarely early adopters and even less frequently known for creativity. Hence, the need for this discussion.

However, no discussion of trade names is complete without recognizing that many firms will not take the leap. While the case for trade names is clear, an ethical imperative, essential for transparency, accessibility, and modern client engagement, some firms will remain hesitant. If a firm is risk-averse, finds all the "good" names already taken, or wishes to leverage its long history or legacy (even if its name actually is Dewey, Cheatum and Howe), then it must engage in a serious branding campaign around its identity. Such a firm still bears the modern duty to ensure it is properly branded, marketed, recognizable, and approachable to the public. This means deliberate, strategic branding – crafted with purpose and professionalism – not a half-hearted callback to roadside billboards.

This evolving landscape demands that firms start thinking like businesses, conducting trademark searches, securing domain names, and ensuring their brand identity is both distinctive and legally defensible. The shift to trade names is not just about modernizing law firm branding; it is about adapting to a world where intellectual property strategy is now essential to running a successful legal practice.

The legal profession must lead, not lag behind

For centuries, the legal profession has clung to surname-based firm names, feigning the belief that they signal credibility and tradition. In reality, these names have reinforced hierarchy, created barriers for clients, and hindered access to legal services.

Today's consumers do not choose lawyers based on legacy. They seek clarity, relatability, and trust. The firms that thrive are those that align with consumer expectations, not those that rely on outdated prestige. Trade names provide immediate transparency, ensuring that clients know what kind of legal help is available before they even realize they need it.

Meanwhile, non-lawyer competitors and tech-driven platforms have already embraced branding, seeking to dominate legal marketing and capture market share. The legal profession can no longer afford to resist modern branding strategies while outside forces reshape the industry.

The argument against trade names has never been about ethics – it has been about control. Regulators impose rigid restrictions on branding while allowing gimmicky advertising to flourish. True ethical responsibility is not in restricting names but in upholding substantive professional standards and client trust.

Beyond accessibility and ethics, trade names offer firms long-term business advantages. They create lasting brand equity, ensure continuity beyond individual partners, and position firms for success in a rapidly changing legal landscape.

The legal industry has always prided itself on precedent, but precedent should never stand in the way of progress. The choice is clear – law firms can modernize, embrace branding, and take charge of their future, or they can be left behind as consumers turn elsewhere for legal help.

References

1 I am immensely grateful to Doug Peebles and Peebles Creative Group for their invaluable contributions. They undoubtedly sharpened my thinking regarding branding, trade names and how these should apply to law firms in the modern world.

Chapter 15:
Data-driven decision-making – the power of predictive analytics in law firm strategy

By Mori Kabiri, president and CEO, InfiniGlobe LLC

Introduction

For years, law firms have been told the same thing – technology is rapidly evolving, data is growing, and artificial intelligence will reshape legal practice. Yet historically, most firms have been slow to adopt new tools, focusing instead on delivering legal services, expanding, and staying profitable. Although a few forward-thinking firms have experimented with predictive analytics, the real impact of these tools has remained on the horizon –until now, thanks to advancements in AI.

Today, the legal industry is at a pivotal juncture. The convergence of artificial intelligence, machine learning, and vast amounts of structured and unstructured data means predictive analytics is no longer just a buzzword. Compared to other sectors, law firms may have lagged in adoption, but they're on the verge of making predictive analytics a core component of their strategic decision-making.

One key driver of this change is the growing emphasis on metrics. Traditionally, law firms have tracked billable hours, case outcomes, and financial performance. In a data-driven future, these same metrics – powered by predictive analytics – will anticipate trends, forecast litigation success, optimize resource allocation, and enhance client acquisition. Instead of simply describing past performance, metrics will illuminate the path ahead.

In this chapter, we'll explore how firms are moving from collecting data to leveraging it for better decisions. We'll also envision what a law firm could look like in 2030, where predictive analytics inform everything from acquiring clients to shaping litigation strategy and allocating resources.

These projections are based on research, industry patterns, and a measure of intuition. Although no one can predict the future with absolute certainty, the signs are clear – firms that embrace this data-driven shift will gain a significant competitive edge, while those that hesitate may struggle to keep pace.

Before diving in, let's clarify what predictive analytics really entails, examine why this moment is different, and consider how law firms can best prepare for a data-driven future.

Predictive analytics – what it is and why it matters

At its core, predictive analytics is the practice of using data, statistical algorithms, and machine learning techniques to identify patterns and forecast future outcomes. Unlike traditional analytics, which focuses on understanding what happened, predictive analytics help organizations anticipate what is likely to happen next and make more informed decisions.

Predictive analytics isn't new. Industries such as finance, healthcare, and retail have used it for decades to mitigate risks, optimize resources, and improve decision-making. One of the earliest large-scale uses can be traced back to the mid-20th century when financial institutions developed statistical models to assess credit risk. By analyzing customer data, banks and lenders could predict loan defaults and adjust interest rates accordingly. Banks and credit card companies began analyzing spending behaviors and identifying anomalies to flag suspicious transactions before a major breach occurred.

As computing power increased, predictive models became more sophisticated and expanded into other industries. In healthcare, hospitals started forecasting patient admissions based on seasonal trends, historical data, and real-time patient monitoring, ensuring that staffing and medical supplies aligned with anticipated demand. In retail, companies use predictive models to anticipate customer behavior, make recommendations before a customer even searches for a product, and adjust inventory levels to meet future demand. These industries quickly realized that predicting the future wasn't just an advantage – it was a necessity for staying competitive.

A critical component of predictive analytics is the use of metrics and indicators, which are quantifiable measures used to track performance. While businesses have always relied on data, predictive analytics shifts the focus from merely reporting past performance to using metrics to anticipate trends and adjust strategies before problems arise. In finance, metrics like credit risk scores predict loan defaults. In healthcare, patient readmission rates help hospitals anticipate future resource needs. In retail, customer churn rates allow businesses to forecast which customers are likely to stop purchasing and take action before losing them. The key difference between traditional analytics and predictive analytics is that instead of reacting to what has already happened, organizations use data to make proactive decisions about what is likely to happen next.

The widespread adoption of predictive analytics wasn't just about having access to more data – it was driven by competition. Relying on intuition and past experiences alone became too risky. In fast-moving industries, companies that could anticipate future trends and adjust their strategies accordingly gained a clear advantage. Think of a chess player analyzing the board. The more moves into the future they can predict, the better decisions they can make in the present. Businesses that embraced predictive analytics outperformed competitors by making smarter, more strategic decisions based on future trends rather than reacting to past events.

Of course, implementing predictive analytics wasn't easy. It required large amounts of data, complex AI models, and significant computing power. But as technology advanced, the barriers to entry became lower. What was once only accessible to large financial institutions and tech giants is now being implemented in smaller industries, including the legal sector.

Legal metrics and KPIs – the foundation of predictive analytics

Predictive analytics offers law firms the ability to anticipate risks, optimize operations, and improve client outcomes, but its effectiveness hinges on one fundamental element – reliable, well-defined metrics and key performance indicators (KPIs). Without clear, structured data to analyze, even the most advanced AI models will struggle to generate meaningful insights.

For predictive analytics to drive real business outcomes, law firms must first establish a data foundation built on the right KPIs. This means tracking and optimizing metrics that matter – not just generic financial or operational figures, but specific, strategic indicators tailored to a firm's practice areas, clients, and long-term goals.

Some key areas where KPIs will be critical for predictive analytics include:

- *Litigation strategy*. Analyzing historical win/loss rates, judge tendencies, and case duration trends to refine legal strategies.
- *Client profitability and retention*. Using client lifetime value (CLV) metrics to predict which clients are most valuable and which are at risk of disengagement.
- *Operational efficiency*. Measuring time spent on billable vs non-billable work to optimize resource allocation and workload distribution.
- *Financial performance*. Tracking realization and collection rates to forecast revenue trends and adjust pricing strategies.

As law firms move toward a more data-driven future, those that integrate metrics and KPIs into their predictive analytics strategies will have a clear advantage over those that rely on gut instinct or incomplete data. KPIs provide the measurable structure that allows AI to generate insights that lawyers can trust and act upon.

Firms that prioritize defining, tracking, and refining the right legal metrics will not only improve their ability to make informed decisions today but will also position themselves for long-term success in the AI-powered legal industry of tomorrow.

Litigation outcome prediction

In high-stakes disputes, law firms must decide whether to settle for millions or take a case to trial. Traditionally, attorneys rely on human intuition, experience, and a review of facts and evidence to weigh the risks of settlement versus litigation. Predictive analytics, however, introduces a new dimension to this decision-making process. By analyzing similar cases, judge profiles, jury behavior, and court rulings faster and broader than any human, an AI-powered tool might predict an 80 percent chance of winning at trial. Armed with this insight – and after reviewing the reasoning provided by the tool – a firm chooses to litigate and wins. This is not a gamble but a data-driven strategy, illustrating how predictive analytics is transforming legal decision-making.

AI-powered platforms trained on vast amounts of structured and unstructured legal data are becoming essential tools for evaluating litigation risks, refining legal strategy, and advising clients with greater precision. Even at the initial case evaluation phase, predictive models can estimate a 65 percent chance of winning at trial, with potential damages ranging from $100,000 to $300,000. Alternatively, they might predict a 75 percent likelihood of settlement, with expected amounts between $80,000 and $150,000. These insights not only help attorneys set realistic client expectations but also guide decisions on resource allocation, budgeting, and litigation strategy.[1]

While this may sound like a future concept, the reality is approaching quickly. Clients seeking high-performing law firms will soon expect their legal teams to incorporate these tools. Firms that embrace data-backed decision-making will gain a clear competitive advantage, while those relying solely on intuition and experience may find themselves at a disadvantage.

Compliance and risk management

In today's complex regulatory environment, where compliance and risk management have become significant challenges, predictive analytics can provide law firms with deeper insights into potential compliance issues and help mitigate risks for their clients before they materialize.

By analyzing historical compliance data, these tools can identify patterns that signal potential risk areas, allowing firms to take pre-emptive action. For example, AI-driven systems can assess trends in litigation, compliance records, and client behaviors to flag activities that may lead to regulatory breaches. As a result, law firms will shift from being reactive problem-solvers to proactive risk managers, helping clients avoid legal pitfalls before they occur.

As the legal industry continues to evolve, proactive compliance and risk management will become increasingly essential for clients. Firms that adopt these technologies will be better equipped to navigate the complexities of modern legal practice, offering clients a higher level of assurance and positioning themselves as leaders in innovation and compliance excellence.

Internal operations management

Optimizing internal operations has always been a priority for law firms, driving efficiency, cost reduction, and better decision-making. By integrating predictive analytics into internal operations, law firms will transform raw data into actionable insights, promoting continuous improvement and maintaining a competitive edge in an increasingly data-driven industry. Here are some areas where predictive analytics will play a key role in shaping the law firm in the future.

- *Resource allocation and workflow optimization*. Predictive analytics will enable law firms to analyze historical data to forecast future workloads, allowing for strategic resource allocation. By identifying patterns in case types and durations, firms will be able to assign tasks more effectively, ensuring that attorneys and support staff are neither overburdened nor underutilized. This will lead to improved productivity, better efficiency, and higher employee satisfaction.
- *Financial management and budgeting*. By examining past billing records, case expenses, and benchmarking data, predictive models will project future financial needs and assist in budgeting. This includes forecasting cash flow, setting appropriate billing rates, and identifying cost-saving opportunities, allowing firms to maintain profitability while offering competitive pricing models.

- *Talent management and retention*. Predictive analytics will help firms develop strategies to improve work–life balance and retain top talent by analyzing employee performance, workload, and turnover trends. These tools will allow firms to identify key factors contributing to staff attrition and implement targeted initiatives such as professional development programs or workload adjustments to improve job satisfaction and retention.

Law firms that embrace these tools will position themselves as leaders in efficiency and innovation.

Client acquisition and retention

Predictive tools will play an essential role alongside traditional networking and referrals, helping law firms identify, attract, and maintain client relationships. Firms will use these tools to not only bring in new clients but also strengthen their relationships with existing ones.

Predictive client targeting and acquisition

Predictive tools will help law firms identify high-value prospects by analyzing market trends and online behaviors to determine which clients are most likely to require legal services. For example, firms will be able to detect clients experiencing rapid growth or facing regulatory challenges, allowing them to proactively offer specialized legal services before issues arise. Using micro-segmentation, firms will ensure that marketing resources are allocated effectively, and outreach efforts are personalized based on industry, legal needs, and engagement history.[2]

Client relationship management

AI-powered predictive tools will analyze client interaction histories – such as meeting recaps, communication patterns, and service feedback – to anticipate client needs and preferences. By identifying early warning signs of dissatisfaction or disengagement, firms will be able to take proactive measures to enhance client retention and long-term relationships. For example, predictive models might flag clients considering switching firms based on billing trends, communication frequency, and past case outcomes. With this insight, firms can intervene early by offering strategic advice, scheduling check-in meetings, or tailoring legal solutions to strengthen client loyalty before it's too late.

Optimizing legal service offerings

Predictive analytics will enable firms to anticipate emerging client needs by examining regulatory changes, industry shifts, and litigation trends. This will allow firms to develop new legal services ahead of demand, ensuring they stay competitive and relevant. For instance, if AI identifies a rising trend in cybersecurity litigation, firms can proactively develop legal strategies and targeted marketing content, positioning themselves as thought leaders and capturing client demand before competitors react.

Challenges and obstacles

While predictive analytics promise to revolutionize law firm operations, client relationships, and legal strategy, the path to widespread adoption is not without challenges. Here are some thoughts.

Data privacy and security risks

Implementing predictive analytics requires aggregating and analyzing sensitive client data, raising ethical and regulatory concerns. While service providers are becoming more equipped with information privacy measures, compliance with data protection laws will always be a concern, as breaches could lead to reputational damage and legal liability.

Resistance to change and adoption challenges

The legal industry has historically been slow to embrace technological change. Many attorneys and firm leaders still trust intuition and experience over algorithms, leading to skepticism about AI-driven insights. Overcoming this resistance will require training, leadership buy-in, and cultural shifts within firms.

Quality and availability of data

For predictive analytics to work effectively, law firms need high-quality data. However, inconsistent record-keeping, fragmented systems, and unlabeled legal documents pose challenges. Many firms lack centralized data repositories, making it difficult to aggregate, clean, and analyze data at scale.

High implementation costs

Integrating predictive analytics requires investment in data infrastructure, talent, and of course technology, which can be costly. Smaller firms may struggle to justify the expense, while larger firms must carefully balance the cost with expected returns. Without a clear ROI strategy, some firms may hesitate to make the leap.

Ethical and bias concerns

AI-driven predictions are only as good as the data they're trained on. Bias in historical legal data can lead to unfair or skewed predictions, particularly in litigation outcome forecasting. Also, governments and bar associations are increasingly scrutinizing AI's role in decision-making, and future laws may impose restrictions on how predictive analytics can be used in legal practice.[3]

Over-reliance on technology

While predictive analytics provides valuable insights, it should complement – not replace – legal expertise and judgment. Over-reliance on AI without critical human oversight could lead to misinterpretations, flawed legal strategies, or ethical dilemmas. At the end of the day, predictive analytics should be a tool, not a final decision maker. The firm must always be in the driver's seat, reviewing suggestions and making final decisions.

Despite these obstacles, the shift toward predictive analytics is inevitable. Law firms that proactively address these challenges – by investing in secure AI solutions, upskilling legal professionals, and maintaining ethical safeguards – will position themselves ahead of the competition. The firms that resist change may find themselves struggling to keep up in a legal market that is increasingly driven by data, efficiency, and strategic foresight.

Guidelines for small and medium-sized law firms

In terms of cost, complexity, and data readiness, for small and medium-sized law firms, the idea of integrating predictive analytics may seem like a major undertaking. However, firms that take a strategic, phased approach can gradually adopt predictive tools without disrupting their current operations.

Start with small, measurable wins

Instead of aiming for full-scale implementation, firms should begin with a targeted use case – such as analyzing past billing trends for better budgeting or using basic case outcome forecasting to support litigation strategy. Starting small allows firms to see value quickly and build confidence in AI-driven insights.

Conduct a data audit

Since predictive analytics relies on high-quality data, firms should first assess their existing data. Identify:

- Where case, billing, and client data is stored (e.g., case management systems, spreadsheets, or scattered records).
- How structured the data is (clean, digitized vs incomplete, inconsistent formats).
- Gaps in data collection that could hinder AI's effectiveness.

Cleaning and organizing data before adopting predictive tools will increase accuracy and efficiency when the technology is implemented.

Choose the right tools and partners

Law firms don't need to build AI systems from scratch. More and more legal tech providers will offer scalable, cost-effective, predictive analytics solutions tailored for small and mid-sized firms. To start, consider legal research and case analytics platforms that offer basic predictive insights using GenAI.

Invest in training and change management

One of the biggest hurdles to technology adoption in law firms is resistance to change. To ensure successful adoption, firms should encourage a data-driven culture where decisions are supported by analytics rather than just experience. Start a small project that explores new legal tech solutions and introduce them gradually to the firm.

Prioritize security and ethical considerations

Smaller firms often worry about data security and regulatory compliance when adopting AI. Before implementing predictive analytics, firms should ensure client confidentiality by selecting trusted, secure platforms that comply with legal industry standards and stay updated on emerging AI regulations to remain compliant as laws evolve.

Measure success and scale over time

Once a firm implements predictive analytics in one or two areas, it's important to measure impact. Define clear metrics and KPIs, such as improved case outcome accuracy, better financial forecasting, or increased client retention, to track success. If the initial implementation proves valuable, firms can expand predictive analytics to more areas like litigation strategy, compliance, or client engagement.

A competitive advantage, even for smaller firms

Predictive analytics isn't just for large corporate firms – smaller law firms stand to benefit the most by using AI to optimize operations, allocate resources efficiently, and provide data-backed legal advice. The key is to start small, focus on real value, and scale gradually. By taking a step-by-step approach, small and medium firms can future-proof their practice and stay competitive in an increasingly data-driven legal market.

Guidelines for large law firms

Unlike small and medium-sized firms, large law firms have greater resources, larger datasets, and more complex operations. However, implementing predictive analytics at scale comes with its own challenges – such as system integration, organizational resistance, and regulatory scrutiny. To fully capitalize on predictive analytics, large firms should take a structured, strategic approach that aligns with their existing infrastructure, long-term vision, and competitive positioning.

Develop a firm-wide data strategy

Large firms generate vast amounts of case, client, financial, and operational data spread across multiple offices and practice areas. To make predictive analytics effective, firms need a centralized, firm-wide data strategy that ensures:

- Data standardization across offices and systems to avoid fragmented insights.
- Integration of structured and unstructured data (case records, billing, client interactions, legal documents, etc.).
- Real-time access to analytics dashboards for attorneys, partners, and business teams.

To oversee these initiatives, firms are increasingly appointing chief data officers (CDOs) and establishing AI governance committees responsible for data security, analytics strategy, and compliance with emerging AI regulations.

Establish a proof of concept

Instead of rolling out predictive analytics firm-wide, large firms should start with high-impact use cases that offer measurable benefits. Common starting points include:

- Litigation risk assessment to predict case outcomes based on judge rulings, opposing counsel strategies, and jurisdictional trends.

- Resource and staffing optimization to forecast demand for legal services and balance workload distribution.
- Client profitability modeling to identify high-value clients and anticipate future legal needs.

By demonstrating quick wins in these areas, firms can generate momentum for broader adoption and secure buy-in from leadership and attorneys.

Align with business development and client services

For large firms, competition is intensifying, and corporate clients are demanding data-backed legal advice, cost transparency, and greater efficiency. To stay ahead, firms should:

- Use predictive analytics in pricing models to provide more accurate alternative fee arrangements (AFAs) and competitive pricing structures.
- Leverage AI-powered insights to proactively identify emerging legal risks for clients, strengthening trust and differentiation.
- Offer AI-driven legal services as a value-added offering, positioning themselves as tech-forward, data-driven legal partners.

Scale across firm operations

Once firms establish proof of concept in specific areas, the next step is to expand AI-driven insights across the organization. This includes:

- Enterprise-wide knowledge management powered by predictive analytics, helping attorneys instantly access relevant case law, precedents, and best practices.
- Automated compliance and risk monitoring to prevent regulatory breaches and ensure adherence to evolving laws.
- M&A and contract analytics to identify potential risks in complex transactions and optimize deal structures.

Scaling predictive analytics will transform legal operations, allowing firms to make faster, more informed decisions while improving overall efficiency.

The competitive imperative

For large firms, predictive analytics will not just improve efficiency – it will redefine legal service delivery and competitive positioning. Firms that embrace a data-driven culture, invest in AI training, and align predictive analytics with business strategy will establish themselves as leaders in the next era of legal practice.

Those that delay adoption risk losing their competitive edge as clients increasingly prefer firms that offer data-driven insights, proactive risk management, and AI-enhanced decision-making. With legal tech disruptors and alternative legal service providers (ALSPs) gaining ground, firms that fail to adapt may find themselves outpaced by more agile, technology-driven competitors.[4]

By making predictive analytics a core part of their strategy, large law firms will not only future-proof their practice but also gain a decisive advantage in an increasingly competitive, data-driven legal market.

Reinforce the idea that predictive analytics is not just a tool but a mindset shift. Summarizing key lessons learned or providing a brief "roadmap" for incremental adoption could be very impactful.

Conclusion

Predictive analytics is no longer a distant vision – it is becoming a defining force in how law firms operate, compete, and deliver legal services. By 2030, firms that fully embrace data-driven decision-making will outperform those that rely solely on intuition and tradition. Litigation strategies will be refined with AI-driven outcome predictions, compliance risks will be mitigated before they escalate, and client relationships will be proactively managed with predictive insights.

But the firms that truly succeed in this transformation will be those that understand and measure what matters. Predictive analytics are only as powerful as the metrics and key performance indicators (KPIs) that fuel it. Without clear, reliable KPIs, firms will struggle to extract meaningful insights, let alone act on them effectively. The ability to define, track, and optimize the right legal metrics will be the bedrock of any successful data strategy, enabling firms to harness AI and analytics in a way that drives real business outcomes.

For law firms preparing for this shift, the path forward is clear – embrace a culture of data, invest in the right tools, and build a foundation of strong, strategic legal metrics. Those that do will not only thrive in an increasingly competitive and AI-driven market but will also set the standard for the future of legal practice.

References

1 Hallene, A., and Allen, J. M. (16 October 2024) Using AI for predictive analytics in litigation. American Bar Association. www.americanbar.org/groups/senior_lawyers/resources/voice-of-experience/2024-october/using-ai-for-predictive-analytics-in-litigation/

2 SenGupta, R. (9 December 2024) Law firms lean into the business of prediction. *Financial Times*. www.ft.com/content/ec87d146-bf3e-4b10-9272-4a322c60c425

3 Surden, H. (November 2021) Predictive analytics and law. National Courts and Justice Institute. https://ncji.org/wp-content/uploads/2021/11/Symposium-Draft-Surden-Predictive-Analytics-and-Law.pdfa

4 Garg, S. (8 May 2024) No crystal ball needed: Predicting litigation outcomes through data analytics. Legaltech News. www.law.com/legaltechnews/2024/05/08/no-crystal-ball-needed-predicting-litigation-outcomes-through-data-analytics/

Chapter 16: Picture vs movie – the dynamic data revolution in legal practice

By Kassi Burns, senior attorney, King & Spalding LLP, Olga V. Mack, fellow at CodeX, The Stanford Center for Legal Informatics, and Generative AI Editor at law.MIT Computational Law Report, and Adam Rouse, director and senior counsel, e-discovery operations, Walgreen Co.

The law has always been a profession of documents. Contracts, precedents, pleadings, evidence – all traditionally exist as static artifacts, carefully crafted to capture precise moments in time. Legal practice has historically centered around creating and analyzing these fixed points of reference. The lawyer's skill has been measured by the ability to compose the perfect snapshot, the definitive contract, the authoritative brief, and the comprehensive memorandum that captures all relevant considerations at a single moment.

This static, document-centric approach has served the profession well in a world where information itself was primarily static. As we approach 2030, we face a fundamental mismatch between how legal practice has traditionally operated and how information increasingly exists in our digital, interconnected world.

Today's information is not static but dynamic. It flows continuously through interconnected systems, evolving in real-time, and revealing its full meaning not in isolated moments but in patterns that emerge over time.

This chapter examines a transformative paradigm shift now underway in legal practice – the evolution from thinking in "pictures" to thinking in "movies". This shift is not merely technological but conceptual – a fundamental reimagining of how legal information exists and how legal professionals must engage with it to serve clients effectively in the digital age.

Throughout this chapter, we explore how leading legal practitioners and organizations are already navigating this transition. Developing new approaches, technologies, and competencies that embrace the dynamic nature of modern information while maintaining the profession's core values of accuracy, reliability, and trustworthiness is key to the success of adept attorneys. We will envision the law firm of 2030, an organization structured around dynamic information flows rather than static document repositories, with professionals skilled not just in legal analysis but in orchestrating and interpreting the continuous movies of modern legal information.

From snapshots to stories – the evolution of legal data

The traditional "picture" approach to legal data

For centuries, the legal profession has operated through a series of static snapshots. Court decisions, frozen in time as precedent. Contracts that are meticulously drafted to capture a precise moment of agreement. Case files that are carefully assembled as collections of discrete documents. Legal data has traditionally existed as what we might call "pictures" – carefully composed, fixed-in-time representations of legal realities.

Consider the classic leather-bound case reporter on a law library shelf. Each volume represents a collection of judicial snapshots, decisions preserved exactly as they were rendered, unchanging and immutable. These snapshots have formed the backbone of legal reasoning for generations. Law students are taught to analyze these static images, comparing one with another across time but treating each as a discrete, frozen moment.

This picture-based paradigm extends throughout legal practice. A contract is drafted to capture with precision the meeting of minds at a particular moment. A trademark registration fixes intellectual property rights as they exist on filing. A will documents intentions at the time of execution. Even litigation proceeds through a series of snapshots – pleadings, discovery documents, and trial exhibits. All are treated as discrete objects fixed in time.

The emerging "movie" reality

As we move deeper into the digital age, this static paradigm is increasingly at odds with how information exists in the world. Legal data is no longer confined to discrete documents but flows continuously through interconnected systems. The "picture" is giving way to the "movie". A continuous, evolving narrative has developed, capturing not just isolated moments but the full trajectory of legal relationships and obligations. This shift is driven by several technological and social developments, including continuous data generation, collaborative creation, and ambient data collection.

Modern business systems generate continuous streams of data rather than periodic reports. For example, supply chain management systems track goods in real time, and financial transactions flow through payment networks instantaneously. The rapid adoption of Generative AI technologies by businesses across the globe increases the amount of real-time data generation exponentially. Businesses are increasingly relying on Generative AI technologies to not only create new data, but to analyze, summarize, and query the data points created by modern business systems, creating contextual data that must be examined alongside the original to be useful to legal practitioners. These continuous data flows mean that relevant legal information exists not as discrete documents but as ongoing processes.

We have increasingly moved towards a work product creation mindset of collaborative efforts. Legal work itself increasingly takes place on platforms that capture not just final documents but the entire process of their creation. Multiple participants can access a single document and edit it asynchronously, minimizing version control issues and maximizing editing turnaround capabilities. Contract negotiation platforms record every draft, comment, and revision. Case management systems track the evolution of legal strategies. These tools transform legal work from the production of static outputs to participation in dynamic processes.

The proliferation of sensors and connected devices and their related metadata through the Internet of Things (IoT) means that relevant legal information is increasingly generated automatically and continuously. Building management systems capture environmental data relevant to regulatory compliance. Wearable devices monitor health metrics that may bear on insurance claims or employment matters. While these pieces of data are small, when consolidated across systems and over time, they can quickly grow to millions of data points, which can then be combined and analyzed to support a legal position.

As in any data-driven field, the quality of the information we use determines the value of our results. "Garbage in, garbage out" applies as much to legal practice as to any other domain. The evolution from snapshots to stories represents not just a challenge but an opportunity for the legal profession. By embracing the dynamic nature of modern legal data, we can develop more responsive, effective, and nuanced approaches to legal problems. The static picture will always have its place, but the future belongs to those who can master the moving image – capturing not just isolated moments but the full narrative of legal relationships in a complex and connected world.

Beyond the frame – legal evidence in motion

The limitations of "picture thinking" in modern legal practice

The law's traditional approach to evidence has been firmly grounded in the "picture" paradigm. Documentary evidence, testimony, and physical exhibits have all been treated as discrete, fixed objects that can be collected, authenticated, and presented. This approach has served the legal system well in a world where information primarily existed in static forms. However, as our digital ecosystems evolve, this paradigm is increasingly unable to capture the reality of how information exists and how events unfold in modern environments.

Consider a workplace harassment case from the pre-digital era versus today. Traditional evidence might include written complaints, witness statements, and personnel files. All of these are static "pictures" that could be collected and presented in court. But today's workplace harassment might play out across multiple digital platforms simultaneously – Slack messages that are edited and deleted, emails with embedded tracking, calendar invitations that change over time, security badge data showing movement patterns, and sentiment analysis from internal communication platforms. None of these exist as a static "picture". They are continuous streams of data that capture behavior over time.

The limitations of "picture thinking" in this context become apparent in several key ways. Context loss can occur. When dynamic information is reduced to static snapshots, crucial context may be completely missed. A message viewed in isolation may appear innocuous, but when viewed as part of a pattern over time, it may reveal a troubling progression. Static evidence captures moments but misses processes and patterns. The timing, sequence, and frequency of events are all often critical to understanding what occurred. These patterns may be invisible when examining only discrete snapshots.

How evidence increasingly resembles a "movie" rather than a "picture"

The nature of evidence itself is undergoing a profound transformation. Rather than existing as discrete, static objects, evidence increasingly takes the form of continuous data streams that capture behavior over time, making this data more like a movie than a series of photographs. This shift is driven by key developments in how digital systems capture and store information.

Modern systems don't just record discrete events but continuously monitor and log activities, sometimes across multiple interconnected systems. Cloud services track every access and modification to documents, and communication platforms preserve not just messages but typing indicators, read receipts, and edit histories. For cross-system tracking, single sign-on solutions create audit trails that span diverse applications and marketing technologies are capable of tracking user activity across websites and platforms. These are all data points that, when combined, can be used by an attorney to craft a compelling story.

Digital systems increasingly preserve not just current states but complete historical records. Code repositories track every commit and branch. Document management systems maintain comprehensive revision histories. These systems transform static documents into dynamic timelines.

Advanced analytics increasingly focus not on discrete actions but on patterns of behavior over time, leveraging these varied and robust points of data. Security systems flag unusual access patterns rather than individual intrusions. Fraud detection systems identify suspicious sequences of transactions rather than single anomalies.

A hypothetical case study from financial compliance illustrates this shift. Traditional fraud detection might have examined individual transactions flagged as suspicious – static snapshots of potentially problematic activity. Modern systems instead analyze patterns across time, identifying sequences of apparently normal transactions that, taken together, reveal coordinated fraudulent activity. This pattern-based approach has proven far more effective but requires thinking in "movies" rather than "pictures", examining the full narrative rather than isolated moments.

Legal implications when evidence exists as a continuous stream

The transformation of evidence from discrete objects to continuous streams creates profound challenges for legal systems designed around the "picture" paradigm. When evidence takes the form of ongoing data flows rather than static documents, preservation dilemmas potentially arise. The duty to preserve evidence may become dramatically more complex in dynamic environments, raising difficult questions about whether preservation requires freezing entire systems in time, and thereby potentially disrupting crucial business operations that depend on real-time data processing. Organizations could face the impossible choice between complying with legal obligations and maintaining essential functions.

These challenges extend to proportionality considerations in discovery. The volume and complexity of dynamic data streams create intense proportionality pressures that were inconceivable in traditional discovery contexts. While capturing, preserving, and analyzing continuous data from multiple interconnected systems may be technically possible, the costs can be prohibitive even for well-resourced litigants. Courts struggle to apply traditional proportionality tests to these new realities, often lacking frameworks to balance the probative value of dynamic evidence against the burden of its preservation and production.

Further complicating matters are the technical comprehension gaps throughout the legal system. Few judges, attorneys, or juries possess the technical sophistication necessary to understand complex dynamic data systems without substantial expert assistance. This creates significant risks of misunderstanding or misinterpretation when such evidence is presented in court. Expert witnesses become increasingly essential, not merely to analyze evidence but to explain its very nature to legal decision-makers. As evidence evolves from static "pictures" to dynamic "movies", the legal system must develop new competencies and frameworks to ensure fair and accurate adjudication.

These challenges are not merely technical but go to the heart of how legal systems establish facts and may be used to render judgments. The rules of civil procedure, evidence, and professional responsibility, all developed in a world of static evidence, must now evolve to accommodate dynamic data reality.

E-discovery – from snapshots to time-lapse

Electronic discovery – the process of identifying, collecting, and producing electronically stored information (ESI) in legal proceedings – has undergone a remarkable transformation that mirrors the broader shift from "picture" to "movie" perspectives. This evolution has unfolded across four distinct generations.

The first generation – digital pictures (1990s)

E-discovery emerged as a response to the growing prevalence of digital documents in business environments. The approach treated electronic documents as direct analogues to paper – discrete files to be collected and reviewed as static objects. Email messages were collected as individual items, with minimal attention to threading or context. Word processing documents were processed without their revision histories. The goal was simply to gather digital versions of what had previously been paper documents.

The second generation: organized snapshots (2000s)

As electronic information proliferated, e-discovery evolved to handle larger volumes and more diverse types of ESI. The Federal Rules of Civil Procedure amendments in 2006[1] formally recognized the distinct challenges of electronic discovery. This generation introduced concepts like deduplication, email threading, and metadata preservation. However, the fundamental paradigm remained essentially static, albeit a more organized collection of snapshots. Collection typically involved creating forensic images of storage media or extracting specific file types at a particular point in time.

The third generation – time-lapse photography (late 2010s and 2020s)

As digital systems became more complex and interconnected, e-discovery began to incorporate more dynamic perspectives. This approach resembles time-lapse photography, capturing systems at multiple points in time to reveal changes and developments. Technologies emerged to track document versions, visualize email communication patterns, and identify timeline inconsistencies. Tools began to focus not just on the content of individual documents but on the relationships between them and their evolution over time.

The fourth generation – continuous capture (present and future)

Today, we are witnessing the emergence of a fourth generation of e-discovery that truly embraces the "movie" paradigm – the continuous capture of data flows rather than periodic sampling. This approach recognizes that modern information systems generate continuous streams of data that cannot be adequately understood through static collection.

Modern e-discovery increasingly focuses on capturing processes rather than just artifacts, behaviors rather than just objects, and patterns rather than just content. This shift requires not just technological evolution but a fundamental reconceptualization of what evidence is and how it should be handled in legal proceedings.

Data curation – the intentional selection, organization, and maintenance of information – becomes increasingly critical in this context. As the volume and variety of potentially relevant data grows exponentially, legal professionals must become more discerning about what data is most valuable and how it should be preserved and presented. The challenge is no longer just finding the exact needle in a needlestack but determining which pile of needles contains the most relevant ones and how those needles can be arranged to tell a story over time.

The law firm of 2030 – directors of legal narratives

Organizational structures built around data flows

The law firm of 2030 will bear little structural resemblance to its 2020 predecessor. While traditional firms organized themselves around practice areas and document-centric workflows, the successful legal organization of 2030 will structure itself around dynamic data flows that capture the continuous nature of legal information.

Traditional law firm structures evolved in a world of paper documents and discrete matters. Practice groups formed around bodies of substantive legal knowledge, with information shared primarily through formal mechanisms like memoranda, meetings, and training sessions. Document management systems essentially replicated this siloed structure in digital form, organizing information hierarchically by matter, client, or practice area.

By 2030, leading legal organizations will organize as flexible networks optimized for information flow. These forward-thinking firms will structure themselves around dynamic teams that form and dissolve in response to specific client needs, with expertise and information flowing continuously across traditional departmental and hierarchical boundaries. This approach will represent a fundamental shift from the rigid practice group structures that dominated the profession for decades.

The organizational design of these firms will orient primarily around client industries and needs rather than traditional legal specialties, creating integrated teams that maintain continuous awareness of client contexts and can respond with agility to emerging challenges. These teams will develop deep industry knowledge alongside legal expertise, allowing them to anticipate issues before they emerge.

Reporting relationships and team structures will be deliberately designed to optimize the flow of information and insights throughout the organization, removing bottlenecks and encouraging cross-pollination of ideas. This will mean flatter hierarchies and more transparent information sharing than has been traditional in the legal profession.

Within this new organizational paradigm, specialized continuous monitoring groups will emerge, focused specifically on tracking legal developments, regulatory changes, and client-specific concerns in real time. These groups will serve as "early warning systems" that allow firms to respond proactively rather than reactively to changes in the legal landscape or client environments.

Complementing these monitoring functions, advanced firms will develop dedicated cross-matter analytics teams focused on identifying patterns across matters, clients, and legal domains. These specialized units will generate valuable insights that would remain invisible within traditional practice silos. By leveraging artificial intelligence and data science to extract meaning from the firm's collective experience, these teams will create a virtuous cycle of continuous learning and improvement that elevates the entire organization's capabilities.

Instead of static repositories, law firms will treat their internal knowledge and data as a continuously flowing stream of information. Dynamic, constantly updated, and responsive to evolving needs. Advanced technology systems will act like intelligent filters within this continuous stream, automatically categorizing, tagging, summarizing, and connecting insights drawn from real-time interactions, client communications, case outcomes, and external market developments. Lawyers will seamlessly navigate this live information environment, effortlessly accessing timely precedents, relevant expertise, and critical insights exactly when they are needed. This stream-based approach will not only accelerate the speed of decision-making but also significantly improve accuracy, collaboration, and responsiveness across the entire organization.

Technology infrastructure supporting continuous information processing

The technology foundation of leading legal organizations in 2030 will have evolved dramatically from current systems. Rather than document-centric platforms designed primarily for storage and retrieval, these firms will operate on dynamic systems optimized for continuous information flow and pattern recognition.

At the core of the 2030 law firm will be a "continuous awareness platform" integrating several key capabilities that work in concert to transform how legal information is processed and utilized. These systems will continuously and automatically capture relevant information from multiple sources – email communications, virtual meetings, drafting sessions, research activities, court filings, regulatory updates, and client business systems – creating a comprehensive information environment that requires minimal manual input from attorneys and staff.

Once captured, this information will be processed in real-time rather than periodically, with sophisticated analysis tools identifying significant patterns, anomalies, risks, and opportunities that require attention. This represents a fundamental shift from the batch-processing approach that has dominated legal technology, moving to a model where insights are generated continuously as information flows through the system. These platforms will maintain temporal awareness, tracking how information evolves over time, identifying emerging trends, and preserving comprehensive histories that allow legal professionals to understand not just the current state but the complete trajectory of matters, relationships, and legal developments.

Building on this foundation of continuous analysis across matters and domains, these systems will develop increasingly sophisticated predictive capabilities. By recognizing patterns that would be invisible to human observers, they will identify likely developments and potential issues before they become problems, allowing legal teams to shift from reactive to proactive approaches. The most advanced platforms will learn continuously from outcomes, refining their predictive models to achieve ever-greater accuracy and usefulness.

Despite these technological advances, significant challenges remain in balancing information flow with essential privilege protections. The seamless movement of data across traditional boundaries creates complex confidentiality concerns that require sophisticated solutions. Law firms must develop dynamic privilege screens and access management systems that can identify sensitive information in real-time, apply jurisdiction-specific rules, and create ethical walls that adjust automatically as team compositions change. This challenge is intensified by evolving cyber threats targeting legal organizations. Firms that fail to address these issues risk ethical violations and liability exposure, creating ongoing tension between information accessibility and the fundamental obligation to protect client confidences.

This technology infrastructure will transcend traditional organizational boundaries through secure, permissioned connections to client business systems, direct integration with court filing systems and regulatory databases, and sophisticated interfaces with external data sources. By incorporating news feeds, market information, scientific developments, and social trends, these systems will provide rich contextual awareness extending far beyond traditional legal information. The result will be a technological ecosystem that not only processes legal information more efficiently but fundamentally transforms how legal professionals understand, analyze, and respond to the dynamic legal environments they navigate.

Creating value through orchestrating and interpreting dynamic data narratives

In a world of information abundance, leading firms will create value through the generation of insights from complex information flows. Superior pattern recognition capabilities will distinguish elite firms, allowing them to identify meaningful correlations between seemingly unrelated events, recognize early indicators of emerging issues, and detect subtle shifts in regulatory approaches before they become obvious to competitors. These firms will develop advanced capabilities in predictive modeling and scenario development, helping clients navigate uncertain futures rather than merely responding to existing conditions.

The ability to identify non-obvious connections across domains, jurisdictions, and time periods will reveal insights invisible to those working only with static information. As legal information becomes increasingly complex and technical, firms that excel at translating specialized insights into actionable business guidance will create distinctive value for clients seeking not just legal analysis but strategic direction.

Firms will pursue several distinct strategies for competitive differentiation in this environment. One strategy will focus on industry integration, differentiating through a deep understanding of specific sectors and seamlessly combining legal expertise with sophisticated industry knowledge. Another strategy will emphasize process excellence, creating value through exceptional efficiency and reliability in managing complex legal workflows with minimal friction and maximum predictability.

A final strategy will have firms differentiating themselves through proprietary technology capabilities that enable unique insights or exceptional service delivery efficiency beyond what standardized platforms can provide. Across all these approaches, the ability to integrate diverse talent (legal specialists, technologists, industry experts, and process designers) into cohesive teams will provide a sustainable competitive advantage as the complexities of legal work increasingly require multidisciplinary solutions.

Embracing the director's role

The transformation of legal information from static documents to dynamic flows represents both the greatest challenge and the greatest opportunity the legal profession has faced in generations. Law firms that remain wedded to static paradigms, continuing to organize themselves around document repositories rather than information flows, focusing on periodic deliverables rather than continuous awareness, will find themselves increasingly marginalized.

The most successful legal organizations of 2030 will have fundamentally reimagined themselves as directors of legal narratives rather than producers of legal documents. They will create value not primarily through the creation of static work products but through the orchestration and interpretation of dynamic information flows. Yet even as legal practice transforms, the core values that have long defined the profession remain essential. The commitment to accuracy, reliability, and trustworthiness becomes not less important but more critical as information becomes more dynamic and complex.

The challenges posed by dynamic data cannot be overstated. Legal professionals must develop innovative solutions to preservation dilemmas that arise when evidence exists as continuous streams rather than discrete objects. They must navigate increasingly complex proportionality considerations when the full capture of dynamic systems would be technically overwhelming and economically unfeasible. Perhaps most fundamentally, the profession faces a significant technical literacy gap, with many practitioners, judges, and juries struggling to comprehend the complex technical realities underpinning dynamic evidence. Addressing these challenges will require not merely technological solutions but a fundamental reimagining of legal education, procedural rules, and evidentiary standards.

The picture may be worth a thousand words, but the movie tells the whole story. For legal professionals preparing for 2030 and beyond, learning to work with the whole story, with its context, connections, and evolution over time, will be essential not just for technological relevance but for delivering the comprehensive understanding and guidance that clients increasingly require in a complex, rapidly changing world.

This is the promise and the challenge of the dynamic data revolution in legal practice – a transformation already underway that will fundamentally reshape how we understand and practice law in the decades to come.

References

1 Federal Rules of Civil Procedure amendments in 2006: www.uscourts.gov/forms-rules/records-rules-committees/superseded-rules/federal-rules-civil-procedure-2006

Chapter 17:
Data use and misuse

By Brian Fox, partner, PwC

One of the most important mind shifts of the 2020s was the realization that all our vast, expanding, and evolving technology infrastructure is merely a conduit for the delivery of data. Not even *information*, mind you – not yet – but *data*, whose quality, provenance, context, and timeliness dictate whether any actual information is delivered. In the early days of data management and data governance, we were all quick to point out the difference between data and information, and we were right to do so. What has arrived since is the clarity that there is a gap between our data as it exists today and the information we seek to extract from it – a big gap.

We've also come to understand that the content of the data we hold is not necessarily fully owned by us. Private data, protected data, and controlled data all involve constituencies that have a say in how that data is used, and they expect us to be able to demonstrate that we've heard them and cared for their concerns. The complexity and significant resources necessary to service those concerns are challenges left to us to solve.

Further, it is increasingly becoming the case that our data outputs are being received as if they come with a guarantee of completeness, accuracy, and timeliness. Especially in our customer interactions, our engagement with regulators and to our senior management, the quality and accuracy of our data is assumed in a way that does not fully comport with how data lives in most of our messy and complex enterprise environments. Being asked to attest to the accuracy of reports involving data from hundreds or even thousands of source systems is becoming more and more common as the pressure increases to gain real control over the minute manipulations and calculations happening in tiny snippets of code developed years ago and buried deep in our technology environments.

Nevertheless, the message is clear – the world expects us to know and control our data. The complexity and scale of the data challenge is real, but with the advent of GenAI, machine learning, and the ubiquity of search, it is no longer sufficient to say that our environments are too disparate, too complex, and too siloed to be controlled. What's left is for legal professionals to lead our organizations toward achievement of the new expectation by creating structure and capabilities over our data estates that can pay down the tech debt and bring forth the vital information from our piles of data. Our success in these areas may be the deciding factor in whether we are engaging in data use – or misuse.

The data we hold is not fully owned by us

One of the most significant trends in law affecting business in the last decade is the expansion and proliferation of statutes controlling the use and flow of data. Privacy law being most obvious, hundreds of jurisdictions around the world have developed laws dictating requirements around the protection of personally identifiable information as well as the consequences for failing to protect it. The articulation of consumer data rights was the next wave, ranging from rights to access data collected about you to rights "to be forgotten" or to have your data corrected. Some of the statutes also addressed what are now being called consumer preferences, where consumers opt out of the sale or distribution of their personal data from companies that have collected it to third parties. The trendline across these areas is increasing transparency to consumers about what is being collected along with increasing engagement with consumers to solicit their preferences and respect them.

Most interesting about these trendlines is the set of implied capabilities that they expect that companies would have to be able to comply with the requirements explained above. Among those capabilities would be:

- The ability to find the consumer data that they have collected;
- The ability to identify precisely within the consumer data what relates to specific consumers;
- The ability to assemble all such data from myriad systems into a single, comprehensible document that can be provided back to a consumer within a reasonable time frame;
- The ability to delete data related to a specific consumer from all repositories to which it may have proliferated; and
- The ability to know what consumer data is being sold or shared with third parties, through what mechanisms, and being able to stop such sharing or sales for the specific consumers who request it.

As these laws emerged, many (maybe most) companies found themselves not being certain they had any of these capabilities. The race to develop them or passable workarounds has been one of the main thrusts of privacy compliance over the last several years.

Similar challenges arise around the control of export-controlled information, confidential supervisory information, intellectual property, and many other kinds of data. Some data belongs to multiple categories and therefore carries multiple sets of control requirements.

The range of data control requirements seems sure to continue growing, and their granularity is rapidly increasing. The data we hold is not fully owned by us – we must develop the capability to care for the concerns of our co-owners if we want to stay in their good graces and unlock the full potential of our data.

The data quality challenge

Alongside the sometimes-unrealistic expectations of our data co-owners, the expectations of the recipients of our data outputs for impeccable data quality are also escalating rapidly. Reporting delivered to regulators, management, the board, and customers carries with it a near-zero-tolerance expectation for low data quality, which may feel even more overwhelming to meet than even our data privacy obligations.

Some reports are sourced from hundreds or even thousands of upstream sources. They often undergo multiple levels of aggregation, transformation, and enrichment on the path from our systems of record to a final report. Systems use different identifiers, have different classification schemes and codes to consider, and different naming conventions that make aggregation a major challenge. Further, controls at data capture that prevent fat-fingering errors are often insufficient to prevent those kinds of errors from making their way to the final product. Sometimes the front office isn't even aware that a data element they're entering is used in a critical regulatory report. The scale of the problem set is truly overwhelming.

Yet our stakeholders continue to demand that we answer questions about these complex data flows, such as:

- How do you know the report is accurate?
- Is all the data sourced from authoritative sources?
- What issues have you had with the data in the past?
- Have you investigated the root causes of those issues and fully remediated them?
- How are you reducing the need for adjustments made to final reports?

Like the expectations of our co-owners, asking these questions implies that they believe we have a set of capabilities around these complex reports, including:

- Understanding where all the data comes from and how it flows through our systems.
- How the technology transformations work and what calculations and manipulations are occurring.
- Where anomalies exist in our production systems that require specific workarounds or processes to manage.

Gaining insight into these questions is foundational to meeting the data quality expectations of our data consumers. But how do companies even approach a problem at this scale?

Attacking the problem at both ends

We can see that expectations surrounding the granular control of data are increasing across numerous dimensions and show no signs of letting up. Further, the more time goes on and technology improves, the less people believe that the complexity of our enterprises is an insurmountable barrier to avoiding data misuse. While it is likely the case that most people don't really understand the sheer scale and complexity of data flows in large corporate enterprises, it seems to also be the case that they believe big companies should be able to manage it. As such, it's important that we devise a practical approach to making progress against these lofty goals.

The approach that the most successful companies have taken is in two directions:

1. Build structure, context, and governance over your key data flows as they are today.
2. Work to simplify, streamline, and re-engineer your data toward a lower-risk, more straight-through data model.

Building structure, context, and governance means deploying people, process, and technology in a way that visualizes and contextualizes data flows in ways that permit the insertion of controls. Building a foundation of these capabilities provides a way to begin to understand complex data flows that create key reports, model inputs, or support critical processes.

Simplify, streamline, and re-engineer is about rethinking your key data flows to untangle overly complex legacy systems and reimagine them in a simplified, better curated, and more versatile model. Sometimes it's easier to rebuild a report from scratch than it is to try to unwind a data flow that was designed years ago and involves a codebase that few are familiar with.

Working on both of these capabilities at the same time has a multiplier effect on the level of control you gain over your data. Your capability to see, understand, and monitor data increases while you build your governance structure, and at the same time your data is becoming simpler, better curated, and better engineered.

Building structure, context, and governance

The basic components of a data governance program create a foundation of knowledge that helps all stakeholders understand and evaluate the way data flows into their key data outputs. The basic components are as follows:

- *Data catalog*. A repository of metadata that provides business context, system, and ownership information to help technology and business owners understand what data elements mean and whether they are fit for purpose for particular use cases. Done well, they help bridge the communication gap that often exists between technology professionals, the business, and data consumers in functional areas like finance or risk.
- *Data lineage*. A data set that contains information about the provenance and manipulation of data elements across a data flow. Lineage is usually visualized as a bunch of tables with lines linking data elements in a source table to their destination tables as they move through a data flow. Lineage also can include transformations, end-user computing sources like Excel spreadsheets, and enrichment steps. Lineage is extremely time-intensive to create manually and can quickly go stale if it's not supported by technology to keep it current.
- *Data quality rules and monitoring*. These are capabilities to set tolerances on certain data elements or data sets and monitor the data as it flows for values that fall outside those tolerances and may indicate a data issue. Rules and monitoring are used to help detect and prevent bad data before it reaches your critical outputs.
- *Data classification*. These are capabilities to scan and label data containing certain content to be used as a trigger for controls. Classification can be used to detect personally identifiable information, other kinds of sensitive data, and can utilize techniques like exact data matching to look for known data that requires protection but is hard to identify with a rule.

Some key things to consider as you design your data governance program:

- *Focus on your data outputs*. For most companies, your data risk lies in your ultimate data outputs – think reports, model inputs, data feeds into critical applications. Building an inventory of these outputs and risk-ranking them gives you a great way to focus your energy on the data risks that are most serious for you.
- *Explore tooling in all these areas*. Many data governance activities are extremely cumbersome to perform manually – especially data lineage – and are even harder to keep current. The state of data governance tooling is better than it's ever been, and the right tooling will make the difference between a program that is sustainable and one that is not.
- *Investigate how your reports get created today*. It is sometimes the case that the technology you use to create your reporting today includes some of the capabilities you are seeking to build in your program. Engage with your technology professionals and see what may already be available!

These capabilities, among others, create visibility and a knowledge base that incrementally builds your company's visibility into key data flows and hence your ability to place controls.

Simplify, streamline, and re-engineer

While you're building your structure and visibility, and as you learn more about your data, taking the time to re-think how you store and deliver data is only logical. The better structured and curated your source data is, the easier and less error-prone your data flows will be. In a complex enterprise it can seem overwhelming to redesign data flows that cross hundreds of systems and multiple business units – and it is certainly no small feat. However, it is also overwhelming to create a control framework over such data flows and, as we've already seen, the pressure to do so is only going to increase.

Making data flows simpler, more streamlined, and more centralized can only benefit the effort to impose control. In the data governance field, you often hear the truism, "It is never going to be easier than it is today". Your data is only going to get more complex and more interconnected. Taking the time to unwind the tech debt, and to plan, structure, and empower your data now is the surest path to control and insight later. So how are others tackling it?

Some of the most interesting approaches to data simplification being pursued today are ideas that have been around for a while but are being implemented in a new way. Three of those include implementing Data mesh, use of Knowledge graphs, and development of dedicated reporting environments to re-platform reports.

Data mesh

Data mesh is an architecture concept that has been around for over 20 years and is a data-centric approach to segmenting your data in logical "data products" that build data quality into them by design. The result is a centralized environment – sometimes called a Data Marketplace – with curated data products that can be accessed in a controlled way on a self-service basis.

Think of it as stocking a pantry of baking ingredients in a clearly labeled way so that, whether you're baking a cake or making cookies, the ingredients in the pantry are easy to find and easy to access. If you need organic butter for a particular recipe, you can dive into the documentation to check all the specifications, and if the right type is not there, you can ask for it to be added.

Your data marketplace can work in a similar way. In many regulatory reports in financial services, for example, aggregations of financial products make up a significant and complex cohort of the highest risk data on the report. Pre-aggregating them in a data product can eliminate all the risks of those aggregations for any data consumer that might need them.

Building up a library of these data products over time is a great way to incrementally simplify your data flows without having to re-design production systems or disrupt your business. You can also deploy marketplaces in hyperscale environments to gain access to the power and performance of the cloud.

Knowledge graphs

Graph theory has been around since the 1960s, but the last 20 years have seen a significant emergence of graph technology in data applications. Graph databases are structures that are extremely efficient at organizing data that is highly interconnected. One of their most interesting uses in data governance is as an abstraction layer that maintains linkages, relationships, and interconnections between data that gives users important context about the data that permits more efficient decision making. Graphs can also be used to model data in ways that create controlled consumption, similar to the way that Data mesh works.

Creating context through relationships

Graphs can take two things that don't have any natural connection in your enterprise and connect them in ways that are useful. For example, you could have data you've labeled as PII (through some of the mechanisms we talked about earlier), and you could have data about servers that are physically maintained in different countries – two completely different data sets. By creating relationships between the two, your graph can help illustrate dynamically where your PII data crosses from a server in one country to a server in another – a cross-border event that may need review by your privacy office. You can do this without having to change either of the underlying data sets.

Data modeling

Graphs can also be used to create models that operate in a similar way to the data products mentioned above in the Data mesh context. Instead of a data product like loans, you can create a graph entity that carries properties, events, and attributes of a loan, and ingest data through the graph entity to control for all the aggregation risks we talked about above. Modeling through a graph helps create what are sometimes called Canonical Data Models or CDMs, which are a fantastic foundational basis for enhanced data quality.

Re-platforming reports

Both Data mesh and Knowledge graphs represent approaches to data governance that arise from an important question that doesn't get asked often enough: "Before I go create lineage, cataloging, and data quality rules on the convoluted data flows I have, should I just re-build the data output from scratch?" This is not a crazy question to ask. It is often the case that companies find that it would have been easier to rebuild the report from scratch rather than attempt to put visibility and control into the dozens of hops, thousands of lines of code, and hundreds of spreadsheet inputs (sometimes called end-user computing or EUCs) that some of these reports involve. It may be the case that you could rebuild the report in a much simpler, more automated, and better documented way that would lend itself to better control by design – and it might even be faster.

To this end, some companies abandoned the idea of creating structure, context, and governance on the existing flows, and elected to rebuild each data output in a dedicated environment designed for high-risk data. With such an approach, you could include a Data mesh or a Knowledge graph, or both, as you re-engineer the data flow. Also, building the reports using modern extract-transform-load (ETL) platforms can give you data lineage nearly for free while also bringing automation and better speed of execution. Thinking holistically about where your effort is best placed is entirely appropriate to the scale of the problem and can better ensure your multi-year efforts bear the fruit that is expected.

Conclusion

As we've seen, the world expects us to know and control our data. In many cases, our ability to do so will be the measure of whether our data use cases are considered appropriate data use – or misuse. These expectations imply capabilities over our data that are well beyond what currently exists, especially in our largest, most complex organizations. However, unless we think concerns about data privacy, data security and data quality are going to diminish over time (and we don't!), then we have to get to work. By 2030, there will be no patience for failures to manage the data under our care.

The book of work is daunting, but it can be attacked in logical ways that incrementally build capability and control. Working from both ends – building structure, context, and governance capabilities on one side while simplifying, streamlining, and re-engineering on the other – will accelerate progress and position us to talk confidently about how we manage data.

It will also put us in an excellent position to use our data to its fullest and take maximum advantage of AI, which every company wants. We must remind our leaders that AI is only as good as the data that feeds it.

Our data estates came to be what they are through decades of evolution, mergers, tech changes, and process overhauls, and it won't be unwound overnight. It is worth stepping back and thinking big to make sure our efforts will make lasting change while the spotlight is on us. The legal profession can be a catalyst for this change by demonstrating how all the diverse statutes and regulations point to the need to know and control our data – and make it a call to action.

Chapter 18:
The geopolitical climate and law

By Jane C. Allen, partner, legal business solutions, PwC

The concept and discipline of "geopolitics" arguably dates back to the early 1900s. While the centers of power may have shifted in that time, and the complexity of the variables involved, the focus on geopolitics has never been greater as law and economics are inextricably intertwined.

As of the end of 2024, the geopolitical climate was increasingly complex and volatile, at a rate of change faster than seen in previous years and decades. At the beginning of 2025 we saw a number of increasingly controversial changes in government administrations, some with more exceptional circumstances than others, in the US, Europe, and beyond, paired with complex societal factors.

Nationalism and associated policies are increasing at speed. Rather than tempered or incremental shifts, we're seeing complete or near "roll backs" of previous legislation. Corporate power and influence continue to increase, while labor associations and regulations diminish. We have seen more polarizing views, a decline in centrist leadership and collaboration, and changes in how the public consumes and trusts (or distrusts) channels of information via traditional or social media. Perhaps most troubling is the fundamental erosion of the Rule of Law, which appears to be gaining precedence.

As we look toward 2030, the ability to have a confident line of sight into the future is even less likely than before. The economy and capital markets may serve as the sole barometer, and restraining force, to keep certain movements in check.

While geopolitical awareness has always been part of the chief legal officer and general counsel's oversight for global companies, rarely did it arise so frequently front and center or outside the government/regulatory affairs team. In recent years, however, Legal has needed to manage challenges such as the Russian–Ukraine war, cybersecurity threats from nation states, data sovereignty, and increasing regulations and inquiries as a way to keep foreign entities at bay and in check.

Today, geopolitical forces and actions are front and center, with cascading effects into the business supply chain and partners, sales and service engagements with government entities, contractual terms that may include references to climate efforts or diversity, workforce and recruitment efforts that may refer to women, LGBTQ+, minorities or diversity, website and public communications, and more. The latest wave of tariffs is sending shockwaves across the globe, and the full domino effect of intended and unintended consequences has yet to be seen. As of this writing, how much further this will extend is unknown, but areas such as tax classifications and the funding of philanthropic and charity work appear at risk of becoming a target.

This new wave of geopolitical disruption has shifted legal leadership from anticipating what's lying around the corner to navigating a perpetual onslaught, often with little to no time to prepare, and in domains not previously anticipated. Layer on heightened consideration of "brand perception" from actions, where even the choice of law firm may draw scrutiny, and not only are legal leaders in a whole new world of how they need to operate, but new ways of evaluating situations, sometimes with less time than ever for careful consideration.

Relying on past precedence isn't necessarily as helpful or determinant as it once was.

Do you continue to engage the same law firms, or other vendors or suppliers, who may have capitulated to recent geopolitical pressures? Is the greatest erosion of the Rule of Law now reflected in recent defiant actions to in-country judicial systems and courts?

Legal leaders must now navigate business decisions and communications with heightened sensitivity to how they are perceived by various stakeholders. This includes alignment with the company's stated mission and purpose, as well as awareness of how narratives – whether in traditional or alternative media – can shape economic outcomes and financial performance. What we do see – and have perhaps resigned ourselves to at this stage – is that the years to 2030 are likely to bring further deterioration of the Rule of Law.

In effect, effective geopolitical navigation is the new business resilience. And we're likely only getting started. From an operational and tactical perspective, legal leaders will need to focus on what they can control and reframe their thinking and advice on matters with this new lens.

The majority of legal functions of private and public institutions, from emerging growth to long established entities, have long expressed a capacity challenge with increasing urgency. Traditional protection and risk management of companies has grown more complex with new domains of regulations (e.g., privacy and data, content, AI, cyber, sustainability, etc.) that emerge differently across the world. Businesses have become more technology- and data-centric in their assets and how they operate, requiring different and new ways to govern. And businesses have entered new markets, new products, and new ventures and M&As that require new and additional areas of legal expertise.

This has resulted in Boards and Management expecting a different breed of general counsel – one that is just as focused on value creation and paving the way for corporation transformation and growth efforts, in addition to traditional protection and responsive efforts to litigation, regulatory changes, commercial support, IP, employment, privacy, and records. Like CEO turnover, we have seen an uptick in chief legal officer and general counsel turnover that brings a new strategic lens to how the legal function supports the organization, and different models in which to operate legal services.

These leadership changes have happened in parallel with many corporate "transformation" or efficiency efforts to drive improved ways of working and unlock margins for ultimate shareholder performance and expectations, or support capital investment into strategic growth areas. SG&A (Selling, General and Administrative) expenses – often referred to as "back office" functions – have been the primary focus of such efforts.

Historically, legal functions were largely able to avoid such efforts due to the reactive and often unpredictable nature of legal matters, as well as the unique and also manual way lawyers provide advice and expertise tailored to each situation. That narrative began to shift several years ago with pushes for greater standardization, ability to leverage technology, and a focus on onshore and offshore Centers of Excellence, or managed services providers, capable of executing at scale and at cheaper rates without the need for additional headcount.

Let's look at some predictions of where we're headed in 2030 in the legal domain as a direct result of current geopolitical forces and trends.

Changes in strategy

With the eroding Rule of Law and deregulation trends already underway, legal leaders are going to need to work with C-suite leaders and either validate or – more likely – determine a refreshed and more multi-dimensional risk tolerance in how they approach risk, legal matters, and regulation. Is the organization now willing to take on more risk in certain domains or geographic regions? Will some products and services or higher risk behaviors and potential consequences be considered simply the price of doing business? As access to business and legal data becomes more sophisticated and measurable, will a new cost–benefit model emerge – one where the threshold for risk exposure is far higher than in the past? And how will these choices be perceived by employees, business partners, shareholders, and customers? Will the reputational impact ultimately outweigh the perceived gains from a less rigorous Legal and Compliance posture? This review of risk tolerance is also going to need to happen on a much more frequent basis, but also with the longer term in sight. If the pendulum swings back, how will your organization and actions be judged by regulators and beyond?

Changes in execution

As companies are likely to continue to push hard on back office functions overall, to minimize expenses and invest in new products, services, and mergers and acquisitions, Legal and Compliance are likely to be under more pressure to reduce costs – even after many have undertaken major efforts in recent years. Even with greater focus and better demonstration of direct value add to the business, this is likely to intensify. With this, the boundaries of where legal advice are in fact needed may see some movement and decrease. If companies are willing to take on risk, they will require more generalized approaches and applications of developed playbooks to execute against categories of issues rather than individualized legal analysis. Some of this is already done with paralegals, especially in contracting functions that can execute more quickly and cheaply with offshore teams of non-lawyers executing against pre-determined playbooks that outline negotiation priorities, fallbacks, and guardrails.

Self-service and automation has to date typically been limited to work such as NDAs, routing of routine claims, things of an "FAQ" nature, and lower-exposure and lower-complexity work. This will dramatically increase – in part driven by necessity and by innovation as risk tolerances decrease. While Generative AI has been slow to be implemented into legal organizations, the clear evidence and expectation is that this will rise like a hockey stick by 2030.

The notion of a more outsourced legal and compliance function overall has been discussed for many years, yet not often seen outside of start-ups and niche sectors that operate domestically with very little regulation. There are likely to be companies that will push the boundaries here and ultimately decide on a nearly fully outsourced legal function, with perhaps only a few internal legal and compliance leaders to establish core and sophisticated strategy and light project management of law firms and consulting/ALSP providers.

On top of all this, legal functions will have to make decisions faster and likely under duress, with more unplanned events occurring. Cyber and privacy response "tabletop" exercises have long been good practice in order to make decisions and execute potentially "bet the company" actions with little time and less than complete information and data. These scenarios will increase as more geopolitical changes meet the threshold of a business resilience matter and require crisis management muscle in how to operate effectively.

Legal data science

Given the complex geopolitical environment, coupled with technology and market changes, lawyers will have to leverage data in their analysis in far more sophisticated ways to enhance their efforts. Those who have dragged their feet on the basics will soon find themselves not only less impactful but potentially negligent in the future, given the ability of Generative AI to be able to retrieve and summarize information faster, and find nuances and patterns in data that individuals simply cannot do on their own. Legal judgement and advice will be directly paired with data insights from the results of data science algorithms and ever-growing processing power.

Today, more mature legal functions are developing vast legal data lakes to capture all regulations, compliance obligations, and regulatory inquiries and responses from around the globe in which they operate. Tomorrow they will have this data, the data of known actions of competitors, vendors, and customers, actions of political and regulatory leaders from around the globe, and "profile" algorithms of key constituents such that scenario planning for legal advice and judgment can be executed at scale, more informed than ever. More scenarios of sweeping change, and where time equates to potential for significant losses or ability for competitors to quickly take advantage when you are on your backfoot will require legal leaders to have the right advisors and data, and make sound decisions as swiftly as possible, without the need to consider a wider array of factors and unusual circumstances.

A number of global entity law departments have added the role of "chief legal data officer", "director of legal data" or similar to show a focused and more mature strategy towards leveraging data for the legal function and the business. This trend will be far more advanced than those managing legal systems, carrying out ad hoc reporting and analytics or even those beginning to build consolidated legal data lakes.

Convergence of disciplines, and changes in education and talent

Just as these world stage topics are converging and cannot be viewed in isolation, so are traditional legal practice areas. Cyber, privacy, artificial intelligence, intellectual property, and commercial law are already often inter-mingled, and expertise from all are often required for thoughtful decision-making. We will see more legal leaders wearing multiple hats, overseeing larger teams.

Additionally, we are already seeing law schools, headed by executive education programs, move quickly to address and develop curriculum around generative AI in the legal domain. The past 30 years have had a slow, yet continued narrative of the legal function lagging far behind other corporate functions in the use of technology. Spikes in progress include e-discovery and document review technologies, contract management advancement, and now generative AI. In order for the next generation of lawyers – and frankly for existing ones – to remain relevant, they will require not only more working knowledge of technology and data science, but greater study in geopolitics and financial acumen. This goes beyond how the legal function and each matter is scoped, delivered, and the associated costs and levers to manage. Lawyers will need to have confident knowledge and detailed understanding of the products and services their company creates and sells. This will include a more intimate understanding of pricing dynamics, supply chains and parts, labor, and market trends, combined with detailed accounting as to how this translates to financial reporting, profits, and margin.

Growing legal function oversight

Recent trends show legal functions overseeing a growing number of corporate functions overall, including compliance, risk, cyber, and sustainability. For similar efficiency reasons and fuzzier boundaries of compliance, corporate legal functions are likely to continue to absorb and ultimately oversee more corporate functions.

In the coming years we're likely to see similar trends, with the possible addition of human resources in the mix. The focus of centralization for efficiency and cost savings, in addition to grouping together aspects that ultimately tie to mandated activities and risk management, will continue to drive this force as geopolitics continues to be the overarching headline as it touches upon more and more domains.

Changes in the law firm landscape

The law firm landscape in recent times has been the subject of its own industry under transformation as well. Consolidations and mergers will continue in pursuit of greater market dominance and operational synergies, but much of the change is happening behind-the-scenes. Internal efficiency efforts are accelerating to automate client conflict checks and onboarding processes, whilst increased usage of generative AI is aiding basic work (and improved margins), and shifts in business models and compensation structures to finally respond to corporate clients' persistent demand for alternative fee arrangements (AFAs).

The news headlines in 2025 have highlighted unprecedented pressure from the US government administration to influence, if not actually force, actions, in some cases to what appears to be direct retribution for advocating for certain organizations or individuals in the past. While caving to such demands may be the immediate reaction to short-term survival and revenue preservation, it will remain to be seen how this is viewed by clients at large in the long run.

More important is the magnitude and reverberations this sends throughout the legal domain of the fabric and integrity of the legal system and law. Lawyer ethics and advocacy are intertwined. If the fabric of legal representation principles such as duty to the court, independence, acting in good faith, honesty and integrity are in jeopardy, certainly the Rule of Law is.

Focus on health and stress management

It was during the COVID-19 years that the concept of the mental and physical health of attorneys first started to gain traction, with a corresponding regularity in the headlines. Many thought this was a long overdue dialogue, especially for lawyers operating in crisis-prone areas or under mounting pressures, shifting timelines, and expanding into unfamiliar domains of expertise. As today's geopolitical landscape intensifies, these stressors are becoming even more prevalent, affecting both lawyers' professional responsibilities and their personal lives. As a result, we're seeing a rise in open discussions around stress, mental health, and burnout. Legal professionals – whether in-house, at law firms, or in legal consulting roles – must address these issues more openly. This means offering meaningful support services and requiring leaders to dismantle lingering stigmas in a profession where stoicism, endurance, and crisis management are still too often worn as badges of honor and pathways to advancement.

While the road to 2030 appears to be tumultuous, the challenges will help bring opportunities, continued prominence, need, respect, and interest in the legal domain, and finally accelerate modernization of the practice of law that has long been dragging its feet. The predictions outlined above are all within the control of legal leaders now and will enhance the practice of law regardless.

On the other side of 2030 we will find a more tech-enabled and automated legal practice by default, in which lawyers' time is spent on complex and advanced topics and legal advice. It will be an industry that is far more dynamic and contains more multi-disciplinary educated lawyers (whether via traditional law school and/or through intense job experience) who are not only intellectually motivated but more poised for other C-suite leadership in their career progression. Should the geopolitical pendulum swing back toward greater stability, these legal professionals – hardened by challenge and seasoned in crisis – will be well-positioned to help their organizations seize new opportunities and contribute meaningfully to restoring and strengthening the global Rule of Law.

Chapter 19:
Giving clients what they want (as well as what they need)

By Joanne Brook, Lionshead Law

"If we leave it to professionals themselves to reinvent their workplace, are we asking the rabbits to guard the lettuce?"[1]

Richard Susskind posed this question some years ago in his book, *The Future of the Professions*. This is a fair question to ask as this chapter aims to answer the question, "What do clients want?". Lawyers are good at assuming that because we are experts in the field we advise on, we know our clients' expectations when they consult us. Many in the profession also retain the view that lawyers will always be needed and, as lawyers are the main providers of legal services, they can dictate how legal services are delivered. Both of these assumptions are increasingly reckless positions to take. In this chapter, we consider the views stated by lawyers in various recent professional surveys and white papers about the challenges they perceive and expectations they have around how legal services will be delivered. We then map what the clients we surveyed have said they expect of the law firm of 2030.

Looking back to move forward

Back in 2015, as Cloud and SaaS delivery began to gain pace and big data was beginning to expand into use-cases across service industries, most legal practices believed that the primary applications for this technology would be outsourcing practice management, evidence, research, contract review and other routine matters, freeing lawyers to focus on "complex" legal work where specific knowledge was favored over bulk. To some extent, this is what happened. According to Oxford University,[2] growth in the non-SRA regulated legal services sector that supports legal firms has outpaced growth in the SRA regulated sector threefold.[3] ABSs and unregulated companies offering lawtech support services were able to launch quickly and make inroads into areas of law where shortening the pipeline and fast review and response times are key. Working from that foundation, those non-regulated business have expanded and now also compete with the law firms they set out to support.

With the introduction of complex AI systems for document creation, document review, evidence assessment, workflow improvement, and provision of direct legal advice, however, the tech-crunching is not being undertaken external to law firms, it now sits firmly within them. In the law firm of 2030, the idea of carving up legal work horizontally so that partners are the top of the pyramid, supported by an expansion in stratified layers of assistants and paralegals, is likely to have finally been dislodged. In its place is a Venn diagram of legal work where every task requires *"a mix of legal expertise, process and technology"*.[4] All elements intersect, are of equal importance, and are interdependent. Where technology is this embedded in firms, their ethos, their working practices, and their output is led by legal innovators and data specialists who see the need for change in the profession and in the demands made on law firms by clients, have anticipated the changes necessary, and formulated how that can be achieved.

To give clients what they want, as well as what they need for the future law firm of 2030, we have to understand the appetite within the broader legal profession for change and innovation.

Legal soundings from firms

In 2021, the SRA commissioned Oxford University to provide an overview of the "state of the market" of use of technology and innovation in law firms.[5] The basis for commission was the SRA's priority to *"actively support the adoption of legal technology and other innovation"*. Oxford University surveyed 900 firms and analyzed data from various tech databases to conclude its work. It summarized that, *"Legal services providers see technology and innovation as a way to improve the quality and efficiency of service delivery, and to satisfy unmet legal needs"*. The report also recognized that, *"Barriers take the form of lack of financial capital, lack of staff with appropriate expertise, and regulatory uncertainty"*.

Similar obstacles had been identified in the Legal Services Board's 2018 study.[6] Although this report was published before the launch of AI in legal practices, it reviewed "lawtech" such as chatbots deployed to answer legal queries, automated document assembly, and digital comparison tools for document review which were all available (although fewer than one in seven firms who responded indicated that they used these technologies).

In both studies, lawyers stated a firm intention to adopt new technology and to change working methods in their professional practices. In the 2018 study,[7] legal services providers who believed that "the availability of new technology or ICT developments" had an influence in driving their service development activities were three times more likely to implement delivery innovation than those lawyers who believed that technology creates ethical problems for lawyers. That latter category of lawyers who foresaw ethical issues were only half as likely to adopt innovations for their practices against the base line of lawyers who were not expecting to change their practices at all in the timeframe scoped. What was interesting in the 2018 study was that lawyers who agreed technology can make legal services cheaper were three times more likely to innovate than those who believed the driver for adoption of new legal technology would be that their clients expected them to (again only 1.5 times more likely to actually implement changes than not to).

Moving forward to the 2021[8] study and attitudes had shifted. There are myriad reasons why but the most obvious must be the seismic shift in working practices when orders to "stay at home" and "shelter in place" drove lawyers (whose work continued) to work from home during the COVID-19 pandemic, and proved definitively to practice managers that flexible and hybrid working did not diminish productivity. Four years on, and the top five stated reasons for adopting legal technology were to "improve service quality" (72 percent of total respondents), "improve efficiency of workflows" (71 percent), "allow staff to work more flexibly" (44 percent), "reduce the overall cost of service delivery" (33 percent), and "increase security and compliance" (22 percent). These figures reveal a subtle shift away from implementing technology solutions simply to drive down cost and meet client expectation, to more lawyer-centric uses, with increased job-satisfaction being factored in. The ground has shifted as both generic communication technology has been adopted as inherent to practice and availability of lawtech has become accessible for all practitioners.

As new technologies have catapulted lawyers forward in their ability to do more, faster, and with more efficiency, we should reflect whether they have also enabled lawyers to do their work more accurately and with better outcomes from clients.

The Lawyers on Demand 2025 global survey[9] highlights that legal teams are *"dealing with a seemingly impossible contradiction"* where the processes and structure that are supposed to help them manage caseloads is often adding to their pressure. It recognizes that before lawyers can *"embrace and employ transformative technologies... they must first reclaim the capacity to support them"*. Practitioners are all too conscious of the demands of those dual-despots, compliance and case management, and here lies the perennial problem – lawyers want to innovate for efficiency, but doing so seems to require them to already be sufficiently efficient to do so. The paradox in gaining increasing access to on-point data that can assist lawyers to do their job more comprehensively, is that such access can lead to data-overload and decreased productivity. In the PWC Law Firms' Survey 2024,[10] the top 11-100 law firms in the UK responded overwhelmingly (more than 50 percent) that they believe AI will have a negative impact on their business. The reasons for this were concerns that use of AI would be seen by clients as a reason for fees to be reduced, whereas investment would be required to implement the technology, upskill staff, and train or recruit to maximize returns on implementation of lawtech. To meet clients' expectations and minimize negative impacts, law firms that want to improve service quality and workflow efficiency (the 70 percent plus majority in the SRA/Oxford University survey),[11] must plan now how human and financial resource can be best matched with transformative technology to achieve this for the law firm of 2030.

In the Great Reinvention survey,[12] 46 percent of lawyers surveyed *"overwhelmingly"* identified AI as the pre-eminent driver of future change in law firms. A new category of concern for well over a third (39 percent) of the lawyers responding to the PWC survey[13] was the "reduction in client's demand for legal work through automation of legal work... driven by the increased adoption of GenAI tools".

We know that AI poses a threat to how law is practiced and to jobs within the legal profession. We know it poses an existential threat to the Rule of Law too. AI is not yet ready to be left to make autonomous legal decisions, but the pace of change suggests it soon could be. Currently, there are grave issues with reliability in AI that could undermine trust in legal outcomes and transparency in Law. Stanford University's Human-Centered Artificial Intelligence and Stanford RegLab's 2024 paper[14] noted that, in legal AI, false biographies and fake case law ("hallucinations") abound. Hallucination rates ranged from 64-88 percent in response to specific legal queries put to new LLMs, or put bluntly, more often than not, AI makes it up. The Stanford RegLab's 2024 headline comment is that the AI *"lacks self-awareness about their errors and tend to reinforce incorrect legal assumptions and beliefs"*. It is not just in general practice use that AI use has been called out – bogus and fake case law and authorities have begun to be cited and have crept into the courts as submissions in evidence.[15]

The SRA identified this as a known (but not new) factor in its November 2023 Risk Outlook Report[16] and cautioned even then that *"there is evidence that people may place more trust in computers than in humans"*[17] and that *"errors by an AI system could affect many more people than errors by a single person could"*. The SRA warned that, *"The high output of an AI system also makes it harder to supervise effectively"*.[18] Stanford HAI was blunter, saying, *"These findings raise significant concerns about the reliability of LLMs in legal contexts"*. This reminds us that AI is often not simply a case of plug and play, but that the ever-increasing data deluge leads to a workload crisis that leaves scant space for general practitioners where BigLaw and niche firms push specificity, expertise, and empathy but early innovators are still left paying for their bespoke AI system that has become open access for other firms and unregulated businesses.

The law firm of 2030 – what clients want

Having identified what lawyers perceive as risks and threats, we move to the opportunities for lawyers by asking what it is that clients want from the law firm of 2030. To help understand what it is that clients want from their future lawyers, I approached a number of my clients to ask them. Those who felt most qualified to reply were ones who work in technology and in professional service industries. I opened an online survey and asked the following five questions to which I invited (anonymized) short and long responses. The percentages that follow and the comments are taken directly from the responses received.

1. Who advises you. Which professional advisors do you instruct regularly?

To assess the authority of the answers from the respondents, we first asked for a general indication of which professionals they regularly instructed – "lawyers, accountants or other professionals"? All respondents directly instructed professionals in the course of their work, 44 percent of respondents regularly instruct external lawyers, 33 percent also instructed accountants and the remaining 22 percent were "other" professionals such as IT specialists.

2. The work split. What matters do you engage legal advisors for the most?

The two largest categories were "general legal advice" (17 percent) and "commercial contracts" (also 17 percent). Here, the "general advice" was making enquiries such as legal considerations about how current and proposed work is undertaken, and testing proposals from a legal perspective. "Commercial contracts" work was requests to review contracts and advise on specific terms and risk analysis. The next largest category was compliance and regulatory matters (13 percent).

Interestingly, the responses from business about what they engage lawyers for most frequently mirror the categories lawyers responding to the Great Reinvention[19] questionnaire identified as areas for operational innovation in their own firms and work (namely, contract management innovation – 48 percent, and compliance and risk management – 42 percent). M&A and employment matters both nudged towards ten percent, family office and personal matters provided nine percent of the instructions, with litigation and also debt collection at seven percent of instructions. IT and IP, planning and property made up the smallest categories with only seven percent of respondents instructing external lawyers on these matters.

These smaller categories of work may be skewed by respondents from very large multi-national organizations who have in-house legal counsel to deal with the majority of these types of matters and so only exceptionally is external legal resource instructed. The low percentage of M&A advice is reflective of the respondents' (predominantly) SME size. These businesses are the most immediately vulnerable to economic uncertainly and where mergers and acquisitions have stagnated and therefore fewer instructions in this area are given. The top 50 law firms who service "BigLaw" all saw record profit growth and all firms in the top 100 by size have enjoyed PEP growth year-on-year so as M&As are still buoyant, one would expect the percentage of respondents who instruct lawyers on such matters to increase across a wider group of respondents. If we look at the largest law firms (surveyed by PWC)[20] who service M&A work in the arena of their expectation of change to address clients' upcoming legal needs and expectations, in the PWC survey *"only four percent and two percent of Top 100 firms stated they were extremely concerned about the speed of technological change and clients reducing demand through automation of legal work".* This may be reflective of their practice structure, but could also indicate an overconfidence in the firms' infallibility!

3. Client engagement. What do you dislike about engaging lawyers?

Six out of ten (60 percent) of repsondents felt lawyers are too expensive and perceived legal services as more costly than other professional advisors.

Twenty percent of respondents believed that the "value add" from legal advice was worse than from other professionals, and the majority thought it was the same as or better than other professional advice (40 percent the same value-add, 40 percent felt legal advice provides "added value" more than other professions). Considering this response from an alternative perspective, it can just as easily be reflected that 60 percent of respondents thought that there was no value-add from lawyers or that it was not better than other professionals. Legal advice from lawyers *should* be as valued (and even more so) than other professionals and clients have a right to expect that the advice received offers useful insight, experience, and expertise, which provides added value to the response.

4. Business threats. What do you consider the biggest challenge to your business in the next five years?

By far the largest category identified AI as being a threat to their business (63 percent of respondents). Within that category, 28 percent said that fakes and AI hallucinations were likely to discredit the work in their industry and/or devalue their business and destabilize them economically or reputationally. Work being taken in-house and, as a sub-category, being carried out by technology solutions such as AI was perceived as a threat by 27 percent of respondents.

Economic uncertainty and budget constraints (such as "hire-freeze" and spending embargos) were the next largest categories of perceived threats, with 36 percent of respondents noting each of these elements as threats to address. Some respondents mentioned a change in globalization and a recalibration of location for manufacturing and sales arising from geopolitical factors and the sovereign debt crisis (nine percent). This is not considered a sub-category of "Economic uncertainty", as it is not solely monetary but almost reflects an underlying perception of "change" in both the way services are procured and how they are delivered, as well as the shift from centralization of technology supply from the US to other platforms and suppliers. At the time of writing, Trump's tariff gamble to either force manufacturing back to the US and increase revenue for the US Treasury, or to re-base the USD and lower its borrowing, fuels that sense of uncertainty for all businesses. Law is perhaps unique in that being nationally decreed and applied, its services are generally provided in situ (if virtually), but whilst its own output may be somewhat insulated from tariffs and trade wars, of course its clients (and their ability to instruct lawyers and complete deals) is not.

In longer responses, clients acknowledged that businesses must *"embrace AI", "enhance leadership resilience", "adapt to new work cultures"*, and *"integrate transformation strategies"*. Clients perceive *"unprecedented challenges driven by AI disruption"* but saw that *"Success will depend on balancing technological advancements with the human element"* where necessary, to secure their own continuation. Where tech-suppliers responded, they noted a developing *"rift"* between their customers' intentions and expectation of their adoption and use of AI and suppliers' own use policies. There also appears to be a widening gap in expectations of delivery of ownership of technology. This is not unexpected as generally in every leap forward first adopters often try to control and own the output they have helped originate and funded development of, and therefore feel invested in.

In many respects, the "threats" perceived by business mirrored those expressed by lawyers. In the Law Firms Survey[21] PWC notes, *"Many firms are still unable to deliver the pace of technological change, get the best use of technology once implemented or drive long term adoption"*.

5. What do clients want from the law firm of 2030?

- Clients want help to navigate change.
- They do not want ever increasing and opaque pricing.
- Clients want to know that engaging a lawyer will give enhanced output and better results.
- Clients do not necessarily need help from a human lawyer.

Human lawyers are no longer the only access point to law and legal advice. The legal profession is not the gate keeper to law, the courts, and judges, and it is not the only trusted oracle of justice. The keys to the vast repositories of legal knowledge and judgment set down are accessible on request from AI driven law-tech. In Part 1 of this book, we considered the transformative power of AI for the legal profession. Legal engagement has always been based on human relationships and trust. As the most human-like interface in tech, AI is the "natural" successor to traditional practice, whilst at the same time being the most transformative of it.

One client wondered if lawyers would become the portals to "access the great AI of law" where charges were $50,000 an hour for "all the answers you need", but the AI was like some Wizard of Oz where users never really know what is behind the screen but trust it because "It is Oz". This blind trust harks back to the days of "putting oneself in the hands of lawyers" or "throwing oneself on the justice of the courts" – that it is not reflective of current practice does not, however, mean it might not be the future of it.

Clients were asked the question, "Would you trust AI to...". Below are the answers.

Would you trust AI to...?	% Yes	% Not sure	No	Not yet
Draft a binding legal contract	45.5%	18.2%	9.1%	27.3%
Summarize legal documents and advise on them	81.8%	0%	0%	18.2%
Negotiate settlement in a dispute on your behalf	18%	18%	37%	27%
Give a considered and correct judgement in a civil court (NB not a criminal case)	18%	37%	18%	27%
Make financial awards based on evidence submitted	9%	36%	19%	36%
Draft laws	45.5%	9%	36.5%	9%

The answers are suggestive of the areas of legal engagement where there is the most price sensitivity, and potentially, where most clients already have used some form of AI and so score the value of lawyers' input lower. Summarizing documents and drafting them already have their place in the general toolkit of business. ChatGPT can summarize a contract for anyone with access to an account and Google Gemini can provide an outline and output for anyone with access to the internet.

A surprise response is that AI would be trusted (almost) as often as not to draft new law. This is perhaps the "AI guarding the (micro) chips" equivalent of Susskind's "rabbits guarding the lettuce" analogy. It is insightful in that it does suggest that as the drafting process is one that few people engage with, the sacrifice made in handing it over to a machine with the attendant lack of transparency is not so keenly felt and responsibility for it may be ceded more willingly to a "trusted" machine.

The "human" engagements of negotiation and financial settlement unsurprisingly score lowest in terms of trust. It could be that humans trust humans to do these jobs for them, but the question for the law firm of 2030 is "For how long?". As training data becomes more robust and outputs more akin to "human" judgements, or better still, better than human ones, and as hallucinations are curtailed, a system that easily crunches all available data on the opponent and applies game strategies to map scenarios will inevitably be able to analyze all possible outcomes and present the best negotiation position.

AI's ascendancy does not mean the demise of lawyers, but it invariably does mean a sea-change in practice.

We are human lawyers in a human world and can only operate on that basis. Lawyers cannot compete with algorithms that we have no input into and technology that operates in a black box (even if the front-end has been made bespoke for use by us and our clients). To have a place at the table, you need to be in the room where it happens. Our clients expect us to know how to use the technology they are introducing to their businesses and have answers to how to use it better. Adopting it is the best way to achieve this and speed the transition when *all* that is needed is to change.

References

1 *The Future of the Professions: How Technology Will Transform the Work of Human Experts*, Richard Susskind, Daniel Susskind, 2015, OUP.

2 *Technology And Innovation In Legal Services*, www.sra.org.uk/globalassets/documents/sra/research/full-report-technology-and-innovation-in-legal-services.pdf

3 *Ibid.*, p.54.

4 *Vertically Integrated Legal Service*, Harvard Law School's Center on the Legal Profession, 2021, https://clp.law.harvard.edu/knowledge-hub/magazine/issues/integration-in-legal-services/vertically-integrated-legal-service/

5 *Technology and Innovation in Legal Services*, Final Report for the Solicitors Regulation Authority. Mari Sako and Richard Parnham, with contributions from

John Armour, Ian Rodgers, and Matthias Qian. University of Oxford, www.sra.org.uk/globalassets/documents/sra/research/full-report-technology-and-innovation-in-legal-services.pdf

6 https://legalservicesboard.org.uk/wp-content/media/Innovation-survey-2018-report-FINAL-2.pdf

7 *Ibid.*, p.48.

8 www.sra.org.uk/globalassets/documents/sra/research/full-report-technology-and-innovation-in-legal-services.pdf at pages 5-9

9 https://cdn.prod.website-files.com/6706d0c620be3bd3a6954c8e/67ee48f342e9e33b39690f8e_BM.SP0108.B%20-%20LOD%20Global%20Survey%20Report_2024%205.pdf

10 https://image.uk.info.pwc.com/lib/fe31117075640475701c74/m/1/Law+Firms+Survey+2024_FINAL+version.pdf

11 www.sra.org.uk/globalassets/documents/sra/research/full-report-technology-and-innovation-in-legal-services.pdf at p 5-9

12 *Ibid.*

13 PWC Law Firm Survey 2024, "Innovate, adapt, protect", Law Firms' Survey 2024, as above.

14 https://hai.stanford.edu/news/hallucinating-law-legal-mistakes-large-language-models-are-pervasive

15 *Harber v. Commissioners for His Majesty's Revenue and Customs* (2023) UKFTT 1007 (TC)

16 www.sra.org.uk/sra/research-publications/artificial-intelligence-legal-market/

17 www.sciencedaily.com/releases/2021/04/210413114040.htm

18 AI Safety Summit 2023, Capabilities and Risks from Frontier AI: https://assets.publishing.service.gov.uk/media/65395abae6c968000daa9b25/frontier-ai-capabilities-risks-report.pdf

19 https://cdn.prod.website-files.com/6706d0c620be3bd3a6954c8e/67ee48f342e9e33b39690f8e_BM.SP0108.B%20-%20LOD%20Global%20Survey%20Report_2024%205.pdf

20 PWC Law Firm Survey 2024, "Innovate, adapt, protect", Law Firms' Survey 2024, as before.

21 *Ibid.*

About Globe Law and Business

Globe Law and Business was established in 2005. From the very beginning, we set out to create legal books that are sufficiently high level to be of real use to the experienced professional, yet still accessible and easy to navigate. Most of our authors are drawn from Magic Circle and other top commercial firms, both in the United Kingdom and internationally.

Our titles are carefully produced, with the utmost attention paid to editorial, design and production processes. We hope this results in high quality publications that are easy to read and a pleasure to own.

In 2021, we were very pleased to announce the start of a new chapter for Globe Law and Business following the acquisition of law books under the imprint Ark Publishing. Our law firm management list is now significantly expanded with many well-known and loved Ark Publishing titles.

We are also pleased to announce the launch of our online content platform, Globe Law Online, which allows for easy access across firms. Details of all titles included can be found at www.globelawonline.com. Email glo@globelawandbusiness.com for further details and to arrange a free trial for you or your firm.

We'd very much like to hear from you with your thoughts and ideas for improving what we offer. Please do feel free to email me on sian@globelawandbusiness.com. Happy reading and thank you for your time.

Sian O'Neill
Managing director
Globe Law and Business
www.globelawandbusiness.com

www.ingramcontent.com/pod-product-compliance
Ingram Content Group UK Ltd.
Pitfield, Milton Keynes, MK11 3LW, UK
UKHW051508160525
458554UK00006B/4

9 781837 230853